PUBLIC LANDS: USE AND MISUSE

PUBLIC LANDS: USE AND MISUSE

WILLIAM E. NEELEY
EDITOR

Nova Science Publishers, Inc.
New York

Library of Congress Cataloging-in-Publication Data

Public lands : use and misuse / William E. Neeley (editor).
p. cm.
Includes index.
ISBN 13 978-1-60021-352-6
ISBN 10 1-60021-352-9
1. Public lands--United States--Management. 2. Public lands--United States--Planning. 3. Conservation of natural resources--United States. 4. United States. Bureau of Land Management. I. Neeley, William E.
HD221.P83 2006
333.730973--dc22 2006022752

Published by Nova Science Publishers, Inc. ✦New York

CONTENTS

PREFACE

There is a great amount of debate concerning the establishment and use of public lands. While there is a desire for recreational areas and parks, there are also considerations for the preservation of wilderness and wildlife. National parks must determine rules regarding the use of off road vehicles, personal watercrafts, snowmobiles and the implementation of hiking trails. This book examines the growing diversity of recreation on federal lands and the resulting impact on the environment.

Chapter 1 - One major element of the energy debate is whether to approve energy development in the Arctic National Wildlife Refuge (ANWR) in northeastern Alaska, and if so, under what conditions, or whether to continue to prohibit development to protect the area's biological recreational, and subsistence values. ANWR is rich in fauna, flora, and commercial oil potential. Its development has been debated for over 40 years, but sharp increases in gasoline and natural gas prices from late 2000 to early 2001, terrorist attacks, further increases in 2004-2006, and infrastructure damage from hurricanes have intensified the debate. Few onshore U.S. areas stir as much industry interest as the northern area of ANWR. At the same time, few areas are considered more worthy of protection in the eyes of conservation and some Native groups. Current law forbids oil and gas leasing in the Refuge.

On March 16, 2006, the Senate passed S.Con.Res. 83, the FY2007 budget resolution. Its sole reconciliation instruction was to the Senate Committee on Energy and Natural Resources, and it assumed revenues from leasing in ANWR.

During the first session, the Senate Budget Committee reported a title in S. 1932 (reconciliation) to open ANWR; supporters designed it to meet the savings target and Senate procedural restrictions on matters included in reconciliation bills. According to press reports, the insistence of a group of Republican Members led to the removal of ANWR provisions from the House version of reconciliation (H.R. 4241) before floor consideration. The House then substituted its text for the Senate version of S. 1932. The difference on ANWR was a major issue in conference. The conference report (H.Rept. 109- 362) omitted ANWR development. The House and Senate passed different versions of the report. Neither contained ANWR provi- sions, nor did the final bill (P.L. 109-171).

Development advocates then added ANWR development to the conference report for the Defense appropriations bill (H.R. 2863). The House passed the conference report with the ANWR provision, but the ANWR title was removed from the bill (P.L. 109-148) after failure of a cloture motion in the Senate.

Development advocates argue that ANWR oil would reduce U.S. energy markets' exposure to crises in the Middle East; lower oil prices; extend the economic life of the Trans Alaska Pipeline; and create jobs in Alaska and elsewhere in the United States. They maintain that ANWR oil could be developed with minimal environmental harm, and that the footprint of development could be limited to a total of 2,000 acres.

Opponents argue that intrusion on this ecosystem cannot be justified on any terms; that economically recoverable oil found (if any) would provide little energy security and could be replaced by cost-effective alternatives, including conservation; and that job claims are exaggerated. They maintain that development's footprints, being scattered across the landscape, would have a greater impact than is implied by a limit on total acreage. They also argue that limits on foot- prints have not been worded to apply to extensive Native lands in the Refuge, which could be developed if the Refuge were opened.

Chapter 2 - The 109th Congress is considering issues related to the public lands managed by the Bureau of Land Management (BLM) and the national forests managed by the Forest Service (FS). The Administration is addressing issues through budgetary, regulatory, and other actions. Several key issues of congressional and administrative interest are covered here.

Energy Resources. The Energy Policy Act of 2005 affects energy development on federal lands in a variety of ways. Significant new regulations are expected in response to the law, including changes to the federal oil, gas, and coal leasing programs and application of environmental laws to certain energy-related agency actions.

Wild Horses and Burros. Controversial changes to the Wild Free-Roaming Horses and Burros Act of 1971 gave the agencies authority to sell certain old and unadoptable animals and removed the ban on selling wild horses and burros and their remains for commercial products. BLM has resumed animal sales with provisions to prevent their slaughter. Bills have been introduced to overturn the changes (H.R. 297/S. 576) and to foster adoptions and sales (H.R. 2993/S. 1273).

Wilderness. Many wilderness recommendations for federal lands are pending. Questions persist about wilderness review and managing wilderness study areas (WSAs). Bills to designate areas have been introduced, and the 109th Congress may address wilderness review and WSA protection.

Wildfire Protection. President Bush's Healthy Forests Initiative, the Healthy Forests Restoration Act, and other provisions may help protect communities from wildfires by expediting fuel reduction. Some believe that more effort is needed; others are concerned that current and additional streamlining will increase timber sales and damage the environment. Legislation for research and post-fire rehabilitation of federal lands is being considered. The 109th Congress also has held hearings on fire protection and on litigation over fuel treatments and use of fire retardant.

Other Issues. The Administration and Congress are addressing other issues as well, including grazing management, hardrock mining, FS NEPA categorical exclusions, national forest roadless areas, federal land sales, and R.S. 2477 rights of way.

Chapter 3 - Approximately 30% of the land in the United States is under the control of federal land managers. Much of this public land is rich in paleontological [fossil] resources. Concern has been expressed over the management, conservation, and protection of these resources.

There is no comprehensive statute or management policy for the protection or management of fossils located on federal lands. Federal authority for the management of such resources may be derived from a number of general statutes relating to the protection of public properties. The applicability of some of these statutes, such as the Antiquities Act and the Archeological Resources Protection Act, is uncertain or limited. General authority for fossil protection also may be derived from general criminal theft statutes dealing with the theft of government property and from certain site-specific statutes. There may also be certain regulatory authority which is provided by the statutes governing each agency's operations.

In May 2000, the Secretary of the Interior released a comprehensive report concerning the management of fossils which are located on federal and Indian lands. The report was prepared at the request of Congress and it is considered to be the authoritative study of fossils on these lands. It has served as an impetus for federal legislation. The report outlined seven principles for the effective management of fossils which are located on federal land.

Legislative activity concerning the protection of fossils located on federal lands has occurred in both the 107th and 108th Congresses. There have been two types of legislation: one type deals with specific fossil resources at a particular location; the other type provides comprehensive management and protection authority for fossils located on federal lands. In the 108th Congress, the Senate passed S. 546, the Paleontological Resources Preservation Act. The bill has been referred to two House committees. H.R. 2416, a similar bill, has been introduced in the House. The two bills provide a comprehensive approach to the management of fossils on federal lands, providing uniform definitions, public programs, specific prohibitions, permit procedures, and civil and criminal penalties. The bills would not modify the general mining or reclamation laws, or apply to lands other than federal lands.

Chapter 4 - Congress enacted the Wilderness Act in 1964. This Act created the National Wilderness Preservation System, reserved to Congress the authority to designate wilderness areas, and directed the Secretaries of Agriculture and of the Interior to review certain lands for their wilderness potential. The Act also designated 54 wilderness areas with 9 million acres of federal land. Congress began expanding the Wilderness System in 1968, and today, there are 649 wilderness areas, totaling more than 105 million acres, in 44 states. Numerous bills to designate additional areas and to expand existing ones are introduced and considered in every Congress.

The Wilderness Act defined wilderness as an area of generally undisturbed federal land, but did not establish criteria or standards to determine whether an area should be designated, because of differing perceptions of wilderness and because of the varying purposes of wilderness. In general, wilderness areas are undeveloped, and commercial activities, motorized access, and roads, structures, and facilities are prohibited in wilderness areas. However, in response to conflicting demands, Congress has granted both general exemptions and specific exceptions to the general standards and prohibitions.

The federal government owns about 29% of the land in the United States, although the proportion in each state varies widely. Four federal agencies — the Bureau of Land Management, National Park Service, and Fish and Wildlife Service in the Department of the Interior and the Forest Service in the Department of Agriculture — manage most of the federal lands. These agencies manage the 106 million acres of designated wilderness, as well as many other lands. In addition, they have are protecting another 46 million acres as possible additions to the Wilderness System, and are reviewing the wilderness potential of additional lands.

In total, more than 23% of all federal land, and nearly 7% of all land in the United States, has been designated as wilderness or is being protected as possible wilderness. Alaska, because of its size and relatively pristine condition, dominates wilderness statistics — more than 54% of designated wilderness is in Alaska. In total, nearly 16% of all land (federal, state, private, and other) in Alaska has been designated as wilderness. In contrast, 4% of all land in the United States outside Alaska has been designated as wilderness.

Chapter 5 - The use of snowmobiles in national parks has been controversial because of their potential impacts on wildlife and the absence of standards for their emissions and noise. This report focuses on the latter set of issues.

Congress has addressed snowmobile issues primarily through provisions in appropriations bills. On November 20, 2004, the House and Senate approved the conference report on H.R. 4818, the Consolidated Appropriations Act, 2005 (P.L. 108-447). Among its many provisions, the bill establishes winter use rules for Yellowstone and Grand Teton National Parks, allowing up to 720 snowmobiles daily in Yellowstone and 140 in Grand Teton, during the 2004-2005 winter season. Earlier the House voted twice against amendments to Interior Department appropriation bills that would have prohibited recreational snowmobiling in the two parks.

Most current model snowmobiles emit significant quantities of pollution. In one hour, a typical snowmobile emits as much hydrocarbon as a 2001 model auto emits in about two years (24,300 miles) of driving. On November 8, 2002, the Environmental Protection Agency (EPA) promulgated regulations limiting air emissions from snowmobiles. These regulations would require a 30% reduction in emissions beginning in 2006, with more stringent standards (requiring 50% reductions) effective in 2010 and 2012. The standards were challenged in court by both the snowmobile manufacturers and environmental groups and were vacated in part and remanded to EPA in part by the Court of Appeals for the D.C. Circuit, June 1, 2004. EPA has not promulgated any standards for snowmobile noise.

Regarding national parks, the National Park Service has allowed snowmobile use in 43 units of the park system, in many cases in apparent violation of Executive Orders from the Nixon and Carter years. Outside of Alaska (where snowmobiles are permitted in most national parks by law), the most popular national park for snowmobiling has been Yellowstone, which saw more than 76,000 snowmobile visits in the 1999-2000 winter season. Under the Clinton Administration, the National Park Service decided that the emissions and noise from snowmobiling were incompatible with protecting the park, and promulgated rules that would have phased out snowmobiles from Yellowstone, with a complete ban beginning in the winter of 2003-2004. The Bush Administration revisited these rules in settlement of a lawsuit, and announced modifications in March 2003. The modifications would have allowed 950 cleaner, quieter snowmobiles to enter Yellowstone Park per day. These rules and the Clinton Administration action have been the subject of conflicting court rulings: a federal court in Wyoming has vacated and remanded the Clinton Administration's phase-out, while a federal court in the District of Columbia has vacated and remanded the Bush Administration rules.

Efforts to reduce snowmobile emissions and noise remain contentious. This report discusses snowmobile access to the parks, snowmobile emissions, and the new EPA standards, and concludes with a discussion of legislative proposals in the 107th and 108th Congresses. It will be updated as events warrant.

Proposals by the National Park Service to enforce long-standing policy that regulates the use of snowmobiles in national parks have raised a number of questions regarding the current and potential regulation of such vehicles. National Park System units account for only about 3% of the land mass of the United States and possess few trails and roads suitable for snowmobiles, compared to areas available on other federal lands; but — for both proponents and opponents — the question of snowmobile access to the parks has taken on a far greater importance. To the snowmobile industry and to many in communities neighboring national parks, "Snowmobiling is an important part of the economic engine that supports northern communities, winter tourism."[1] To environmental groups, snowmobiling "is one of the most environmentally devastating recreational activities permitted by the Park Service .... resulting in adverse impacts to Park wildlife, air and water quality, vegetation, Park ecology, and Park users."[2] Underlying the debate are broader questions concerning regulation of emissions and noise from the vehicles and the degree to which restrictions may serve as a precedent or stigma affecting snowmobile and motorized recreation[3] use more generally.

Chapter 6 - The growing and diverse nature of recreation on federal lands has increased the challenge of balancing recreation with other land uses, and balancing different types of recreation. Motorized recreation has been particularly controversial, with issues centering on access and environmental impacts. The 109th Congress is considering legislation and conducting oversight on issues involving recreation on federal lands, including traditional recreational pursuits and newer forms of motorized recreation. The Administration is addressing these issues through budgetary, regulatory, and other actions. Several prominent issues are covered in this report.

Motorized Recreation in the National Forests and on BLM Land. The use of off-highway vehicles (OHVs) on Forest Service (FS) and Bureau of Land Management (BLM) lands has been particularly controversial. Both agencies decide the extent of allowed OHV use through their planning processes. The FS finalized new regulations (Nov. 9, 2005) governing OHV use that require designating roads, trails, and areas open for OHV use and prohibit OHV use outside the designated system. The BLM is addressing transportation issues through national strategies and other guidance. A July 13, 2005, House Resources joint subcommittee hearing examined motorized recreation use on federal lands. The FY2007 Administration budget request would cut FS recreation management by 3% and trails funding by 19%, and BLM recreation management by 2%. The House-passed Interior appropriations bill restored or increased funding for these accounts.

Personal Watercraft and Snowmobiles. Personal watercraft (PWC) and snowmobile use in National Park Service (NPS) units has fueled debate over the balance between recreation on, and protection of, park lands and waters. Regulatory actions restricting use of these vehicles have been especially controversial. The NPS currently is evaluating PWC and snowmobile use in several areas. Service-wide management policies encompassing motorized and non-motorized recreation are being reviewed.

Aircraft Overflights. Grand Canyon National Park is at the center of a conflict over whether to limit air tours over national parks to reduce noise. The NPS and the Federal Aviation Administration (FAA) continue to work to implement a 1987 law that sought to reduce noise at Grand Canyon, and a 2000 law that regulates overflights at other park units. Recent regulations require air tour operators to seek authority to fly over park units; the agencies then must develop Air Tour Management Plans at those park units. Further, the FAA is developing final safety regulations for commercial air tours nationally.

The National Trails System. While designation of trails is often popular, issues remain regarding funding, expansion, and quality of trails. The 109th Congress is considering a variety of trail measures, including adding routes to the National Trail System, authorizing studies of routes for possible additions to the system, and authorizing land acquisitions from willing sellers. Legislation has been introduced to create a new category of trails, called National Discovery Trails.

Other Issues. Other federal land recreation issues of interest to the 109th Congress include recreational uses within the National Wildlife Refuge System, recreation at federal water sites (Army Corps of Engineers and Bureau of Reclamation), recreation fees, and Grand Canyon Colorado River management.

Chapter 7 - The roadless areas of the National Forest System have received special management attention for decades. In part to recognize the importance of national forest roadless areas for many purposes and in part because making project decisions involving roadless areas on a forest-by-forest basis was resulting in controversy and litigation that consumed considerable time and money, the Clinton Administration established a new nationwide approach to the management of the roadless areas in the National Forest System. A record of decision (ROD) and a final rule were published on January 12, 2001, that prohibited most road construction and reconstruction in 58.5 million acres of inventoried forest roadless areas, with significant exceptions. Most timber cutting in roadless areas also was prohibited, with some exceptions, including improving habitat for threatened, endangered, proposed, or sensitive species, or reducing the risk of wildfire and disease. With some exceptions, the new prohibitions would have applied immediately to the Tongass National Forest in Alaska.

The Bush Administration initially postponed the effective date of the roadless area rule, then decided to allow it to be implemented while proposing amendments. However, the Federal District Court for Idaho preliminarily enjoined its implementation. The Ninth Circuit reversed the Idaho district court, but on July 14, 2003, the Federal District Court for Wyoming again permanently enjoined implementation of the Rule. This holding is still on appeal to the 10th Circuit, but now may be moot. A final rule "temporarily" exempting the Tongass National Forest (Alaska) from the roadless rule was published December 30, 2003. On July 16, 2004, a new general roadless rule was proposed and a new final rule was published on May 13, 2005. The new rule eliminates the need for a separate Tongass rule, and replaces the Clinton roadless rule with a procedure whereby the governor of a state may petition the Secretary of Agriculture to promulgate a special rule for the management of roadless areas in that state, and make recommendations for that management. The new rule contains no standards by which the Secretary is to review a state's recommendations, and does not address the weight to be given to the views of local residents versus those of out-of-state residents with an interest in the public lands.

A new final forest planning rule was also published on January 5, 2005. The rule does not address roadless areas at all, but does require review of areas that might be suitable for wilderness designation when plans are revised.

This chapter traces the development and content of the roadless area rules and directives, describes the statutory background, reviews recent events, and analyzes some of the legal issues.

Chapter 8 - The Land and Water Conservation Fund (LWCF) has been the principal source of monies for four federal agencies — the National Park Service, Bureau of Land Management, Fish and Wildlife Service, and Forest Service — to acquire recreational lands since 1965. The LWCF also funds a matching grant program to assist states (and localities) in acquiring recreational lands and developing facilities. The fund accumulates $900 million annually from designated sources. Congress allocates these funds through appropriations each year.

Current congressional issues include (1) deciding the amount to appropriate each year to each of the four federal agencies, and to the state grant program; (2) identifying which lands should be acquired; and (3) determining whether LWCF funds should be appropriated for additional related purposes. The primary context for debating these issues is Interior appropriations legislation, which is tracked in CRS Report RL32893.

In: Public Lands: Use and Misuse
Editor: William E. Neeley, pp. 1-17

ISBN: 978-1-60021-352-6

Chapter 1

ARCTIC NATIONAL WILDLIFE REFUGE (ANWR): CONTROVERSIES FOR THE 109TH CONGRESS*

M. Lynne Corn, Bernard A. Gelb and Pamela Baldwin

SUMMARY

One major element of the energy debate is whether to approve energy development in the Arctic National Wildlife Refuge (ANWR) in northeastern Alaska, and if so, under what conditions, or whether to continue to prohibit development to protect the area's biological recreational, and subsistence values. ANWR is rich in fauna, flora, and commercial oil potential. Its development has been debated for over 40 years, but sharp increases in gasoline and natural gas prices from late 2000 to early 2001, terrorist attacks, further increases in 2004-2006, and infrastructure damage from hurricanes have intensified the debate. Few onshore U.S. areas stir as much industry interest as the northern area of ANWR. At the same time, few areas are considered more worthy of protection in the eyes of conservation and some Native groups. Current law forbids oil and gas leasing in the Refuge.

On March 16, 2006, the Senate passed S.Con.Res. 83, the FY2007 budget resolution. Its sole reconciliation instruction was to the Senate Committee on Energy and Natural Resources, and it assumed revenues from leasing in ANWR.

During the first session, the Senate Budget Committee reported a title in S. 1932 (reconciliation) to open ANWR; supporters designed it to meet the savings target and Senate procedural restrictions on matters included in reconciliation bills. According to press reports, the insistence of a group of Republican Members led to the removal of ANWR provisions from the House version of reconciliation (H.R. 4241) before floor consideration. The House then substituted its text for the Senate version of S. 1932. The difference on ANWR was a major issue in conference. The conference report (H.Rept. 109- 362) omitted ANWR development. The House and Senate passed different versions of the report. Neither contained ANWR provisions, nor did the final bill (P.L. 109-171).

Development advocates then added ANWR development to the conference report for the Defense appropriations bill (H.R. 2863). The House passed the conference report with the ANWR provision, but the ANWR title was removed from the bill (P.L. 109-148) after failure of a cloture motion in the Senate.

Development advocates argue that ANWR oil would reduce U.S. energy markets' exposure to crises in the Middle East; lower oil prices; extend the economic life of the Trans

* Excerpted from CRS Report IB10136, Updated May 16, 2006

Alaska Pipeline; and create jobs in Alaska and elsewhere in the United States. They maintain that ANWR oil could be developed with minimal environmental harm, and that the footprint of development could be limited to a total of 2,000 acres.

Opponents argue that intrusion on this ecosystem cannot be justified on any terms; that economically recoverable oil found (if any) would provide little energy security and could be replaced by cost-effective alternatives, including conservation; and that job claims are exaggerated. They maintain that development's footprints, being scattered across the landscape, would have a greater impact than is implied by a limit on total acreage. They also argue that limits on foot- prints have not been worded to apply to extensive Native lands in the Refuge, which could be developed if the Refuge were opened.

Most Recent Developments

The Senate passed the FY2007 budget resolution (S.Con.Res. 83; yeas 51, nays 49, Roll Call #74; no written report) on March 16, 2006. Its sole reconciliation instruction (§201) directed the Committee on Energy and Natural Resources to reduce budget authority by an amount equal to predicted revenues from ANWR development. The move, if retained in the final resolution, would facilitate inclusion of ANWR development in a reconciliation bill; reconciliation bills are not subject to Senate filibusters. The House budget resolution, as reported (H.Con.Res. 376, H.Rept. 109-402), did not have ANWR language, nor direction for the House Resources Committee. Recent increases in gasoline pump prices have added to calls for ANWR development.

Background and Analysis

The Arctic National Wildlife Refuge (ANWR) consists of 19 million acres in northeast Alaska. It is administered by the Fish and Wildlife Service (FWS) in the Department of the Interior (DOI). Its 1.5-million-acre coastal plain is viewed as one of the most promising U.S. onshore oil and gas prospects. According to the U.S. Geological Survey (USGS), the mean estimate of *technically* recoverable oil is 7.7 billion barrels (billion bbl), and there is a small chance that, taken together, the fields on this federal land could hold 10.7 billion bbl of *economically* recoverable oil (at $55/bbl in 2003 dollars). That amount would be nearly as much as the single giant field at Prudhoe Bay, found in 1967 on the state-owned portion of the coastal plain west of ANWR, now estimated to have held almost 14 billion bbl of economically recoverable oil. (See "Oil," below, for further discussion.)

The Refuge, especially the nearly undisturbed coastal plain, also is home to a wide variety of plants and animals. The presence of caribou, polar bears, grizzly bears, wolves, migratory birds, and other species in this wild area has led some to call the area "America's Serengeti." The Refuge and two neighboring parks in Canada have been proposed for an international park, and several species found in the area (including polar bears, caribou, migratory birds, and whales) are protected by international treaties or agreements. The analysis below covers, first, the economic and geological factors that have triggered interest in development, then the philosophical, biological, and environmental quality factors that have generated opposition to it.

The conflict between high oil potential and nearly pristine nature in the Refuge creates a dilemma: should Congress open the area for energy development or should the area's ecosystem continue to be protected from development, perhaps permanently? What factors should determine whether to open the area? If the area is opened, to what extent can damages be avoided, minimized, or mitigated? To what extent should Congress legislate special management of the area if it is developed, and to what extent should federal agencies be allowed to manage the area under existing law?

Basic information on the Refuge can be found in CRS Report RL31278, *Arctic National Wildlife Refuge: Background and Issues*, by M. Lynne Corn (coordinator) (hereafter cited as "CRS Report RL31278"). For legal background, see CRS Report RL31115, *Legal Issues Related to Proposed Drilling for Oil and Gas in the Arctic National Wildlife Refuge (ANWR)*, by Pamela Baldwin (hereafter cited as "CRS Report RL31115"). State lands on the coastal plain are shown at [http://www.dog.dnr.state.ak.us/oil/products/maps/maps.htm]. An extensive presentation of development arguments can be found at [http://www.anwr.org], sponsored by a consortium of groups. Opponents' arguments can be found variously at [http://www.alaskawild.org/], [http://www.dfait-maeci.gc.ca/can-am/washington/shared_env/default-en.asp], [http://www.protectthearctic.com/], or [http://www.tws.org/OurIssues/Arctic/index.cfm?TopLevel=Home].

Legislative History of the Refuge

The energy and biological resources of northern Alaska have been controversial for decades, from legislation in the 1970s, to a 1989 oil spill, to more recent efforts to use ANWR resources to address energy needs or to help balance the federal budget. In November 1957, an application for the withdrawal of lands in northeastern Alaska to create an "Arctic National Wildlife *Range*" was filed. On December 6, 1960, after statehood, the Secretary of the Interior issued Public Land Order 2214 reserving the area as the "Arctic National Wildlife Range." The potential for oil and gas leasing was expressly preserved.

In 1971, Congress enacted the Alaska Native Claims Settlement Act (ANCSA, P.L. 92-203) to resolve all Native aboriginal land claims against the United States. ANCSA provided for monetary payments and created Village Corporations that received the surface estate to roughly 22 million acres of lands in Alaska, including some in the National Wildlife Refuge System. Under §22(g) of ANCSA, these lands in Refuges were to remain subject to the laws and regulations governing use and development of the particular Refuge. Kaktovik Inupiat Corporation (KIC, the local corporation) received rights to three townships in the coastal plain of ANWR (and a fourth was added later). ANCSA also created Regional Corporations which could select subsurface rights to some lands and full title to others. Subsurface rights in Refuges were not available.

The Alaska National Interest Lands Conservation Act of 1980 (ANILCA, P.L. 96-487, 94 Stat. 2371) renamed the Range as the Arctic National Wildlife Refuge, and expanded the Refuge, mostly south and west, to include another 9.2 million acres. Section 702(3) designated much of the original Refuge as a wilderness area, but not the coastal plain, nor the newer portions of the Refuge. Instead, Congress postponed decisions on the development or further protection of the coastal plain. Section 1002 directed a study of ANWR's "coastal plain" (therefore often referred to as the "1002 area") and its resources. The resulting 1987 report was called the *1002 report* or the Final Legislative Environmental Impact Statement (FLEIS). ANILCA defined the "coastal plain" as the lands specified on an August 1980 map

— language that was later administratively interpreted as excluding many Native lands, even though these lands are *geographically* part of the coastal plain.

Section 1003 of ANILCA prohibited oil and gas development in the entire Refuge, or "leasing or other development leading to production of oil and gas from the range" unless authorized by an act of Congress. (For more history of legislation on ANWR and related developments, see CRS Report RL31278; for legal issues, see CRS Report RL31115. For specific actions, including key votes, see CRS Report RL32838, *Arctic National Wildlife Refuge: Legislative Actions Through the 109th Congress, First Session*, by Anne Gillis, M. Lynne Corn, Bernard A. Gelb, and Pamela Baldwin.)

Actions in the 109th Congress, First Session. As explained below, the ANWR debate has taken two basic routes in the 109th Congress: (a) reconciliation bills (S. 1932 and H.R. 4241) under the budget process, which cannot be filibustered; and (b) other bills (H.R. 6 and H.R. 2863, an energy bill and Defense appropriations, respectively) which can be.[1] (See *Omnibus Energy Legislation*, below.) The FY2006 Senate budget resolution (S.Con.Res. 18) passed by the Senate Budget Committee included instructions to the Senate Committee on Energy and Natural Resources to "report changes in laws within its jurisdiction sufficient to reduce outlays by $33,000,000 in FY2006, and $2,658,000,000 for the period of fiscal years 2006 through 2010." This resolution assumed that the committee would report legislation to open ANWR to development, and that leasing would generate $2.5 billion in revenues for the federal government over five years. An amendment (S.Amdt. 168) on March 16 to remove these instructions was defeated (yeas 49, nays 51, Roll Call #52). The House FY2006 budget resolution (H.Con.Res. 95, H.Rept. 109-17), while instructing the House Resources Committee to provide somewhat smaller reductions in outlays, did not include assumptions about ANWR revenues.

The conference agreement (H.Con.Res. 95, H.Rept. 109-62) approved by the House and Senate on April 28, 2005, contained reductions in spending targets of $2.4 billion over FY2006 to FY2010 for the House Resources and Senate Energy Committees that would be difficult to achieve unless ANWR development legislation were passed. The inclusion of the Senate target particularly set the stage for including ANWR development legislation in a reconciliation bill, since reconciliation bills cannot be filibustered (i.e., they require only a simple majority, rather than 60 votes to invoke cloture).

Under the Congressional Budget Act of 1974 (CBA, Titles I-IX of P.L. 93-344, as amended, 2 U.S.C. §§601-688), while the target reductions of the budget resolutions are binding on the committees, the associated assumptions are not. The Senate Energy and Natural Resources Committee did choose to meet its target by recommending ANWR legislation, and the Budget Committee incorporated the recommendation as Title IV of S. 1932, the Deficit Reduction Act of 2005.[2] The House Resources Committee included ANWR legislation, and other spending reductions and offsetting collections, thereby more than meeting the Committee's targets. These measures were incorporated by the House Budget Committee into an omnibus reconciliation bill. However, before the House bill came to the floor, considerable opposition to the ANWR provision developed among a number of Republicans, 24 of whom signed a letter to the Speaker opposing its inclusion. The provision was removed before floor consideration; S. 1932 (with the text of H.R. 4241 inserted in lieu — minus an ANWR provision) passed the House on November 18, 2005 (yeas 217, Nays 215; Roll call #601). ANWR was a major issue in conference. In the end, the conference report (H.Rept. 109-362) omitted ANWR development, and the President signed the measure on February 8, 2006 (P.L. 109-171).

ANWR in the Defense Appropriations Bill. As Congress moved toward the December recess, and the chance of an agreement on reconciliation with an ANWR provision seemed to fade, Senator Stevens (Chair of the Defense Appropriations Subcommittee) added an ANWR development title to the "must-pass" FY2006 Defense appropriations bill (H.R. 2863) in conference. Senators opposing ANWR were forced to choose between filibuster of the popular measure or acquiescing to opening the Refuge. Members began a filibuster, and a cloture motion failed (yeas 56, nays 44, Roll Call #364). While the conference report was approved, the relevant two Divisions (C and D) were removed through House and Senate passage of S.Con.Res. 74, correcting the enrollment of the bill (P.L. 109-148).

Omnibus Energy Legislation. The House Resources Committee considered and marked up its portion of the omnibus energy bill on April 13, 2005, before the bill was introduced. The provisions approved by the committee were then incorporated into the House version of H.R. 6, introduced on April 18. The House passed H.R. 6 on April 21 (yeas 249, nays 183, Roll Call #132). The Senate passed its version of H.R. 6 on June 28, 2005 (yeas 85, nays 12, Roll Call #158). The Senate version contained no ANWR development provisions. The ANWR title was omitted in the final measure (P.L. 109-58).

Actions in the 109th Congress, Second Session. The Senate passed the FY2007 budget resolution (S.Con.Res. 83; yeas 51, nays 49, Roll Call #74; no written report) on March 16, 2006. Its sole reconciliation instruction (§201) directs the Committee on Energy and Natural Resources to reduce budget authority by an amount equal to predicted bonus bids, royalties, and rental revenues from ANWR development. According to press reports, Senators hoped that such a reconciliation bill, perhaps with ANWR as its sole subject, might lead to sufficient bipartisan support in the House to counterbalance opposition of the 24 Republican Members who opposed its inclusion in a larger reconciliation measure in the first session. The House Budget Committee did not include such an instruction in its budget resolution (H.Con.Res. 376, H.Rept. 109-402) on March 29, 2006, and to date the House has not passed a budget resolution.

The Energy Resource

The developed parts of Alaska's North Slope suggest promise for ANWR's prospects. Oil-bearing strata extend eastward from structures in the National Petroleum Reserve-Alaska through the Prudhoe Bay field, and may continue into and through ANWR's 1002 area.

Oil. Estimates of ANWR oil potential, both old and new, depend upon limited data and numerous assumptions about geology and economics. Recent interest has centered especially on parts of the 1002 area west and north of the Marsh Creek anticline, an area which comprises roughly a third of the 1002 area. (See **Figure 5** in CRS Report RL31278.) The most recent government geologic study of oil and natural gas prospects in ANWR, completed in 1998 by the USGS,[3] found an excellent chance (95%) that at least 11.6 billion bbl of oil are *present* on federal lands in the 1002 area. (For comparison, annual U.S. oil consumption from all sources is about 7.5 billion bbl.)

But the amount that would be *economically* recoverable depends on the price of oil, and crude oil prices have increased substantially in the last two years, bringing roughly $70 per barrel in the futures market in mid-May 2006. In its latest assessment, USGS estimated that, at $55/bbl in 2003 dollars, there is a 95% chance that 3.9 billion bbl or more could be economically recovered and a 5% chance of 10.7 billion bbl or more.[4] These estimates reflect field development practices introduced and cost and price changes since USGS's 1998 assessment. Roughly one-third more oil may be under adjacent state waters and Native lands — areas that could be difficult to develop economically without access through federal land or a lifting of the statutory prohibition on oil and gas development in the Refuge.

The U.S. Energy Information Administration estimated that, at a relatively fast development rate, production would peak 15-20 years after the start of development, with maximum daily production rates of roughly 0.015% of the resource. Production at the slower rate would peak about 25 years after the start of development, at a daily rate equal to about 0.0105% of the resource. Peak production associated with a *technically* recoverable resource of 5.0 billion bbl at the faster development rate would be 750,000 bbl per day, roughly 4% of current U.S. petroleum consumption (about 20.5 million bbl per day). (For economic impacts of development, see CRS Report RS21030, *ANWR Development: Economic Impacts*, by Bernard A. Gelb.)

Natural Gas. Large quantities of natural gas are also estimated to be in the 1002 area. Being able to sell this gas probably would enhance prospects of the 1002 area and the rest of the North Slope — oil as well as gas. However, there currently is no way to deliver the gas to market. Higher gas prices in the last few years increased interest in the construction of a pipeline to transport natural gas from the North Slope to North American markets —directly and/or via shipment in liquefied form in tankers. The 108th Congress acted to facilitate such a pipeline (P.L. 108-324).

Advanced Technologies. As North Slope development proceeded after the initial discovery at Prudhoe Bay, oil field operators developed less environmentally intrusive ways to develop arctic oil, primarily through innovations in technology. New drilling bits and fluids and advanced forms of drilling — such as extended reach, horizontal, and "designer" wells — permit drilling to reach laterally far beyond a drill platform, with the current record being seven miles at one site in China. (See CRS Report RL31022, *Arctic Petroleum Technology Developments*, by Bernard A. Gelb, M. Lynne Corn, and Terry R. Twyman, for more information.)

Reducing the footprints of development has been a major goal of development. Improved ice-based transportation infrastructure can serve remote areas during the exploratory drilling phase on insulated ice pads. However, for safety reasons, use of ice roads and pads may be limited in the more hilly terrain of the 1002 area; gravel structures could be required for greater safety. In addition to ice technology, industry has been experimenting with essentially modified offshore platforms mounted on supporting legs to hold exploration rigs above the tundra. These rigs may offer access for exploration in areas lacking sufficient water or too hilly to permit ice technology. At the same time, warming trends in arctic latitudes have already shortened winter access across the tundra and led to changes in the standards for use of ice roads; if these trends continue, heavy reliance on ice technology could be infeasible. Rigid adherence to ice technology (instead of gravel construction) might put some marginal fields out of reach due to the high cost of exploration, development, or operation. Accelerated warming in polar areas is also making ice technology problematic and might force greater reliance on gravel structures. Moreover, fields that begin with few roads may expand their gravel road network as the field expands.

Because it is held as a model of modern development, the history of the Alpine field, located along the border of the National Petroleum Reserve-Alaska (NPRA) west of Prudhoe Bay, is relevant. Run by ConocoPhillips, it was considered innovative because of the short road connecting the two initial pads, and the lack of connection with the remainder of North Slope development, except in winter via ice road. However, with the approval of five additional pads, the expansion of the field will add roughly 27.5 miles of gravel roads to the existing 3 miles of roads, and create 1,845 acres of disturbed soils, including 316 acres of gravel mines or gravel structures.[5] Approximately 150 miles of roads would be constructed if the field were fully developed. If ANWR development follows a similar pattern, it is unclear whether energy development could be held to a stringent limit on road or other gravel construction and still allow producers to have access to otherwise economic fields.

Proponents of opening ANWR note that these technologies would mitigate the environmental impact of petroleum operations, but not eliminate it. Opponents maintain that facilities of any size would still be industrial sites and would change the character of the coastal plain, in part because the sites would be spread out in the 1002 area and connected by pipelines and (probably) roads.

A March 2003 report by the National Academy of Sciences (NAS) highlighted impacts of existing development at Prudhoe Bay on arctic ecosystems. Among the harmful environmental impacts noted were changes in the migration of bowhead whales, in distribution and reproduction of caribou, and in populations of predators and scavengers that prey on birds. NAS noted beneficial economic and social effects of oil development in northern Alaska and credited industry for its strides in decreasing or mitigating environmental impacts. It also said that some social and economic impacts have not been beneficial. The NAS report specifically avoided determining whether any beneficial effects were outweighed by harmful effects.

The Biological Resources

The FLEIS rated the Refuge's biological resources highly: "The Arctic Refuge is the only conservation system unit that protects, in an undisturbed condition, a complete spectrum of the arctic ecosystems in North America" (p. 46). It also said "The 1002 area is the most biologically productive part of the Arctic Refuge for wildlife and is the center of wildlife activity" (p. 46). The biological value of the 1002 area rests on the intense productivity in the short arctic summer; many species arrive or awake from dormancy to take advantage of this richness, and leave or become dormant during the remainder of the year. Caribou have long been the center of the debate over the biological impacts of Refuge development, but other species have also been at issue. Among the other species most frequently mentioned are polar bears, musk oxen, and the 135 species of migratory birds that breed or feed there. (For more information on biological resources of the 1002 area, see CRS Report RL31278.)

An updated assessment of the array of biological resources in the coastal plain was published in 2002 by the Biological Research Division of USGS.[6] The report analyzed new information about caribou, musk oxen, snow geese and other species in the Arctic Refuge, and concluded that development impacts would be significant. A follow-up memo[7] on caribou by one of the authors to the Director of USGS clarified that if development were restricted to the western portion of the refuge (an option that was being considered by the

Administration), the PCH would not be affected during the early calving period, since the herd is not normally found in the area at that time. Any impacts that might occur when the herd subsequently moves into the area were not discussed in the memo.

FWS has recently begun a review to determine whether polar bears should be listed as threatened under the Endangered Species Act (71 *Fed. Reg.* 6745, Feb. 9, 2006). Among the information to be considered are the effects of accelerated polar climate change on polar bears and their prey (primarily seals), threats to denning habitat, and effects of oil and gas development. The listing of polar bears could have a significant impact on energy development in ANWR, since the FLEIS stressed the unusual importance of the 1002 area as a location for dens of pregnant female polar bears.

In a larger context, many opponents of development see the central issue as whether the area should be maintained as an intact ecosystem — off limits to development — not whether development can be accomplished in an environmentally sound manner. In terms that emphasize deeply held values, supporters of wilderness designation argue that few places as untrammeled as the 1002 area remain on the planet, and fewer still on the same magnificent scale. Any but the most transitory intrusions (e.g., visits for recreation, hunting, fishing, subsistence use, research) would, in their view, damage the integrity and the "sense of wonder" they see in the area. The mere knowledge that a pristine place exists, regardless of whether one ever visits it, can be important to those who view the debate in this light.

Major Legislative Issues in the 109th Congress

Some of the issues that have been raised most frequently in the current ANWR debate are described briefly below. In addition to the issue of whether development should be permitted at all, key aspects of the current debate include restrictions that might be specified in legislation, including the physical size — or footprints — of development; the regulation of activities on Native lands; the disposition of revenues; labor issues; oil export restrictions; compliance with the National Environmental Policy Act, and other matters. (References below to the "Secretary" refer to the Secretary of the Interior, unless stated otherwise.) The analysis below describes the ANWR title (the "House bill") of the reconciliation recommendations as submitted by the House Committee on Resources (and later dropped before floor consideration), the provisions of Division C of the conference report on H.R. 2863 (the "Defense bill"), and §4001 of S. 1932, the Senate reconciliation bill (the "Senate bill"). Because of the lack of detail in §4001, many aspects of ANWR leasing would be left to administrative decisions, with levels of public participation in some instances curtailed along with judicial review, as noted below.

Environmental Direction. If Congress authorizes development, it could address environmental matters in several ways. Congress could impose a higher standard of environmental protection because the 1002 area is in a national wildlife refuge or because of the fragility of the arctic environment, or it could legislate a lower standard to facilitate development. The choice of administering agency and the degree of discretion given to it could also affect the approaches to environmental protection. For example, Congress could make either FWS or BLM the lead agency. It could include provisions requiring use of "the best available technology" or "the best commercially available technology" or some other general standard. Congress could also limit judicial review of some or all of a development program, including standards and implementation.

The House bill as reported would have named BLM as the lead agency. Section 6107(a) would require the Secretary to administer the leasing program so as to "result in no significant adverse effect on fish and wildlife, their habitat, and the environment, [and to require] the application of the best commercially available technology...." Section 6103(a)(2) would also have required that this program be done "in a manner that ensures the receipt of fair market value by the public for the mineral resources to be leased." It is unclear how the two goals of environmental protection and fair market value are to relate to each other (e.g., if environmental restrictions might make some fields uneconomic). Subsections 6106(a)(3) and (5) would require lessees to be responsible and liable for reclamation of lands within the Coastal Plain (unless the Secretary approves other arrangements), and the lands must support pre-leasing uses or a higher use approved by the Secretary. There were requirements for mitigation, development of regulations, and other measures to protect the environment. These included prohibitions on public access to service roads, and other transportation restrictions. Other provisions might also affect environmental protection. (See "Judicial Review," below.) The Defense bill (§7) was similar to the House bill. The Senate bill (§4001(b)(1)(B)) directed the Secretary to establish and implement an "environmentally sound" leasing system, but did not provide further direction.

The Size of Footprints. Newer technologies permit greater consolidation of leasing operations, which tends to reduce the size and the environmental impacts of development. One aspect of the debate in Congress has focused on the size of the footprints in the development and production phases of energy leasing. The term *footprint* does not have a universally accepted definition, and therefore the types of structures falling under a "footprint restriction" are arguable (e.g., the inclusion of exploratory structures, roads, gravel mines, port facilities, etc.). (See CRS Report RL32108, *North Slope Infrastructure and the ANWR Debate*, by M. Lynne Corn.) In addition, it is unclear whether exploratory structures, or structures on Native lands, would be included under any provision limiting footprints. (See CRS Report RS22143, *Oil and Gas Leasing in the Arctic National Wildlife Refuge (ANWR): The 2,000-Acre Limit*, by Pamela Baldwin and M. Lynne Corn, for a discussion of an acreage limit.) The new map accompanying the Senate bill includes the Native lands in the Coastal Plain leasing area, but how the federal leasing program will apply to those lands is not clear. See *New Maps*, below.

Development advocates have emphasized a limit on the acreage of surface disturbance, while opponents have emphasized the dispersal of not only the structures themselves but also their impacts over much of the 1.5 million acres of the 1002 area. One single consolidated facility of 2,000 acres (3.1 square miles) would not permit full development of the 1002 area. Instead, full development of the 1002 area would require that facilities, even if limited to 2,000 acres in total surface area, be widely dispersed. Dispersal is necessary due to the limits of lateral (or extended reach) drilling: the current North Slope record for this technology is 4 miles. If that record were matched on all sides of a single pad, at most about 4% of the Coastal Plain could be developed from that pad. Even if the current world record (seven miles) were matched, only about 11% of the 1002 area could be accessed from a single compact 2,000-acre facility. In addition, drilling opponents argue that energy facilities have impacts on recreation, subsistence, vegetation, and wildlife well beyond areas actually covered by development.

The House bill as reported (§6107(d)(9)) would have provided for consolidation of leasing operations to reduce environmental impacts of development. House §6107(a)(3) further would have required, "consistent with the provisions of section 6103" (which include ensuring receipt of fair market value for mineral resources), that the Secretary administer the leasing program to "ensure that the maximum amount of surface acreage covered by production and support facilities, including airstrips and any areas covered by gravel berms or piers for the support of pipelines, does not exceed 2,000 acres on the Coastal Plain." The terms used were not defined in the bill and therefore the range of structures covered by the restriction is arguable (e.g., whether roads, gravel mines, causeways, and water treatment plants would be included under this provision). In addition, the wording may not apply to structures built during the exploratory phase. An essentially identical provision (§4001(f)) is found in the Senate bill and the Defense bill (§7(a)(3)). The Defense bill also called for facility consolidation (§7(d)(4)) and for the Secretary to develop a consolidation plan (§7(f)).

Native Lands. ANCSA resolved aboriginal claims against the United States by (among other things) creating Village Corporations that could select surface lands and Regional Corporations that could select surface and subsurface rights as well. Kaktovik Inupiat Corporation (KIC) selected surface lands (originally approximately three townships) on the coastal plain of ANWR, but these KIC lands were administratively excluded from being considered as within the administratively defined "1002 Coastal Plain." A fourth township was added by ANILCA, and is within the defined Coastal Plain. The four townships, totaling approximately 92,000 acres, are all within the Refuge and subject to its regulations. The Arctic Slope Regional Corporation (ASRC) obtained subsurface rights beneath the KIC lands pursuant to a 1983 land exchange agreement. In addition, there are currently thousands of acres of conveyed or claimed individual Native allotments in the 1002 area that are not expressly subject to its regulations. Were oil and gas development authorized for the federal lands in the Refuge, development would then be allowed or become feasible on the nearly 100,000 acres of Native lands, possibly free of any acreage limitation applying to development on the federal lands, depending on how legislation is framed. The extent to which the Native lands could be regulated to protect the environment is uncertain, given the status of allotments and some of the language in the 1983 Agreement with ASRC. None of the current bills address development on the Native lands in ANWR. (See also CRS Report RL31115, and *New Maps*, below.)

New Maps. Both the House and Senate have created new maps of the "Coastal Plain" that will be the subject of leasing. (See CRS Report RS22326, *Legislative Maps of ANWR*, by M. Lynne Corn and Pamela Baldwin (hereafter cited as "CRS Report RL22326").) The Coastal Plain was defined in §1002 of ANILCA as the area indicated on an August, 1980 map. This map is now missing. An administrative articulation of the boundary was authorized by §103(b) of ANILCA, and has the force of law. This legal description was completed in 1983 (48 Fed. Reg. 16838), but questions also surround this description. (See CRS Report RL31115.) The description excluded three Native townships from the articulated Coastal Plain. Some bills in various Congresses also have excluded these same Native lands by referring to the 1980 map and the administrative description. However, if the 1980 map is missing, evaluating whether the administrative description properly excluded the Native lands is impossible, and, as noted, the fourth Native township (selected later) was not excluded from the Coastal Plain by that description.

The Senate Energy Committee bill (§4001(a)) provided a new map, dated September 2005, to accompany its submission to the Budget Committee for reconciliation. This map includes all Native lands in the "Coastal Plain"(see Figure 1 in CRS Report RS22326). However, the bill text remains unchanged and it is not clear what extent of federal control of Native lands was intended or accomplished by the map change. For example, language is retained that "notwithstanding any other provision of law" directs a 50/50 revenue split between the state of Alaska and the federal government, thereby possibly giving rise to Native claims for compensation for revenues from their lands. If this provision was not intended to apply to Native lands, it is not clear whether other provisions also might not apply. Also, some of the terms in the 1983 Agreement call for an express congressional override to negate their effects, and the text of the bill does not discuss the Native lands. The Defense bill also used a USGS map dated September 2005 (§2(4)); it is not clear whether the map is the same as the one referred to in the Senate bill.

The House also adopted a new map, dated October 25, 2005. It appears to follow the 1983 administrative articulation of the Coastal Plain — it excludes the three Native townships, but leaves the fourth within the Coastal Plain to which the leasing provisions would arguably apply.

Revenue Disposition. Another issue is whether Congress may validly provide for a disposition of revenues formula other than the 90% state - 10% federal split mentioned in the Alaska Statehood Act. A court in *Alaska v. United States* (35 Fed. Cl. 685, 701 (1996)) indicated that the language in the Statehood Act means that Alaska is to be treated like other states for federal leasing *conducted under the Mineral Leasing Act* (MLA), which contains (basically) a 90%- 10% split. Arguably Congress can establish a *non-MLA* leasing regimen — for example, the separate leasing arrangements that govern the National Petroleum Reserve-Alaska, where the revenue sharing formula is 50/50, but this issue was not before the court in this case and hence remains an open issue.

Several sections of the House bill as reported related to revenues. Section 6109 would have provided that 50% of adjusted revenues be paid to Alaska, and the balance be deposited in the U.S. Treasury as miscellaneous receipts, except for a portion to assist Alaska communities in addressing local impacts of energy development. Under §6103(a), the Secretary was to establish and implement a leasing program *under the Mineral Leasing Act*, yet "notwithstanding any other provision of law," §6112 directed a revenue sharing program different from that in the MLA. Given the wording of the Alaska Statehood Act, establishing a leasing program "under the MLA," yet providing for a different revenue disposition, could raise validity questions. If a court struck down the revenue-splitting provision, the court would then have to determine if that provision was *severable* — whether Congress would have enacted the rest of the statute without the flawed provision. If a court both struck down the revenue-sharing provision and found it to be severable, then Alaska could receive 90% of ANWR revenues. In a different subtitle, §6514 would create the Federal Energy Natural Resources Enhancement Fund and apply a portion of moneys received under the revenues section of the MLA to certain wildlife and habitat purposes. It is not clear whether moneys from ANWR leasing would be eligible for this use, since leasing in ANWR, while under the MLA, would have special revenue-splitting provisions.

The Senate bill does not expressly state that leasing would be under the MLA. "Notwithstanding any other provision of law," it directs receipts from leasing and operations "authorized under this section" to be divided equally between the state of Alaska and the federal government. This wording may avoid a conflict with the Alaska Statehood Act. Because of the change in the Senate definition of "Coastal Plain" and the accompanying map, the bill may include revenues from Native lands in the 50/50 split. The Defense bill (Division D, §1) also provided for a 50/50 split, and the Division contained various provisions for distribution of certain percentages of the federal share to various purposes, including hurricane relief. In addition, §14 of Division C contained a severability provision that provided explicitly that if any portion of either Division C or D were held to be *unconstitutional*, the remainder of the two divisions would not be affected. It is not clear to what provisions the severability language might apply. As discussed, there may be validity issues regarding the revenue split, but those issues may rest on contractual interpretations, rather than constitutional concerns. However, if ANWR development is a part of a revenue-raising bill and the 50/50 revenue split were struck down, Alaska would receive 90% of the ANWR revenues and fewer federal funds would be available for programs premised on the 50% federal share. In these circumstances, a court might address the severability issue aside from the constitutional context.

Project Labor Agreements (PLAs). A recurring issue in federal and federally funded projects is whether project owners or contractors should be required, by agreement, to use union workers. PLAs establish the terms and conditions of work that will apply for the particular project, and may also specify a source to supply the craft workers. Proponents of PLAs, including construction and other unions, argue that PLAs ensure a reliable, efficient labor source, help keep costs down and ensure access for union members to federal and federally funded projects. Opponents, including nonunion firms and their supporters, believe that PLAs inflate costs, reduce competition, and unfairly restrict access to those projects. There is little independent information to sort out the conflicting assertions.

The House bill (§6106(b)) as reported would have directed the Secretary to require lessees in the 1002 area to "negotiate to obtain a project labor agreement" — "recognizing the Government's proprietary interest in labor stability and the ability of construction labor and management to meet the particular needs and conditions of projects to be developed...."

The Defense bill (§6(b)) contained similar provisions, but the Senate bill had no similar provision.

Oil Export Restrictions. Export of North Slope oil in general, and any ANWR oil in particular, has been an issue, beginning at least with the authorization of the Trans Alaska Pipeline System (TAPS) and continuing into the current ANWR debate. The Trans Alaska Pipeline Authorization Act (P.L. 93-153, 43 U.S.C.§1651 et seq.) specified that oil shipped through it could be exported, but only under restrictive conditions. When California prices fell in the mid-1990s, causing complaints from California and North Slope producers, Congress amended the MLA to provide that oil transported through the pipeline may be exported unless the President finds, after considering stated criteria, that exports are *not* in the national interest (P.L. 104-58, 30 U.S.C. §185(s)). North Slope exports rose to a peak of 74,000 bbl/day in 1999, or 7% of North Slope production. These exports ceased voluntarily in May 2000, and have since been minimal. If Congress wished to limit export of oil from the 1002 area by applying the restriction to oil transported through TAPS, the restriction might not be effective. Oil shipment via tanker could become practical if current warming trends in the Arctic continue and if crude oil prices provide sufficient incentive.

Recent proposed bans on export of ANWR oil have not been tied to shipment through TAPS. The House bill as reported (§6106(a)(8)) would have prohibited any export of oil produced in the 1002 area as a condition of a lease. The Senate bill (§4001(g) contained a similar provision, as did the Defense bill (§12). However, inasmuch as other North Slope oil is allowed to be exported, it would appear that prohibiting the export of ANWR oil could be moot: producers aiming to tap the export market would substitute other North Slope oil to meet the demand.

NEPA Compliance. The National Environmental Policy Act of 1969 (NEPA, P.L. 91-190; 43 U.S.C. §§4321-4347) requires the preparation of an environmental impact statement (EIS) to examine major federal actions with significant effects on the environment, and to provide public involvement in agency decisions. The last full EIS examining the effects of leasing development in ANWR was completed in 1987, and some observers assert that a new EIS is needed to support development now. NEPA requires an EIS to analyze an array of alternatives, including a "no action" alternative. Some development supporters would like to see the process truncated, in light of past analyses and to hasten production. Development opponents, and NEPA supporters, argue that the 19-year gap and changed circumstances since the last analysis necessitates a thorough update, and stress the flaws they found in the 1987 FLEIS.

Section 6103(c) of the House bill as reported would have deemed the 1987 FLEIS to satisfy NEPA requirements with respect to prelease activities and the development and promulgation of leasing regulations, and requires the Secretary to prepare an EIS of all other actions authorized by the subtitle before the first lease sale. Consideration of alternatives is to be limited to two choices, a preferred leasing action and a "single leasing alternative." (Generally, an EIS must analyze several alternatives, including a "no action" alternative.) Compliance with the subsection is deemed to satisfy all requirements to analyze the environmental effects of proposed leasing. The Defense bill (Division C, §3(c)) was essentially identical. S. 1932 (§4001(c)) had similar provisions, but did not expressly require an EIS for leasing.

Compatibility with Refuge Purposes. Under current law for the management of national wildlife refuges (16 U.S.C.§668dd), and under 43 C.F.R. §3101.5-3 for Alaskan refuges specifically, an activity may be allowed in a refuge only if it is compatible with the purposes of the particular Refuge and with those of the Refuge System as a whole. Section 6103(c) of the House bill as reported, the Defense bill (§3(c)), and §4001(c) of S. 1932 state that the energy leasing program and activities in the coastal plain are deemed to be compatible with the purposes for which ANWR was established and that no further findings or decisions are required to implement this determination. This language appears to eliminate the usual compatibility determination processes. The extent of leasing "activities" that might be included as compatible is debatable and arguably might encompass necessary support activities, such as construction and operation of port facilities, staging areas, and personnel centers.

Judicial Review. Leasing proponents urge that any ANWR leasing program be put in place promptly and argue that expediting, curtailing, or prohibiting judicial review is desirable to achieve that goal. Judicial review can be expedited through procedural changes such as reducing the time limits within which suits must be filed, avoiding some level of review, curtailing the scope of the review, or increasing the burden imposed on challengers. The House bill as reported (§6108) required that any complaints seeking judicial review be filed within 90 days. Sections 6108(a)(1) and (a)(2) appeared to contradict each other as to whether suits are to be filed in "any appropriate district court" or in the Court of Appeals in

Washington, DC. The Defense bill (§8(a)) specified the latter. The House bill (§6108(a)(3)) would also have limited the scope of review by stating that review of a secretarial decision, including environmental analyses, would be limited to whether the Secretary complied with the terms of the ANWR subtitle, that it would be based on the administrative record, and that the Secretary's analysis of environmental effects is "presumed to be correct unless shown otherwise by clear and convincing evidence to the contrary." This standard is unclear, but in this context arguably would make overturning a decision more difficult. S. 1932 and the Defense bill are similar, but required complaints to be filed only in the U.S. Court of Appeals in Washington, DC (§4001(c) and §8(a) respectively). The Senate bill omitted the presumption concerning the Secretary's analysis of environmental effects.

Special Areas. Some have supported setting aside certain areas in the coastal plain for protection of their ecological or cultural values. This could be done by designating the areas specifically in legislation, or by authorizing the Secretary to set aside areas to be selected after enactment. The FLEIS identified four special areas that together total more than 52,000 acres. The Secretary could be required to restrict or prevent development in these areas or any others that may seem significant, or to select among areas if an acreage limitation on such set-asides is imposed. The House bill as reported (§6103(e)) would have allowed the Secretary to set aside up to 45,000 acres (and names one specific special area) in which leases, if permitted, would forbid surface occupancy. As mentioned above, the FLEIS identified four special areas that together total more than 52,000 acres, so the Secretary would be required to select among these areas or any others that may seem significant. Section 6103(f) also stated that the closure authority in the ANWR title is to be the Secretary's sole authority, which might limit possible secretarial actions under the Endangered Species Act. The Defense bill (§3(e)) was essentially identical. The Senate bill had no provision for special areas.

Non-Development Options. Several options are available to Congress that would either postpone or forbid development, unless Congress were to change the law. These options include allowing exploration only, designating the 1002 area as wilderness, and taking no action. Some have argued that the 1002 area should be opened to exploration first, before a decision is made on whether to proceed to leasing. Those with this view hold that with greater certainty about any energy resources in the area, a better decision could be made about opening some or all of the 1002 area for leasing. This idea has had little support over the years because various interests see insufficient gain from such a proposal. (CRS Report RL31278 discusses the pros and cons of this approach.)

Another option is wilderness designation. Energy development is not permitted in wilderness areas, unless there are pre-existing rights or unless Congress specifically allows it or reverses the designation. Wilderness designation would tend to preserve existing recreational opportunities and related jobs, as well as the existing level of protection of subsistence resources, including the Porcupine Caribou Herd. Under ANILCA and the 1983 Agreement, development of the surface and subsurface holdings of Native corporations in the Refuge is precluded as long as oil and gas development is not allowed on the federal lands in the Refuge. Because current law prohibits development unless Congress acts, the no action option also prevents energy development. Those supporting delay often argue that not enough is known about either the probability of discoveries or about the environmental impact if development is permitted. Others argue that oil deposits should be saved for an unspecified "right time." H.R. 567 and S. 261 would designate the 1002 area as part of the National Wilderness System.

LEGISLATION

P.L. 109-58 (H.R. 6, Barton)

An omnibus energy act; Title XXII opens ANWR coastal plain to energy development. Introduced April 18, 2005; considered and marked up by Committee on Resources April 13, 2005 (no report). Considered by House April 20-21, 2005. Markey/Johnson amendment (H.Amdt. 73) to strike ANWR title rejected (yeas 200, nays 231, Roll Call #122) April 20. Passed April 21, 2005 (yeas 249, nays 183, Roll Call #132). Passed Senate, with no ANWR development provision, June 28, 2005 (yeas 85, nays 12, Roll Call #158). Conference agreement omits ANWR title; signed by the President August 8, 2005.

P.L. 109-148 (H.R. 2863)

Provides for Defense appropriations. Conference report (H.Rept. 109-359) filed December 18, 2005 (Division C & D provided for ANWR development and revenue disposition). Cloture motion on filibuster on ANWR provision failed December 21, 2005 (yeas 56, nays 44, Roll Call #364). S.Con.Res. 74 corrected enrollment of the bill to delete Divisions C and D. Passed Senate December 21, 2005 (yeas 48, nays 45, Roll Call. #365). Passed House December 22, 2005 on voice vote. Signed by President, December 30, 2005.

P.L. 109-171 (S. 1932)

Omnibus budget reconciliation; Title IV would have provided for ANWR development. Introduced, referred to Committee on Budget, and reported October 27, 2005 (no written report). Passed Senate November 3, 2005 (yeas 52, nays 47, Roll Call #303). Passed House (amended) November 18, 2005. (For House action, see also H.R. 4241.) Title IV dropped in conference. House approved conference report (H.Rept. 109-362; yeas 212, nays 206, Roll Call #670). Senate approved report with an amendment (yeas 51, nays 50, Roll Call #363), December 21, 2005. House agreed to Senate amendment (yeas 216, nays 214, Roll Call #4), February 1, 2006. Signed by President, February 8, 2006.

H.Con.Res. 95 (Nussle)

FY2006 budget resolution, included spending targets for Committee on Resources. Introduced, referred to Committee on Budget, and reported March 11, 2005 (H.Rept. 109-17). Passed House March 17, 2005 (yeas 218, nays 214, Roll Call #88). Passed (amended) Senate in lieu of S.Con.Res. 18 (no report). April 28, 2005, House approved conference report (H.Rept. 109-62; yeas 214, nays 211, Roll Call #149), and Senate approved conference report (yeas 52, nays 47, Roll Call #114).

H.Con.Res. 376 (Nussle)

FY2007 budget resolution, included spending targets for Committee on Resources. Introduced, referred to Committee on Budget, and reported March 31, 2006 (H.Rept. 109-402). Considered by Committee of Whole House April 6, 2006.

H.R. 4241 (Nussle)

FY2006 budget reconciliation. Title to open ANWR struck before floor consideration. Introduced November 7, 2005; passed House November 18, 2005 (yeas 217, nays 215, Roll Call #601). Inserted in lieu of the text of S. 1932.

S.Con.Res. 18 (Gregg)

FY2006 budget resolution; includes spending targets for Committee on Energy and Natural Resources. Introduced January 31, 2005; referred to Committee on Budget. Reported March 10, 2005 (no written report). Cantwell amendment (S.Amdt. 168, relating to ANWR) defeated March 16, 2005 (yeas 49, nays 51, Roll Call #52). Passed Senate March 17, 2005 (yeas 51, nays 49, Roll Call #81). Senate incorporated measure in H.Con.Res. 95 as an amendment; passed H.Con.Res. 95 in lieu.

S.Con.Res. 83 (Gregg)

FY2007 budget resolution; direction for cuts in mandatory spending targets only for Committee on Energy and Natural Resources. Introduced and reported by Committee on Budget on March 10, 2006 (no written report). Passed Senate March 16, 2006 (yeas 51, nays 49, Roll Call #74).

For Additional Reading

National Academies of Science. *Cumulative Environmental Effects of Oil and Gas Activities on Alaska's North Slope* (March 2003). 452 p. (See [http://www.nas.edu/].)

Nellemann, C. and R. D. Cameron. *Cumulative Impacts of an Evolving Oil-field Complex on the Distribution of Calving Caribou.* Canadian Jour. of Zoology. 1998. Vol. 76, p.1425.

U.S. Department of the Interior. Bureau of Land Management. *Overview of the 1991 Arctic National Wildlife Refuge Recoverable Petroleum Resource Update.* Washington, DC, April 8, 1991. 2 maps.

U.S. Department of the Interior. Fish and Wildlife Service, Geological Survey, and Bureau of Land Management. *Arctic National Wildlife Refuge, Alaska, Coastal Plain Resource Assessment.* Report and Recommendation to the Congress of the United States and Final Legislative Environmental Impact Statement. Washington, DC, 1987.

U.S. Department of the Interior. Geological Survey. *The Oil and Gas Resource Potential of the Arctic National Wildlife Refuge 1002 Area, Alaska.* 1999. 2 CD set. USGS Open File Report 98-34.

U.S. Department of the Interior. Geological Survey. *Arctic Refuge Coastal Plain Terrestrial Wildlife Research Summaries.* Biological Science Report USGS/BRD/BSR-2002-0001.

U.S. Department of the Interior. Geological Survey. "Evaluation of additional potential development scenarios for the 1002 Area of the Arctic National Wildlife Refuge." Memorandum from Brad Griffith, Assistant Leader, Alaska Cooperative Fish and Wildlife Research Unit, to Charles D. Groat, Director, U.S. Geological Survey. April 4, 2002.

U.S. Department of the Interior. Geological Survey. *Economics of 1998 U.S. Geological Survey's 1002 Area Regional Assessment: An Economic Update.* USGS Open File Report 2005-1359. Washington, DC, 2005.

U.S. General Accounting Office. *Arctic National Wildlife Refuge: An Assessment of Interior's Estimate of an Economically Viable Oil Field.* Washington, DC. July, 1993. GAO/RCED-93-130.

U.S. National Energy Policy Development Group. *National Energy Policy.* Washington, DC. May, 2001.

REFERENCES

[1] For more on the budget process and budget enforcement, see CRS Report RS20368, *Overview of the Congressional Budget Process*; and CRS Report 98-815, *Budget Resolution Enforcement*, both by Bill Heniff, Jr. For ANWR and reconciliation, see CRS Report RS22304, *ANWR and FY2006 Budget Reconciliation Legislation*, by Bill Heniff, Jr., and M. Lynne Corn.

[2] There was some question procedurally as to whether Senate rules would permit ANWR legislation to be part of a reconciliation bill. See CRS Report RL30862, *The Budget Reconciliation Process: The Senate's "Byrd Rule"*, by Robert Keith.

[3] U.S. Department of the Interior, Geological Survey (USGS), *The Oil and Gas Potential of the Arctic National Wildlife Refuge 1002 Area, Alaska*, USGS Open File Report 98-34 (Washington, DC: 1999). Summary and Table EA4.

[4] USGS, *Economics of 1998 U.S. Geological Survey's 1002 Area Regional Assessment: An Economic Update,* Open-File Report 2005-1359 (Washington, DC: 2005).

[5] See Figure 2.4.6-1, Alternative F, Preferred Alternative, in Alpine Satellite Development Plan Environmental Impact Statement, Appendix 3, and p. S-8, S-19, and S-30 of Summary, available at [http://www.alpine-satellites-eis.com/alpeis.nsf/?Open], visited on Dec. 13, 2004. Figures given here do not represent full development of the field over the next 20 years.

[6] U.S. Department of the Interior, Geological Survey, *Arctic Refuge Coastal Plain Terrestrial Wildlife Research Summaries*, Biological Science Report, USGS/BRD/BSR-2002-0001.

[7] Griffith, Brad, Memorandum to Director, USGS, "Evaluation of additional potential development scenarios for the 1002 Area of the Arctic National Wildlife Refuge," April 4, 2002.

In: Public Lands: Use and Misuse
Editor: William E. Neeley, pp. 19-35

ISBN: 978-1-60021-352-6

Chapter 2

BUREAU OF LAND MANAGEMENT (BLM) LANDS AND NATIONAL FORESTS*

Ross W. Gorte and Carol Hardy Vincent

SUMMARY

The 109th Congress is considering issues related to the public lands managed by the Bureau of Land Management (BLM) and the national forests managed by the Forest Service (FS). The Administration is addressing issues through budgetary, regulatory, and other actions. Several key issues of congressional and administrative interest are covered here.

Energy Resources. The Energy Policy Act of 2005 affects energy development on federal lands in a variety of ways. Significant new regulations are expected in response to the law, including changes to the federal oil, gas, and coal leasing programs and application of environmental laws to certain energy-related agency actions.

Wild Horses and Burros. Controversial changes to the Wild Free-Roaming Horses and Burros Act of 1971 gave the agencies authority to sell certain old and unadoptable animals and removed the ban on selling wild horses and burros and their remains for commercial products. BLM has resumed animal sales with provisions to prevent their slaughter. Bills have been introduced to overturn the changes (H.R. 297/S. 576) and to foster adoptions and sales (H.R. 2993/S. 1273).

Wilderness. Many wilderness recommendations for federal lands are pending. Questions persist about wilderness review and managing wilderness study areas (WSAs). Bills to designate areas have been introduced, and the 109th Congress may address wilderness review and WSA protection.

Wildfire Protection. President Bush's Healthy Forests Initiative, the Healthy Forests Restoration Act, and other provisions may help protect communities from wildfires by expediting fuel reduction. Some believe that more effort is needed; others are concerned that current and additional streamlining will increase timber sales and damage the environment. Legislation for research and post-fire rehabilitation of federal lands is being considered. The 109th Congress also has held hearings on fire protection and on litigation over fuel treatments and use of fire retardant.

Other Issues. The Administration and Congress are addressing other issues as well, including grazing management, hardrock mining, FS NEPA categorical exclusions, national forest roadless areas, federal land sales, and R.S. 2477 rights of way.

* Excerpted from CRS Report IB10076, Updated May 2, 2006

MOST RECENT DEVELOPMENTS

- The BLM has begun or completed various actions to implement the Energy Policy Act of 2005, including changes to oil and gas lease acreage limits and lease reinstatement petition procedures, a final EIS on wind energy facilities on BLM lands, and a new EIS on tar sands and oil shale leasing.
- On March 29, 2006, the House Resources Committee ordered reported H.R. 4200, to improve research and expedite post-catastrophe forest recovery activities (including timber salvage); the House Agriculture Committee ordered the bill reported on April 5.
- The Administration has sent to Congress draft legislation to sell National Forest System lands, in furtherance of a proposal in the FY2007 budget request for the Forest Service.

BACKGROUND AND ANALYSIS

The Bureau of Land Management (BLM) in the Department of the Interior (DOI) and the Forest Service (FS) in the Department of Agriculture (USDA) manage 454 million acres of land, two-thirds of the land owned by the federal government and one-fifth of the total U.S. land area. The BLM manages 261.5 million acres of land, predominantly in the West. The FS administers 192.5 million acres of federal land, also concentrated in the West.

The BLM and FS have similar management responsibilities for their lands, and many key issues affect both agencies' lands. However, each agency also has unique emphases and functions. For instance, most BLM lands are rangelands, and the BLM administers mineral development on all federal lands. Most federal forests are managed by the FS, and only the FS has a cooperative program to assist nonfederal landowners. Moreover, development of the two agencies has differed, and historically they have focused on different issues.

History of the Bureau of Land Management

For the BLM, many of the issues traditionally center on the agency's responsibilities for land disposal, range management (particularly grazing), and minerals development. These three key functions were assumed by the BLM when it was created in 1946, by the merger of the General Land Office (itself created in 1812) and the U.S. Grazing Service (created in 1934). The General Land Office had helped convey land to settlers and issued leases and administered mining claims on the public lands, among other functions. The U.S. Grazing Service had been established to manage the public lands best suited for livestock grazing under the Taylor Grazing Act of 1934 (TGA, 43 U.S.C. §§315, et seq.).

Congress frequently has debated how to manage federal lands, and whether to retain or dispose of the remaining public lands. In 1976, Congress enacted the Federal Land Policy and Management Act of 1976 (FLPMA, 43 U.S.C. §§1701, et seq.), sometimes called BLM's Organic Act because it consolidated and articulated the agency's responsibilities. Among other provisions, the law establishes a general national policy that the BLM-managed public lands be retained in federal ownership, establishes management of the public lands based on the principles of multiple use and sustained yield, and generally requires that the federal government receive fair market value for the use of public lands and resources. BLM public land management encompasses diverse uses, resources, and values, such as energy and mineral development, timber harvesting, livestock grazing, recreation, wild horses and burros, fish and wildlife habitat, and preservation of natural and cultural resources.

History of the Forest Service

The FS was created in 1905, when forest lands reserved by the President (beginning in 1891) were transferred from DOI into the existing USDA Bureau of Forestry (initially an agency for private forestry assistance and forestry research). Management direction for the national forests, first enacted in 1897 and expanded in 1960, identifies the purposes for which the lands are to be managed and directs "harmonious and coordinated management" to provide for multiple uses and sustained yields of the many resources found in the national forests — including timber, grazing, recreation, wildlife and fish, and water.

Many issues concerning national forest management and use have focused on the appropriate level and location of timber harvesting. In part to address these issues, Congress enacted the National Forest Management Act of 1976 (NFMA; P.L. 94-588) to revise timber sale authorities and to elaborate on considerations and requirements in management plans.

Wilderness protection also is a continuing issue for the FS. The Multiple-Use Sustained-Yield Act of 1960 (16 U.S.C. §528-531) includes wilderness as a use of national forest lands, and possible national forest wilderness areas have been reviewed under the 1964 Wilderness Act as well as in the national forest planning process. Pressures to protect pending wilderness recommendations and other "roadless" areas persist.

Scope of Issue Brief

Many issues affecting BLM and FS lands are similar, and the missions of the agencies are nearly identical. By law, the BLM and FS lands are to be administered for multiple uses, although slightly different uses are specified for each agency. In practice, the land uses considered by the agencies include recreation, range, timber, minerals, watershed, wildlife and fish, and conservation. BLM and FS lands also are required to be managed for sustained yield — a high level of resource outputs in perpetuity, without impairing the productivity of the lands. Further, many issues, programs, and policies affect both agencies. For these reasons, BLM and FS lands often are discussed together, as in this issue brief.

This brief focuses on several issues affecting BLM and FS lands that are of interest to the 109th Congress, and does not comprehensively cover issues primarily affecting other federal lands. For background on federal land management generally, see CRS Report RL32393, *Federal Land Management Agencies: Background on Land and Resources Management*, coordinated by Carol Hardy Vincent. For other information, see the CRS web page at [http://www.crs.gov/].[1]

Energy Resources (by Aaron M. Flynn)

Background. A controversial issue is whether and how to increase access to federal lands for energy and mineral development. A BLM study in 2000 determined that (1) about 165 million acres of federal minerals (24%) have been withdrawn from mineral entry, leasing, and sale, subject to valid existing rights, and (2) mineral development on another 182 million acres (26%) is subject to the approval of the surface management agency and must not be in conflict with land designations and plans. The oil and gas industry contends that entry into currently unavailable areas is necessary to ensure future domestic oil and gas supplies. Opponents maintain that the restricted lands are unique or environmentally sensitive and that the United States could realize equivalent energy gains through conservation and increased exploration elsewhere. (For more, see CRS Report RL33014, *Leasing and Permitting for Oil and Gas Development on Federal Public Domain Lands*, by Aaron M. Flynn and Ryan J. Watson.)

Development of oil, gas, and coal on BLM and FS lands is governed primarily by the Mineral Leasing Act of 1920. Leasing on BLM lands goes through a multi-step approval process. If the minerals are located on FS lands, the FS must perform a leasing analysis and approve leasing decisions for specific lands before BLM may lease minerals. The Energy Policy Act of 2005 (P.L. 109-58) made significant changes to the laws governing federal energy resources, including the management of energy development on BLM and FS lands. Implementation of these changes is discussed below.

Administrative Actions. The Administration has begun to respond to the 2005 Energy Policy Act. For example, BLM is soliciting comments and holding a series of meetings to prepare a report for Congress analyzing agency policy on management of split estates. The report is expected to analyze the rights and responsibilities under existing law of the owner of a mineral lease, the private surface owners, and the federal government. It is also to compare the surface owner consent provisions found in other mining laws to those provisions applicable to federal oil and gas. Finally, the report is to recommend legislative changes necessary to authorize any policy changes the Department wishes to implement.

Pursuant to §352 of the 2005 act, BLM has issued a final rule that may allow the ownership of oil and gas leases covering greater acreages. The law generally limits a single entity to owning leases of up to 246,080 acres in one state. The new regulation exempts the area attributable to producing leases and leases committed to communitization agreements from the overall limitation. A final regulation amending the lease reinstatement petition process has also been issued; now, if a lease is terminated for late or non-payment of rent, a lessee may petition for reinstatement for up to 24 months from the date of termination, an increase from the previous 15-month deadline (71 *Fed. Reg.* 14821, March 24, 2006).

Additionally, in response to §353 and §354 of the Energy Policy Act of 2005, BLM is seeking public comment on two advanced notices of proposed rulemaking. Possible BLM regulations could provide various incentives for development of natural gas hydrates, both onshore and offshore. Others could provide incentives to companies using underground injection of carbon dioxide to increase production from federal oil and gas leases.

BLM has recently completed a final programmatic environmental impact statement (EIS) for developing wind energy facilities on BLM lands (71 *Fed. Reg.* 1768, Jan. 11, 2006). This document will be used to support land management plan amendments providing for wind energy development the western states. The review was undertaken in compliance with

Executive Order 13212 and seeks to comply with congressional directives within the Energy Policy Act of 2005 directing renewable energy development on public lands.

Consistent with §369 of the Energy Policy Act of 2005, BLM has begun a programmatic EIS to support a tar sands and oil shale leasing program for research and development (70 *Fed. Reg.* 73791, Dec. 13, 2005). Regulations to govern this leasing program are also required, and implementation of a commercial leasing program is also underway.

Short of issuing additional regulations, BLM has held meetings and taken a variety of other actions to begin implementation of the Energy Policy Act of 2005, including changes in geothermal leasing (70 *Fed. Reg.* 65933, Nov. 1, 2005) and in oil and gas leasing (70 *Fed. Reg.* 50262, Aug. 26, 2005). Prior to the Energy Policy Act, BLM and FS proposed significant changes to the regulations governing the approval of oil and gas leases (70 *Fed. Reg.* 43349, July 27, 2005). Changes included new requirements for development on split estates, a new approval process for multiple wells based on a single environmental review and Master Development Plan, and additional bonding requirements. The proposal would have also encouraged the use of various best management practices to reduce surface, visual, and wildlife impacts. Because of the passage of the Energy Policy Act, BLM extended the comment period on this proposed rule and may issue a significant revision in the future.

Legislative Activity. On October 7, 2005, the House has passed additional energy policy legislation, the Gasoline for America's Security Act (H.R. 3893). Among other provisions, the bill would require the President to designate federal lands as suitable for refinery construction or expansion and provide an expedited permitting process for refineries sited in the designated area. Additional energy-related legislation has been introduced in response to the Gulf Coast Hurricanes and the ensuing increases in energy prices; various bills (e.g., H.R. 3710, H.R. 4479) would suspend any royalty relief program applicable to oil or natural gas production from federal lands as well as other federal resource production incentives contained in the Energy Policy Act of 2005.

Whether to open the Arctic National Wildlife Refuge (ANWR) to oil and gas development continues to be one of the most contentious issues in the energy debate. Recent efforts to authorize ANWR development through the budget reconciliation process and in the defense appropriations bill were unsuccessful. For more information, see CRS Issue Brief IB10136, *Arctic National Wildlife Refuge (ANWR): Controversies for the 109th Congress*, by M. Lynne Corn. Finally, numerous other bills have been introduced, addressing such issues as geothermal energy access, potash or soda ash royalties, and coal leasing procedures. These bills on specific energy issues are not listed in the "Legislation" section of this report.

Wild Horses and Burros (by Carol Hardy Vincent)

Background. The Wild Free-Roaming Horses and Burros Act of 1971 (16 U.S.C. §§1331, et seq.) seeks to protect wild horses and burros on federal land and places them under the jurisdiction of BLM and the FS. For years, management of wild horses and burros has generated controversy and lawsuits. Controversies include the method of determining the "appropriate management levels" (AMLs) for herd sizes, as the statute requires; whether and how to remove animals from the range to achieve AMLs; alternatives to adoption for reducing animals on the range, particularly fertility control and holding animals in long-term facilities; whether appropriations for managing wild horses and burros are adequate; and the slaughter, or potential for slaughter, of horses. (For background, see CRS Report RS21423, Wild Horse and Burro Issues, by Carol Hardy Vincent)

The 108th Congress enacted changes to wild horse and burro management on federal lands (§142, P.L. 108-447). These changes have intensified controversies. One change directed the agencies to sell, "without limitation," excess animals (or their remains) that essentially are deemed too old (more than 10 years old) or otherwise unable to be adopted (offered unsuccessfully at least three times). Proceeds are to be used for the BLM wild horse and burro adoption program. A second change removed the ban on wild horses and burros and their remains being sold for processing into commercial products. A third change removed criminal penalties for processing into commercial products the remains of a wild horse or burro, if it is sold under the new authority. Also, the law did not expressly prohibit BLM from slaughtering healthy wild horses and burros, as annual appropriations bills had since FY1988. These changes have been supported as providing a cost-effective way to help the agencies achieve AML, to improve the health of the animals, to protect range resources, and to restore a natural ecological balance on federal lands. They have been opposed as potentially leading to the slaughter of healthy animals.

Administrative Actions. On April 25, 2005, BLM suspended sale and delivery of wild horses and burros, due to concerns about the slaughter of some animals sold under the new authority. On May 19, 2005, the agency resumed sales after revising its bill of sale and pre-sale negotiation procedures to protect sold animals from slaughter. For instance, purchasers now must agree not to knowingly sell or transfer ownership of animals to persons or organizations that intend to resell, trade, or give away animals for processing into commercial products. Sales contracts also now incorporate criminal penalties for anyone who knowingly or willfully falsifies or conceals information. Some horse advocates have questioned whether the new penalties would withstand legal challenge because the law provides for the sale of animals without limitation. Also, according to BLM, purchased animals are classified as private property free of federal protection.

There are about 8,200 animals available for sale, with 1,700 having been sold and delivered as of March 2006, according to BLM. The sale price is determined on a case by case basis. Currently, BLM is promoting sales of animals through two new efforts. First, BLM and the Public Lands Council have appealed to BLM grazing permit holders to purchase wild horses and burros. Second, BLM, Ford Motor Company, and Take Pride in America are making a similar appeal to wild horse and equine rescue groups, with the "Save the Mustangs Fund" providing $100 for each animal purchased by these groups. In both cases, the animals would be sold for $10 each and BLM would deliver 20 or more animals purchased by a rancher or rescue group.

As of February 2005, there were about 31,760 wild horses and burros on the range, with the national maximum AML set at 28,186. BLM has been pursuing a multi-year effort to achieve AML. Some critics assert that the current AMLs are set low in favor of livestock. BLM manages another 25,044 animals in holding facilities, as of November 2005. The cost per animal per year in long-term holding facilities is about $500, according to BLM. For FY2007, the President has requested continuing funding for management of wild horses and burros at $36.4 million, with an additional $0.7 million in fees expected to be collected from adoptions.

Legislative Activity. H.R. 297 and S. 576 seek to overturn the changes to wild horse and burro management enacted during the 108th Congress. H.R. 2993 and S. 1273 aim to foster the sale and adoption of wild horses and burros while establishing further protections. Changes include eliminating the limit of four animals per adopter per year; reducing the minimum adoption fee from $125 to $25 per animal; removing the provision that excess, unadoptable animals be destroyed in a humane and cost-effective manner and making them available for sale; imposing a one-year wait period for buyers to obtain title to sold animals; and removing the provision for sale of animals "without limitation." Some opponents fear that additional sales or adoptions could increase the risk of slaughter.

Wilderness (by Ross W. Gorte and Pamela Baldwin)

Background. The Wilderness Act established the National Wilderness Preservation System in 1964 and directs that only Congress can designate federal lands as part of the national system. Designations are often controversial because commercial activities, motorized access, and roads, structures, and facilities generally are restricted in wilderness areas. (See CRS Report RS22025, *Wilderness Laws: Permitted and Prohibited Uses*, by Ross W. Gorte.) Similarly, agency wilderness studies are controversial because many uses also are restricted in the study areas to preserve wilderness characteristics while Congress considers possible designations.

Some observers believe that the Clinton rule protecting national forest roadless areas (discussed below) was prompted by a belief that Congress had lagged in designating areas which "should" be wilderness. Others assert that the Bush Administration — in addressing R.S. 2477 rights-of-way (discussed below), promulgating new guidance to preclude additional, formal BLM wilderness study areas, and eliminating the nationwide national forest roadless area protections of the Clinton Administration — is attempting to open areas with wilderness attributes to roads, energy and mineral exploration, and development, thereby making them ineligible to be added to the Wilderness System.

One significant issue is when the agencies are to review the wilderness potential of their lands. The Wilderness Act directed the review of administratively designated national forest primitive areas and of National Park System and National Wildlife Refuge System lands. *Release language*, in statutes designating national forest wilderness areas, and FS planning regulations (36 C.F.R. §219.7(a)(5)(ii)) provide for periodic review of potential national forest wilderness areas in the agency's planning process. For BLM lands, §603 of FLPMA required the agency to review potential wilderness and to not impair the wilderness character of wilderness study areas (WSAs) "until Congress has determined otherwise." In 1996, then-Secretary Bruce Babbitt used the BLM authority to inventory its lands and resources (§201 of FLPMA; 43 U.S.C. §1711) to identify an additional 2.6 million acres in Utah as having wilderness qualities. The State of Utah challenged the inventory, and in September 2003, DOI settled the case and issued new wilderness guidance (IM Nos. 2003-274 and 2003-275) prohibiting further reviews and limiting the *nonimpairment* standard to the previously designated WSAs. (See CRS Report RS21917, *Bureau of Land Management (BLM) Wilderness Review Issues*, by Ross W. Gorte and Pamela Baldwin.)

Legislative Activity. Many wilderness recommendations remain pending, including some FS areas and many BLM and Park System areas. As shown in the table below, more than 30 bills to designate wilderness areas in more than a dozen states have been introduced; two (for areas in New Mexico and Puerto Rico) have been enacted.

Table 1. 109th Congress Legislation to Designate Wilderness Areas

Bill No.	Bill Title	State	Most Recent Action
H.R. 233/ S. 128	North California Coastal Wild Heritage Wilderness Act	CA	H. Resource hearings 7/14/05 Senate passed S. 128 on 7/26/05
H.R. 362/ S. 156	Ojito Wilderness Act	NM	S. 156 became P.L. 109-94 on 10/26/05
H.R. 539/ S. 272	Caribbean National Forest Act of 2005	PR	H.R. 539 became P.L. 109-118 on 12/1/05
H.R. 567 & S. 261[a]	Udall-Eisenhower Arctic Wilderness Act [no official title to Senate bill]	AK[b]	Both introduced 2/2/05
H.R. 851/ S. 152	Wild Sky Wilderness Act of 2005	WA	H.R. 851 introduced 2/16/05 Senate passed S. 152 on 7/26/05
H.R. 1155	Alaska Rainforest Conservation Act of 2005	AK[c]	Introduced 3/8/05
H.R. 1204	Rockies Prosperity Act	d	Introduced 3/9/05
H.R. 1503	Utah Test and Training Range Protection Act	UT	Title I of P.L. 109-163
H.R. 1774/ S. 882	America's Red Rock Wilderness Act of 2005	UT	Both introduced 4/21/05
H.R. 1975/ S. 942	Virginia Ridge and Valley Act of 2005	VA	Both introduced 4/28/2005
H.R. 2514/ H.R. 3603	Central Idaho Economic Development and Recreation Act	ID	H.R. 2514 introduced 5/19/05 H. Resource hearings 10/27/05
H.R. 3193/ S. 1510	Rocky Mountain National Park Wilderness Act	CO	H.R. 3193 introduced 6/30/05 S. Energy hearings 4/6/06
H.R. 4235/ S. 1971	Browns Canyon Wilderness Act	CO	H.R. 4235 introduced 11/4/05 S. 1971 introduced 11/7/05
H.R. 4587	Colorado Wilderness Act of 2005 Rocky Mountain National Park Wilderness	CO	Introduced 12/16/05
H.R. 4935	and Indian Peaks Wilderness Expansion Act	CO	Introduced 3/9/06
H.R. 5006/ S. 2452	California Wild Heritage Act of 2006	CA	Both introduced 3/16/06
H.R. 5025	Mount Hood Stewardship Legacy Act	OR	H. Resources hearings 4/5/06
H.R. 5059/ H.R. 5062/ S. 2463[e]	New Hampshire Wilderness Act of 2006	NH	House bills introduced 3/30/06 S. 2463 introduced 3/28/06
H.R. 5149/ S. 2567	Eastern Sierra Rural Heritage and Economic Enhancement Act	CA	Both introduced 4/6/06
H.R. 5157/ S. 2565	Vermont Wilderness Act of 2006	VT	Both introduced 4/6/06

[a] Bills are not identical, but designate same acreage as wilderness.

[b] Affects the Arctic National Wildlife Refuge (ANWR).

[c] Affects the Tongass National Forest.

[d] Affects lands in ID, MT, OR, WA, and WY; similar to Northern Rockies Ecosystem Protection Act introduced in previous Congresses.

[e] Bills have the same title, but differ. H.R. 5059 would designate one new wilderness area, while H.R. 5062 would add to an existing area; S. 2463 includes both designations.

The "Legislation" section of this report includes only bills to substantively amend the Wilderness Act or alter wilderness or WSA management. Bills were introduced in the 106th-108th Congresses to prohibit future BLM wilderness reviews and to place time limits on WSA status. No similar legislation has been introduced in the 109th Congress.

Wildfire Protection (by Ross W. Gorte)

Background. Recent fire seasons have killed firefighters, burned homes, threatened communities, and destroyed trees. More acres burned in the 2005 fire season — 8.7 million acres — than in any year since record-keeping began in 1960, and nearly 2.3 million acres have burned already in 2006. Many assert that the threat of severe wildfires has grown, because many forests have unnaturally high fuel loads (e.g., dense undergrowth and dead trees) and increasing numbers of structures are in and near the forests (the *wildland-urban interface*). Reducing fuels on federal lands has been urged to reduce the threats from fire.

In August 2002, President Bush proposed a Healthy Forests Initiative to improve wildfire protection by expediting projects to reduce hazardous fuels on federal lands. The Healthy Forests Restoration Act of 2003 (P.L. 108-148) included many of the proposals in the President's initiative and other provisions. Title I authorized a new, alternative process for reducing fuels on FS or BLM lands in many areas; five other titles indirectly relate to fire protection. (See CRS Report RS22024, *Wildfire Protection in the 108th Congress*, by Ross W. Gorte.)

Administrative Actions. The Bush Administration has made several regulatory changes to facilitate fire protection activities, aside from P.L. 108-148. First, two new categories of actions can be excluded from NEPA analysis and documentation: certain fuel reduction and post-fire rehabilitation activities (68 *Fed. Reg.* 33814, June 5, 2003). Second, the administrative review processes were revised (68 *Fed. Reg.* 33582, June 4, 2003, for the FS; 68 *Fed. Reg.* 33794, June 5, 2003, for the BLM) to clarify that some emergency actions may be implemented immediately and others after complying with publication requirements, and to expand emergencies to include those "that would result in substantial loss of economic value to the Government if implementation of the proposed action were delayed." A U.S. District Court found that these and other regulations violate the legal requirements for public review of FS decisions. (See "Other Issues," below.)

The Administration has made other regulatory changes that could affect fuel reduction, public involvement, and environmental impacts. For example, new categorical exclusions for small timber harvesting projects (68 *Fed. Reg.* 44598, July 29, 2003) and new regulations for FS planning (70 *Fed. Reg.* 1023, Jan. 5, 2005) have been completed. The total impact of the regulatory changes is generally greater discretion for FS action without environmental studies and with fewer opportunities for the public to comment on, or to request administrative review of, those actions.

Legislative Activity. The 109th Congress is overseeing wildfire protection efforts. Several hearings have been held by various committees (House Resources, Senate Energy and Natural Resources, and House Appropriations) on progress in, and various aspects of, wildfire protection. Hearings have addressed the airworthiness of firefighting airtankers and litigation over the use of chemical fire retardant (Forest Service Employees for Environmental Ethics v. U.S. Forest Service, CV 03-165-M-DVM (D. Mt. Sept. 30, 2005)). Other hearings have addressed the litigation over NEPA categorical exclusions (see below) for fuel reduction and post-fire recovery projects.

Bills have been introduced to improve research and expedite action for rehabilitation of areas after catastrophic events. H.R. 4200 and S. 2079 would establish a permanent program to assess significant events affecting forests and allow pre-authorized management activities or use of alternative NEPA arrangements; they would also direct the establishment of appropriate research protocols. H.R. 3973 would establish a three-year pilot program of up to 10 multi-activity projects to rehabilitate lands and resources affected by "uncharacteristic disturbances." The House Resources and Agriculture Committees ordered H.R. 4200 reported on March 29 and April 5, respectively.

Congress also has addressed wildfire protection through appropriations. The FY2006 Interior Appropriations Act (P.L. 109-54) included $2.55 billion for the National Fire Plan. For FY2007, the Administration has requested $2.57 billion, an increase of $23.2 million (1%) from FY2006. The FY2006 appropriations act also required a report on the Biscuit fire (OR) rehabilitation and consideration of the effects of competitive sourcing on wildfire protection. (See CRS Report RL32893, *Interior, Environment, and Related Agencies: FY2006 Appropriations*, coordinated by Carol Hardy Vincent and Susan Boren.) In addition, bills have been introduced to alter firefighter and fire organization compensation and safety practices, and §210 of P.L. 109-58 authorized grants for producing energy from biomass fuels removed from forests to reduce wildfire risks.

Other Issues

Several other federal lands topics are being addressed through legislation or oversight. These include grazing management, hardrock mining, FS NEPA categorical exclusions, FS roadless areas, federal land sales, and R.S. 2477 rights of way.

Grazing Management. (by Carol Hardy Vincent) BLM asserts that changes in grazing regulations are needed to comply with court decisions, increase flexibility of managers and permittees, improve administrative procedures and business practices, and promote conservation. While lauded by some, the reform effort has been criticized by others as unnecessary or harmful. On June 17, 2005, the BLM published a Final Environmental Impact Statement (FEIS) that analyzed the impact of proposed changes as well as two alternatives. On March 31, 2006, BLM published an addendum to the FEIS that analyzed comments of the Fish and Wildlife Service as well as public comment received after the official comment period. The BLM currently is proceeding with final rulemaking. (See [http://www.blm.gov/grazing/].) Some of these changes would (1) allow title to range improvements to be shared by the BLM and permittees, (2) allow permittees to acquire water rights for grazing if consistent with state law, (3) change the definition of "grazing preference" to include an amount of forage, (4) eliminate conservation use grazing permits, (5) extend the time to remedy rangeland health problems, and (6) reduce occasions where BLM is required to consult with the public. BLM did not address some controversial issues, such as revising the grazing fee. BLM expects to return to the consideration of related grazing policy changes when the regulatory process is completed. On September 28, 2005, a Senate subcommittee held an oversight hearing on the regulatory changes and other grazing issues.

Legislation has been introduced to compensate livestock operators on federal lands. H.R. 411 seeks to require federal land management agencies to compensate holders of grazing permits when certain actions reduce or eliminate their permitted grazing, and alternative forage is not available. The bill also would authorize grazing permit holders to sublease their allotments under specified conditions. Other legislation provides for buying out grazing permittees generally or in particular areas, with the allotments then permanently closed to grazing. H.R. 3166 provides for payment to federal grazing permittees who voluntarily relinquish their permits, at a rate of $175 per AUM. The bill also provides for payments to counties in which the relinquished allotments are located, and authorizes permittees to opt for nonuse or reduced use throughout a term. Other examples include H.R. 3701, regarding lands included in Ecosystem Protection Areas that would be created under the legislation, and H.R. 3603, for certain lands in Idaho.

Hardrock Mining. (by Aaron M. Flynn) Reform of the General Mining Act of 1872, the law governing hardrock mining on federal lands, has been proposed in the 109th Congress. The Mining Act authorizes a prospector to locate and claim an area believed to contain a valuable mineral deposit, subject to the payment of certain fees. At such time, mineral development may proceed. Comprehensive legislation to reform the development of these mineral resources, H.R. 3968, has been introduced. Among other provisions, the bill would require a royalty payment based on hardrock mineral production, resolve current disputes regarding the number of acres available for mine-associated mill sites, prohibit patenting — or purchasing — federal lands in most circumstances, and establish new standards for determining which federal lands are available for development.

Significant amendments to the General Mining Act were considered during in budget reconciliation bill, although such provisions were eventually removed. The provisions would have altered the existing discovery requirement to allow fee payments to establish a claimant's right to use and occupy the public lands for mineral development. The proposal would have also repealed the current prohibition on patenting lands encompassed in mining claims. It would have expressly maintained a general requirement that discovery of a valuable mineral deposit precede approval of land patents; however, the provisions would have established several specific circumstances in which title could be purchased without a discovery requirement. Finally, the provisions would have increased the amounts that must be paid to patent lands, setting them at the greater of $1,000 per acre or fair market value.

Forest Service NEPA Categorical Exclusions. (by Pamela Baldwin) The FS has historically identified certain activities as not having significant environmental impacts, and exempted them from analysis and associated public participation under the National Environmental Policy Act of 1969 (NEPA; P.L. 91-190, 43 U.S.C. §§4321-4347), except in extraordinary circumstances. Various statutes and regulations have expanded categorical exclusions, including those for biomass fuel reduction projects (68 *Fed. Reg.* 33814, June 5, 2003), "small" timber sales (68 *Fed. Reg.* 44598, July 29, 2003), and forest plans (70 *Fed. Reg.* 1023, Jan. 5, 2005). The agency also has modified its application of extraordinary circumstances (67 *Fed. Reg.* 54622, Aug. 23, 2002). Previously, the rule appeared to automatically preclude an action from being categorically excluded if extraordinary circumstances were present; the new rule gives the responsible official discretion to determine whether extraordinary circumstances warrant NEPA analysis and public involvement in otherwise exempt projects. Several of the regulations were challenged. On July 2, 2005, a U.S. District Court ruled that five regulations violated the Forest Service Decision Making and Appeals Reform Act (§322 of P.L. 102-381; 16 U.S.C. §1612 note) by excluding decisions from the public comment and appeals process and for other reasons (*Earth Island Institute v. Pengilly*, 376 F.Supp. 2d 994 (E.D. Cal. 2005). The agency initially responded to the ruling by suspending more than 1,500 permits, projects, and contracts. The court issued a clarifying order that allowed many minor activities to go forward as categorical exclusions, now under the name *Earth Island Institute v. Ruthenbeck*.

Roadless Areas of the National Forest System. (by Pamela Baldwin) The Clinton Administration issued several rules affecting roadless areas in the National Forest System (NFS). The principal rule (66 *Fed. Reg.* 3244, Jan. 12, 2001) resulted in a nationwide approach to management that curtailed (but did not eliminate) most roads and timber cutting in roadless areas. National guidance was justified as avoiding the litigation and delays when decisions were made at each national forest. The rule was twice enjoined. The Bush Administration issued a new final rule to replace the Clinton rule and allow governors 18 months to petition the FS for a special rule for roadless areas in all or part of their state (70 *Fed. Reg.* 25654, May 13, 2005). Until such a new regulation in response to a petition is finalized, the FS is to manage roadless areas in accordance with interim directives (69 *Fed. Reg.* 42648, July 16, 2004) that place most decisions with the Regional Forester, and the Chief of the FS, until each forest plan is amended or revised to address roadless area management. This returns decisions on roadless area management to the individual forest plans, basically reversing the Clinton nationwide roadless rule. New FS planning regulations do not address roadless areas, apparently leaving decisions involving them to the project level within each forest, unless a special rule is adopted for a particular state. California, New Mexico, and Oregon have sued to challenge the new roadless area rule. Oregon also petitioned for a rule allowing any state to petition for an expedited restoration of full protections for roadless areas in that state; this petition was denied. Virginia and North Carolina have submitted petitions for a special rule. H.R. 3563 would direct that roadless areas be managed in accordance with the 2001 regulations; S. 2364 would essentially enact the 2001 roadless rule; and S. 1897 would provide stricter protections for roadless areas than the 2001 rule did.

Federal Land Sales. (by Ross W. Gorte and Carol Hardy Vincent) The President's FY2007 budget request includes proposals for federal land sales. For the BLM, the proposal would alter the distribution of proceeds from sales authorized under the Federal Land Transaction Facilitation Act (FLTFA). The proposal also would direct using updated land management plans for determining which lands to sell. Legislation would be needed to effect these changes. The Administration has not offered draft legislation related to BLM land sales and no such legislation has been introduced in Congress to date.

Current FS authorities for selling or otherwise disposing of national forest lands are extremely narrow, so legislation would be needed to authorize the President's proposal. The Administration has sent to Congress draft legislation to sell national forest lands, but related legislation has not been introduced to date. The draft contains criteria for determining lands eligible for sale, such as lands that are inefficient or difficult to manage because they are isolated or scattered. The proceeds would be used to pay for a five-year extension of FS payments under the Secure Rural Schools and Community Self-Determination Act of 2000 (P.L. 106-393). That act created an alternative to the traditional FS 25% payments for county roads and schools, because the decline in timber sales had reduced payments enormously in some areas, but payments under the act expire at the end of FY2006. (See CRS Report RS22004, *The Secure Rural Schools and Community Self-Determination Act of 2000: Forest Service Payments to Counties*, by Ross W. Gorte.) H.R. 517 and S. 267 would reauthorize the 2000 act for five years, but neither includes FS land sales. The House budget resolution for FY2007 (H.Con.Res. 376) includes a reserve fund for reauthorizing P.L. 106-393, which is intended to accommodate such reauthorization as long as it would not increase the deficit for FY2007-FY2011.

Pending legislation pertaining to land sales is not covered in this brief. Such legislation includes proposals to direct disposal of specific sites, grant federal lands to states for state educational purposes, offset acquisitions with disposals, and inventory federal property to identify land no longer required to be in federal ownership.

R.S. 2477: Rights of Way Across Public Lands. (by Pamela Baldwin) In 1866, in an act that became Revised Statute (R.S.) 2477, Congress granted rights of way across unreserved public lands "for the construction of highways." This grant was repealed in 1976, but existing rights were protected. What constitutes construction of highways and whether a qualifying right of way existed by the time of repeal in 1976 can be contentious. These issues are important because possible rights of way may affect the management of federal lands, perhaps degrading their wilderness suitability while increasing access for recreation and other uses. Section 108 of the FY1997 Interior appropriations act (P.L. 104-208) states that final regulations "pertaining to" R.S. 2477 rights of way cannot take effect unless expressly authorized by an act of Congress. On January 6, 2003 (68 *Fed. Reg.* 494), the BLM finalized changes to its regulations for issuing "disclaimers of interest," a procedure to help clear title to property or interests in property with respect to possible interests of the United States. This procedure is to be used to acknowledge R.S. 2477 rights of way, and may constitute regulations "pertaining to" R.S. 2477. A recent case concluded that state law plays a significant role in determining the validity of R.S. 2477 highways, but also cast doubt on the use of administrative disclaimers to disclaim federal title and thereby validate such rights of way. (See *SUWA v. BLM,* 2005 U.S. App. LEXIS 19381 (10th Cir. 2005).) On March 22, 2006, then-Secretary Norton issued guidance on determining R.S. 2477 highways and indicated the disclaimer process would be used. H.R. 3447 in the 109th Congress would establish an administrative process and criteria for resolving R.S. 2477 claims.

LEGISLATION

P.L. 109-58 (H.R. 6 (Barton))

The Energy Policy Act of 2005, among other provisions, amends the Geothermal Steam Act of 1970 and the Mineral Leasing Act, requires the Secretary of the Interior to evaluate the oil and gas leasing process, and shields various energy-related activities on federal lands from review under NEPA. Signed into law August 8, 2005.

H.R. 297 (Rahall); S. 576 (Byrd)

These bills amend the Wild Horses and Burros Act to restore the prohibition on the commercial sale and slaughter of wild horses and burros. H.R. 297, introduced January 25, 2005; referred to Committee on Resources. S. 576, introduced March 9, 2005; referred to Committee on Energy and Natural Resources.

H.R. 411 (Renzi)

The Cattleman's Bill of Rights Act directs compensation for ranchers when federal actions reduce their allowed amount of grazing. Introduced January 26, 2005; referred to Committee on Resources and Committee on Agriculture.

H.R. 517 (Walden)/S. 267 (Craig)

The Secure Rural Schools and Community Self-Determination Reauthorization Act of 2005 reauthorizes modified payments under P.L. 106-393 through FY2013. H.R. 517 reported by House Resources Committee June 9, 2005 (H.Rept. 109-117, Part I). Senate Committee on Energy and Natural Resources held hearings on S. 267 March 8, 2005.

H.R. 2993 (Porter)/S. 1273 (Reid)

These bills foster the sale and adoption of wild horses and burros while strengthening protections. H.R. 2993, introduced June 20, 2005; referred to Committee on Resources. S. 1273, introduced June 20, 2005; referred to Committee on Energy and Natural Resources.

H.R. 3166 (Grijalva)

The Multiple-Use Conflict Resolution Act compensates livestock operators who voluntarily relinquish grazing permits. Introduced June 30, 2005; referred to three committees.

H.R. 3447 (Udall, M.)

The Highway Claims Resolution Act of 2005 establishes an administrative process and criteria to resolve R.S. 2477 claims. Introduced July 26, 2005; referred to Committee on Resources.

H.R. 3563 (Inslee)

The National Forest Roadless Area Conservation Act directs that inventoried roadless areas of the national forests be managed in accordance with the 2001 regulations. Introduced July 28, 2005; referred to Committee on Agriculture and Committee on Resources.

H.R. 3710 (Markey)

Under certain circumstances, the bill directs the suspension of royalty relief programs for oil and natural gas production from federal lands and authorizes resulting revenues to be used for specified hurricane relief and low income energy assistance programs. Introduced September 8, 2005; referred to four committees.

H.R. 3893 (Barton)

The Gasoline for America's Security Act requires, among other things, the President to designate certain federal lands (possibly including BLM or FS lands) as suitable for refinery construction or expansion; an expedited permitting process would be available for a refinery sited in the designated area. Passed House October 7, 2005; referred to Senate Committee on Energy and Natural Resources October 24, 2005.

H.R. 3968 (Rahall)

The Federal Mineral Development and Land Protection Equity Act of 2005 requires a royalty payment based on hardrock mineral production, resolves current disputes over the number of acres available for mine-associated mill sites, prohibits patenting federal lands in most circumstances, and establishes new standards for determining federal lands available for development. Introduced October 6, 2005; referred to Committee on Resources.

H.R. 3973 (Udall, T.)

The National Forests Rehabilitation and Recovery Act of 2005 establishes a three-year pilot program of up to 10 multi-activity projects requested by local groups to rehabilitate and restore lands and resources affected by "uncharacteristic disturbances." Introduced October 6, 2005; referred to Committee on Agriculture and Committee on Resources.

H.R. 4200 (Walden)

The Forest Emergency Recovery and Research Act establishes a permanent program to assess significant catastrophic events affecting forests and allowing pre-authorized management activities or projects using alternative NEPA arrangements. Introduced November 2, 2005; referred to three committees. Resources and Agriculture Committees ordered reported on March 29 and April 5, 2006, respectively.

H.R. 4479 (Higgins)

The emergency Consumer Relief Act of 2005 seeks to reduce energy prices by requiring termination of royalty suspension programs now in place and eliminating various federal resource production incentives in the Energy Policy Act of 2005. Introduced December 8, 2005; referred to six committees.

H.R. 4875 (Udall, M.)/S. 2584 (Salazar)

The Rocky Mountain Forest Insects Response Enhancement and Support (FIRES) Act amends the Healthy Forest Restoration Act of 2003 (P.L. 106-148) to add an insect-affected emergency area in the Rocky Mountain region to priority treatments, and to provide financial assistance for community wildfire protection planning. H.R. 4875 introduced March 2, 2006; referred to Committee on Agriculture, Committee on Resources, and Committee on Ways and Means. S. 2584 introduced April 6, 2006; referred to Committee on Energy and Natural Resources.

S. 1897 (Corzine)

The Act to Save America's Forests provides stricter protection for roadless areas than the 2001 rule did, as part of a larger bill to alter management of federal forestlands. Introduced October 19, 2005; referred to Committee on Energy and Natural Resources.

S. 2079 (Smith, G)

The Forests for Future Generations Act establishes a permanent program to assess significant catastrophic events affecting forests and allowing pre-authorized management activities or projects using EPA alternative arrangements; similar to H.R. 4200. Introduced November 18, 2005; referred to Committee on Energy and Natural Resources.

S. 2364 (Cantwell)

The Roadless Area Conservation Act essentially enacts the 2001 roadless rule; similar in effect (though not in content) to H.R. 3563. Introduced March 2, 2006; referred to Committee on Energy and Natural Resources.

REFERENCES

[1] For brief, general information on natural resource issues, see CRS Report RL32699, *Natural Resources: Selected Issues for the 109th Congress*, by Nicole Carter and Carol Hardy Vincent. Information on FY2006 appropriations for the BLM and FS (and other agencies and programs funded by Interior and Related Agencies appropriations bills) is included in CRS Report RL32893, *Interior, Environment, and Related Agencies: FY2006 Appropriations*, co-coordinated by Carol Hardy Vincent and Susan Boren. For information on park and recreation issues, see CRS Issue Brief IB10145, *National Park Management* coordinated by Carol Hardy Vincent; and CRS Issue Brief IB10141, *Recreation on Federal Lands*, co-coordinated by Kori Calvert and Carol Hardy Vincent. For information on oil and gas leasing in the Arctic National Wildlife Refuge (ANWR), see CRS Issue Brief IB10136, *Arctic National Wildlife Refuge (ANWR): Controversies for the 109th Congress*, M. Lynne Corn, Bernard A. Gelb, and Pamela

Baldwin. For information on local compensation for the tax-exempt status of federal lands, see CRS Report RL31392, *PILT (Payments in Lieu of Taxes): Somewhat Simplified*, by M. Lynne Corn; and CRS Report RS22004, *The Secure Rural Schools and Community Self-Determination Act of 2000: Forest Service Payments to Counties*, by Ross W. Gorte.

In: Public Lands: Use and Misuse
Editor: William E. Neeley, pp. 37-47
ISBN: 978-1-60021-352-6

Chapter 3

PALEONTOLOGICAL RESOURCES PRESERVATION ACT: PROPOSAL FOR THE MANAGEMENT AND PROTECTION OF FOSSIL RESOURCES LOCATED ON FEDERAL LANDS*

Douglas Reid Weimer

SUMMARY

Approximately 30% of the land in the United States is under the control of federal land managers. Much of this public land is rich in paleontological [fossil] resources. Concern has been expressed over the management, conservation, and protection of these resources.

There is no comprehensive statute or management policy for the protection or management of fossils located on federal lands. Federal authority for the management of such resources may be derived from a number of general statutes relating to the protection of public properties. The applicability of some of these statutes, such as the Antiquities Act and the Archeological Resources Protection Act, is uncertain or limited. General authority for fossil protection also may be derived from general criminal theft statutes dealing with the theft of government property and from certain site-specific statutes. There may also be certain regulatory authority which is provided by the statutes governing each agency's operations.

In May 2000, the Secretary of the Interior released a comprehensive report concerning the management of fossils which are located on federal and Indian lands. The report was prepared at the request of Congress and it is considered to be the authoritative study of fossils on these lands. It has served as an impetus for federal legislation. The report outlined seven principles for the effective management of fossils which are located on federal land.

Legislative activity concerning the protection of fossils located on federal lands has occurred in both the 107th and 108th Congresses. There have been two types of legislation: one type deals with specific fossil resources at a particular location; the other type provides comprehensive management and protection authority for fossils located on federal lands. In the 108th Congress, the Senate passed S. 546, the Paleontological Resources Preservation Act. The bill has been referred to two House committees. H.R. 2416, a similar bill, has been introduced in the House. The two bills provide a comprehensive approach to the management of fossils on federal lands, providing uniform definitions, public programs, specific

---

* Excerpted from CRS Report RL32586, Updated September 14, 2004

prohibitions, permit procedures, and civil and criminal penalties. The bills would not modify the general mining or reclamation laws, or apply to lands other than federal lands.

BACKGROUND AND INTRODUCTION

At the present time, considerable interest – commercial, scholarly, and legislative – surrounds fossil resources.[1] This interest is heightening concern among federal land managers, scholars, legislators, and the general public for the protection and management of fossil resources on federal lands. Vast tracts of land under federal management[2] are rich in fossil resources and some of these resources have been, and are being, vandalized and/or stolen. With the growing interest in and commercial value of paleontological resources, resources on federal lands are increasingly jeopardized.[3]

There is somewhat limited statutory and regulatory authority for the protection and management of fossil resources on federal lands. Protection and management authorities and policies vary significantly among federal land management agencies and other federal entities.[4] Also, federal land managers have many other management responsibilities, in addition to the protection of fossil resources, and the staff – law enforcement or paleontological – assigned to the management and protection of fossil resources may be somewhat limited, or at times may be focused on other land management issues.[5]

Caselaw on fossil protection is not well developed and is not necessarily consistent and statutory authority is incomplete. There is no comprehensive legislation regulating federal fossil resources. As there is no comprehensive management and/or protection legislation, the role of law enforcement personnel in the protection of fossils may not be clearly defined.

Legislation is currently pending in the 108th Congress which is intended to improve the protection and management of paleontological resources on federal lands. The proposed Paleontological Resources Preservation Act – S. 546[6] and H.R. 2416[7] – addresses a number of significant protection and management issues. This report examines these issues and provides some background on current laws, regulations, and management practices.[8] The report is limited to issues associated with the federal management of fossils located on federal land. It does not examine any state or local regulation of fossil resources located on state or municipal lands, and it does not consider the regulations, ownership, or control of fossil located on private property. Nor does the report analyze the management of fossils located on Indian lands. The report will be updated as circumstances warrant.

CURRENT AUTHORITY RELATED TO THE PROTECTION AND MANAGEMENT OF PALEONTOLOGICAL RESOURCES WHICH ARE LOCATED ON FEDERAL LANDS

Again, there is currently no comprehensive federal statute concerning the regulation, management, and preservation of fossil resources on federal lands.[9] Fossils in several sites are regulated by site specific statutes[10] and regulations,[11] but the sites represent only a fraction of the federal resources. Portions of some more general laws may apply to fossil protection in limited circumstances, but coverage here remains spotty at best. Some laws that may apply are cited and summarized below. In addition, federal land management agency policies concerning fossil resources vary considerably, which further complicates the management situation.

The **Antiquities Act of 1906 ("Act")**[12] authorizes the President to declare "objects of historic or scientific interest" located on lands owned or controlled by the United States, to be national monuments. Although the statute makes no specific reference to fossils, national monuments have been created in order to protect fossil resources.[13] When fossil resources are in a national monument managed by the National Park Service (as most national monuments are), the relevant regulations, penalties, and prohibitions applicable to the National Park System may be utilized to manage and protect the fossils. Also, presidential declarations aside, certain statutes have created national monuments and have expressly protected fossil resources located within them.[14]

The act provides criminal penalties for any person who removes or destroys any "object of antiquity" without regard to which federal agency manages the lands.[15] A person convicted under this provision may be fined not more than $500 or imprisoned for a period of not more than ninety days, or both.[16] Section 3 of the act: 1) authorizes the Secretaries of the Interior, Agriculture, and the Army to issue permits for gathering objects of antiquity on lands under their jurisdictions, and 2) allows for the gathering of such objects under a permit procedure and under specific guidelines.[17] Regulations have been promulgated which divide jurisdiction over the lands among the three Secretaries.[18]

However, despite the references in the act to "objects of scientific interest," and the use of the act to proclaim national monuments to protect fossils, there is some uncertainty how the act has been applied with respect to fossil resources themselves. No enforcement actions involving application of the act to the removal or destruction of fossil resources as an "object of antiquity" have been located. A court decision, discussed below, has further lessened the effectiveness of the act to protect fossil resources. Still, the act remains the only specific legislation with criminal sanctions that may cover paleontological materials on federal lands.[19]

The **Archeological and Historic Preservation Act of 1974**[20] provides a means for the survey, removal, protection, and preservation of certain resources or data impacted by federally funded construction projects, including dam construction and the alterations of terrain.[21] The legislation provides for the "preservation of historical and archeological data (including relics and specimens)."[22] These provisions are applicable when a federal construction project or federally licensed project, activity, or program may cause the loss or destruction of "significant scientific, prehistorical, historical, or archaeological data."[23] It is unclear whether these provisions apply to fossil resources per se, or whether the fossil resources have to be connected with other historical or archaeological data or resources. As the provisions are rather broadly written, it could be argued that fossil resources might fit into either the "significant scientific" or the "prehistorical" categories. The statute does not provide punitive measures for noncompliance. There appears to be no clear precedent in applying the provisions of this legislation to fossil resources.

The **Archaeological Resources Protection Act of 1979 (ARPA)**[24] protects against the unauthorized removal of archaeological objects located on federal or Indian lands. However, paleontological resources are specifically excluded from the definition of "archaeological resources," for the purposes of the ARPA's coverage, unless the fossil resources are specifically associated with an archaeological site.[25]

The **Federal Cave Resources Protection Act (FCRPA)**[26] may provide some protection for paleontological resources within the context of a protected "cave resource." The FCRPA states that "the term 'cave resource' includes any material or substance occurring naturally in caves on Federal lands, such as animal life, plant life, paleontological deposits, sediments, minerals, speleogens, and speleothems."[27] FCRPA does not define the term "paleontological deposits" nor is the term clarified in regulations. At the same time, FCRPA provides a comprehensive statutory framework for the management and protection of covered resources through 1) management actions,[28] 2) collection and removal of cave resources through a permit process,[29] 3) a listing of prohibited acts and criminal penalties,[30] 4) civil penalties,[31] and 5) authorization to establish a research program.[32]

The general criminal theft provisions of **18 U.S.C. § 641**, which prohibit the conversion, theft, sale, or disposal without authorization of anything of value belonging to the United States, may be applied to the unauthorized removal of fossils from federal lands. The National Park Service's Natural Resources Reference Manual 77 states:

> These statutes [theft of government property law] were first applied to stolen federal fossil resources in the mid-1990's. With a few highly-publicized prosecutions, these statutes could become effective at deterring future theft of fossils on NPS and other federal lands.[33]

One who steals government property or receives stolen property knowing it to have been stolen can be fined under Title 18, imprisoned up to ten years, or both. If the value of the property does not exceed $1,000, the person may be fined under Title 18, imprisoned for not more than one year, or both.

It also may be possible for the United States to protect its fossil resources by instituting a **trespass action** for the unauthorized use of its land and resources. Certain federal statutes address specific types of trespass and provide for associated penalties.[34] For example, 18 U.S.C. § 1863 provides for a fine of not more than $500 or imprisonment for not more than six months or both for whoever "without lawful authority or permission, goes upon any national-forest land which is closed to the public pursuant to lawful regulation of the Secretary of Agriculture. . ." Other federal statutes deal with trespass actions within specific national parks.[35]

However, there is not one general federal statute dealing with trespass to federal property. The most significant source of federal authority to oppose trespass to its property is that which the federal government enjoys as a property owner.[36] At common law, the unauthorized entry of the land of another is a trespass, and the United States can stop trespasses on its lands.[37] The government could seek to recover the value of the public property unlawfully appropriated. However, this course of action does not seem to have been used in the context of the unauthorized taking or use of fossil resources from federal lands. On some federal lands, such as those managed by the Bureau of Land Management, certain state law also may provide an alternative enforcement remedy.[38]

REPORT OF THE SECRETARY OF THE INTERIOR: FOSSILS ON FEDERAL & INDIAN LANDS

The Secretary of the Interior issued a report concerning the current collection, storage, and preservation of fossils in May 2000 pursuant to a request contained in Senate Report 105-227 for the FY1999 Interior and Related Agencies Appropriations Act.[39] The agencies directed by the Senate to assist the Secretary in preparing the report were the Bureau of Land Management, Bureau of Reclamation, and Bureau of Indian Affairs, as well as the Smithsonian Institution. In addition, the U.S. Geological Survey contributed to the report. This report is considered the authoritative study and analysis of the issue.[40]

The federal entities recommended that federal fossil management would be improved by a comprehensive approach for the protection and management of paleontological resources. They further recommended that this approach be guided by seven principles:

Principle 1: Fossils on Federal Lands are a Part of America's Heritage. Actions concerning fossils should reaffirm the current use of federal fossils for scientific, education, and where appropriate, recreational values.[41]

Principe 2: Most Vertebrate Fossils are Rare. Actions regarding fossil management should reaffirm the restriction on collecting vertebrate fossils to qualified personnel. Fossils should remain in federal ownership in perpetuity.[42]

Principe 3: Some Invertebrate and Plant Fossils are Rare. Actions regarding fossil management should reaffirm mission-specific approaches to the management of plant and invertebrate fossils.[43]

Principle 4: Penalties for Fossil Theft Should be Strengthened. Legislative and administrative actions should penalize the theft of fossils from lands under federal jurisdiction in such a way as to maximize the effectiveness of prosecutions and to deter future thefts. In determining penalties, the value of the fossils themselves, as well as any damage resulting from their illegal collection, are to be taken into account. Strategies should emphasize education of federal managers, prosecutors, law enforcement personnel, and the judiciary regarding the value of fossils and the means and techniques for the appropriate protection of fossil resources.[44]

Principle 5: Effective Stewardship Requires Accurate Information. Actions should recognize the need for accumulating and analyzing information about the location of fossils, especially the important role of inventory in the effective management of fossil resources. Increased emphasis on fossil inventory should take into consideration regional approaches across agency lines and utilize modern technology. In protecting fossil inventory, agencies could examine specific issues, such as the impact of erosion on the loss of resources.[45]

Principle 6: Federal Fossil Collections Should be Preserved and Available for Research and Public Education. Actions should affirm the importance of the curation of scientifically valuable fossils as the property of the federal government, but also allow for partnership with non-federal institutions. Approaches should emphasize the use of modern technology to improve fossil curation and access. There should be sharing of information among government agencies and private businesses.[46]

Principle 7: Federal Fossil Management Should Emphasize Opportunities for Public Involvement. Actions should include an emphasis on public education and involvement in the stewardship of fossil resources. Approaches should emphasize the use of technology to increase the public education and awareness of the importance and the benefit of fossil resources.[47]

The report separately considered the management of fossils which are located on Indian lands.[48]

The report set out four management goals to safeguard the intellectual and educational value of fossils and to promote their public benefits:[49]

- The first management objective involves field inventory, monitoring, and protecting of fossils. Because of different levels of acreage, staff, and fossil resources, as well as different legislative mandates, federal land management agencies take somewhat different approaches to performing inventories and monitoring the fossil resources on land that they oversee. Consequently, only a few national parks have completed comprehensive fossil resource inventories.
- The second management object involves collection requirements. The priorities in collecting scientifically significant fossils are based on research and education. Where fossils are located is significant. Agencies must also consider the impact of fossil collection on the entire environment, taking into account such other factors as the presence of endangered species and related cultural resources.
- The third management objective concerns the storage and preservation of fossils. Fossils are placed in museums in order to keep them safe, maintain their physical condition, keep the fossils and the related information together, and make the fossils and their context readily available for study and for present and future educational and interpretative programs.
- The fourth objective of fossil management concerns the management of information. At the present time, there is no systematic approach for sharing fossil related information among agencies. The report recommended that there should be a greater opportunity to exchange information involving fossil resources.

CASELAW

Only a few reported cases deal with fossil resources located on federal lands and related issues, and they do not provide a consistent or a dispositive analysis of the applicability of existing federal preservation laws to fossil resources. The few reported cases tend to be subject- specific and may not have a broad applicability to fossil protection issues. Many prosecutions for fossil theft are not published in the legal case reporting system, so that it is difficult to develop a broad overview of enforcement and legal analysis.

Perhaps the leading case illustrating the state of current law as an enforcement tool is *United States v. Diaz*,[50] which dealt with the application of the Antiquities Act ("Act") in a criminal context. The Ninth Circuit found that the language of the act[51] was unconstitutionally broad. The court noted that the act did not define such terms as "ruin," "monument," or "object of antiquity." The impact of this decision effectively ended the use of the act as a means of prosecution for the theft and/or destruction of archaeological objects located on federal lands throughout the Ninth Circuit, which includes the states of Alaska,

Arizona, California, Hawaii, Idaho, Montana, Nevada, Oregon, and Washington.[52] While the case did not involve fossil resources per se, the court's findings probably ended the possible application of the act to fossil resource protection and management in the above states. The court determined that Congress had inadequately defined the term "object of antiquity," and that the term could have "different meanings to different people."[53] It also found that the term "antiquity" not only referred to the age of an object, but also to a ceremonial function of the object. Therefore, the court determined that the use of undefined terms of uncommon usage in the act was fatally vague, and impeded the statute's ability to provide adequate notice and resulted in a violation of the Due Process Clause of the Constitution.[54]

SUMMARY OF PENDING LEGISLATION

The 2000 Interior Report has served as an impetus for legislation establishing comprehensive management and protection requirements.[55] The bill that has received the most attention in the 108th Congress is S. 546, the Paleontological Resources Preservation Act. S. 546 passed the Senate and has been referred to the House Resources and Agriculture Committee.[56] Following is a summary of the most significant provisions of the legislation.

- Section 2 provides relevant definitions of terms, including "casual collecting," "Secretary," "Federal lands," "Indian lands," "State," and "paleontological resource." The "casual collecting" definition provides a noncommercial exception to allow the random collection of fossil materials from certain federal lands.
- Section 3 directs the Secretaries of Interior and Agriculture ("the Secretaries") to manage and protect paleontological resources on federal land, and to develop plans for inventorying and monitoring such resources. Section 4 directs the Secretaries to establish a program to increase public awareness of paleontological resources.
- Section 5 prohibits an individual from collecting paleontological resources from federal land without a permit. However, casual collecting of common invertebrate and plant paleontological resources for scientific, educational, and recreational uses, without a permit, on certain federal lands is permitted under certain circumstances. Resources collected from federal lands remain the property of the United States.
- Section 6 requires that such resources and related information are to be placed in an approved repository.
- Section 7 makes it a crime to: 1) excavate, remove, or alter a paleontological resource located on federal lands, except in compliance with this act; 2) exchange or receive such a resource, if the person knew or should have known such resource to have been illegally removed from federal lands; or 3) sell or purchase a paleontological resource, if the person knew or should have known such a resource to have been illegally removed from federal lands.
- Section 8 authorizes the assessment of civil penalties.

H.R. 2416,[57] is substantially similar to S. 546. The primary differences are that H.R. 2416:

- Contains a statement of findings and purposes;
- Sets out a different penalty schedule; and
- Contains specific provisions on rock collecting in National Forests.

CONCLUSION

The public lands of the United States possess significant paleontological [fossil] resources. The federal government manages some 30% of the land in the United States, and fossil management is only one of many federal land management responsibilities.

There is no comprehensive statute or management policy for the protection and management of fossils which are located on federal lands. Federal authority for the management of such resources may be derived from a number of statutes relating to the protection of public properties. The application of some of the statutes is uncertain, and the usefulness of the Antiquities Act of 1906 ("Act") is limited, in light of the *Diaz* decision, which found the criminal penalty provisions of the act to be unconstitutionally vague. Generally, the Archaeological Resources Protection Act of 1979 and the Native America Graves Protection and Repatriation Act are not applicable to fossil resources. General authority for fossil protection may be derived from general criminal theft statutes dealing with the theft of government property and from certain specific statutes, such as the Federal Cave Protection Act. There may also be some regulatory authority provided by statutes governing each agency's operations.

In May 2000, the Secretary of the Interior released a comprehensive report concerning the management of fossils located on federal and Indian lands. The report was prepared at the request of Congress, and it is considered to be the authoritative source on federal fossils. It has served as an impetus for federal legislation. The report outlined seven principles for the effective management of federal fossils.

There has been legislative activity in both the 107th and 108th Congresses concerning the protection of fossil resources located on federal lands. There have been two types of legislation: one deals with specific fossil resources at a particular location and the other provides comprehensive management and protection authority for fossils located on federal lands. In the 108th Congress, the Senate passed S. 546, the Paleontological Resources Preservation Act. The bill has been referred to two House committees. H.R. 2415, a similar bill, has been introduced in the House. The two bills provide a comprehensive approach to the management of fossils located on by providing uniform definitions, public programs, specific prohibitions, permit procedures, prohibitions, and civil and criminal penalties. The bills would not modify the general mining or reclamation laws, or apply to lands other than federal lands.

REFERENCES

[1] For the purposes of this report, the terms "fossil resources" and "paleontological resources" are used interchangeably. "Paleontological" and "palentological" are alternative spellings of the same term. The former spelling appears to be the preferred spelling, and is used in the text of this report. It is also the spelling using in pending

federal legislation. Examples of paleontological resources include the remains of organisms which have been preserved by natural processes in the earth's crust, such as the fossilized remains or traces of plant and animal matter. Examples of such resources are available on the National Park Service Paleontology Program website at [http://www2.nature.nps.gov /geology/paleontology/pub/ index.htm].

[2] See CRS Report RL32393, *Federal Land Management Agencies: Background on Land and Resources Management*, coordinated by Carol Hardy Vincent (May 21, 2004)(cited to afterward as "CRS Report RL32393"). The federal government owns 672 million acres (30%) of the nearly 2.3 billion acres of land in the United States. Four federal agencies administer 628 million acres (94%) of this land: Bureau of Land Management has jurisdiction over approximately 262 million acres (38.9%); Forest Service has jurisdiction over approximately 192 million acres (28.7%); Fish and Wildlife Service manages 95 million acres (14.2%); and National Park Service administers about 79 million acres of federal land (11.8%)(plus 5.4 million acres of non-federal land), for a total of 84.4 million federal and nonfederal acres. (CRS Report RL32393 at 2).

[3] *See generally Fossils on Federal and Indian Lands*, May 2000. Prepared at the request of Congress by several consulting federal agencies: Fish and Wildlife Service, Forest Service, National Park Service, Bureau of Land Management, Bureau of Reclamation, U.S. Geological Survey, as well as the Smithsonian Institution. The report is available online at [http://www.doi.gov./fossil/fosilreport.htm].

[4] [4] Three of the "big four" land management agencies are located within the Department of the Interior: Bureau of Land Management; Fish and Wildlife Service; and National Park Service. The fourth, the Forest Service, is in the Department of Agriculture. Other federal entities which have some oversight/management of fossil resources are the Bureau of Reclamation; U.S. Geological Survey; and Department of Defense. The Smithsonian Institution, while not a land management entity, curates a large fossil collection, much which came from federal lands.

[5] For example, a federal land manager may have to deal with such issues as the protection and management of wildlife; the management and protection of mineral and other valuable natural resources; the safety of visitors; the occurrence of natural disasters such as flood, fire, and hurricane; and many other issues. Law enforcement staff in a national park may have to deal with such varied issues as: 1) protection of archaeological, paleontological, and other natural resources; 2) lost or injured visitors; 3) general law enforcement activities such as policing drunk driving, drug trafficking, and other illegal acts.

[6] 108th Cong., 1st Sess. (2003). Passed the Senate on July 17, 2003.

[7] 108th Cong., 1st Sess. (2003).

[8] This report does not consider fossil resources within the context of fossil energy issues. The report does not examine in detail the cultural/historical/tourist interest in fossil resources which visitors to federal lands may have.

[9] Under most circumstances, there is also no federal regulation of fossil resources which are located on private lands or on lands owned by the states or local government units.

[10] See notes 13 and 14.

[11] For example, 36 C.F.R. § 261.2 defines "paleontological resource" within the context of lands managed by the Forest Service; and 36 C.F.R. § 292.41 defines "paleontological resources" within the context of the Hell's Canyon National Recreation Area.

[12] Act of June 8, 1906, ch. 3060, 34 Stat, 225 (1906), codified at 16 U.S.C. §§ 431 to 433.
[13] Dinosaur National Monument, Proc. No. 1313, Oct. 4, 1915, 39 Stat. 1752; Proc. No. 2290, July 14, 1938, 53 Stat. 2454; modified by P.L. 100–701, 102 Stat. 4641 (1988).
[14] Agate Fossil Beds National Monument, Act of June 5, 1965, P.L. 89-33, 79 Stat. 123 (1965).
[15] 16 U.S.C. § 433.
[16] *Id.*
[17] 16 U.S.C. § 432.
[18] 43 C.F.R. §§ 3.1 to 3.17.
[19] Sherry Hutt, Elwood W. Jones & Martin E. McAllister, Archeological Resources Protection 22 (1992)(cited to afterward as "Hutt").
[20] P.L. 93-291, 88 Stat. 174 (1974), codified at 16 U.S.C. §§ 469 to 469c-2.
[21] This legislation originated in the Reservoir Salvage Act, P.L. 86-523, 74 Stat. 220 (1960), which was subsequently expanded and amended as the Archaeological and Historic Preservation Act of 1974.
[22] 16 U.S.C. § 469.
[23] *Id.* at § 469a-1(a).
[24] P.L. 96-95, 93 Stat. 721 (1979), codified at 16 U.S.C. §§ 470AA to 470mm.
[25] 16 U.S.C. § 470bb.
[26] P.L. 100-691, 102 Stat. 4546 (1988), codified at 16 U.S.C. §§ 4301 to 4310.
[27] 16 U.S.C. § 432.
[28] 16 U.S.C. § 4303.
[29] *Id.* § 4305.
[30] *Id.* § 4306.
[31] *Id.* § 4307.
[32] *Id.* § 4310.
[33] NPS Natural Resources Reference Manual, provided by Julia Brunner, NPS Geologic Resources Division , Denver , CO. See [http://www.nature.nps.gov/rm77paleo/Authority.htm].
[34] 18 U.S.C. §§ 1851 to 1863.
[35] For example, 16 U.S.C. § 91 (Mt. Rainier National Park); 16 U.S.C. § 122 (Crater Lake National Park).
[36] *United States v. West*, 232 F.2d 694 (9th Cir. 1956), *cert. denied* 352 U.S. 834 (1956).
[37] *Shannon v. United States*, 160 F.870 (9th Cir. 1908).
[38] A search of state laws where the BLM has land management responsibilities did not disclose any specifically relevant state law concerning fossil resources. However, it is possible that under certain circumstances, a state trespass or other fossil protection law might be applicable. It is well established, that as a property owner, the United States may sue in the states courts under state law to protect its property. *Cotton v. United States*, 52 U.S. (11 How.) 232 (1850).
[39] See note 3.
[40] Telephone call between Douglas Weimer, CRS, and Greg McDonald, paleontological program coordinator, NPS (March 22, 2004). *See also* S. Rep. No. 108-93, at 6 (2003).
[41] Interior Report at 13-15 (page references are to the web version of the report).
[42] *Id.* at pp.15-17.
[43] *Id.* at pp.17-18.

[44] *Id.* at pp. 18-19.
[45] *Id.* at pp. 19-21.
[46] *Id.* at pp. 21-24.
[47] *Id.* at 24-25.
[48] The Bureau of Indian Affairs' (BIA) authority to manage fossil resources located on Indian lands is not mandated by statute and is limited. The federal government does not have the same rights of ownership or control over Indian lands that it exercises over non-Indian lands. The BIA manages fossils as a trust resource and is limited to approving leases of Indian lands or agreements between Indian landowners and third parties for the extraction of fossils.
[49] Interior Report at pp. 8-13 (page references are to the web version of report).
[50] 499 F.2d 113 (9th Cir. 1974).
[51] The statute provides that "Any person who shall appropriate, excavate, injure, or destroy any historic or prehistoric ruin or monument, or any object of antiquity on lands owned or controlled by the Government of the United States..." would be subject to criminal prosecution and punishment.
[52] Jurists, law enforcement personnel, and legal commentators concur that the *Diaz* holding effectively voided certain criminal penalty and enforcement portions of the Antiquities Act in these states. The *Diaz* holding was also a contributing factor to the enactment of ARPA in 1979, since the traditional protection provided by the Antiquities Act was no longer available in the Ninth Circuit. See Hutt at 23-27.
[53] 499 F.2d at 114.
[54] *Id.*
[55] In the 107th Congress, two types of legislation were introduced: 1) site specific legislation to create a particular fossil preserve – H.R. 2385, 107th Cong., 1st Sess. (2002) enacted as P.L. 107-346, 116 Stat. 2896 (2002); and 2) comprehensive legislation to manage, protect, and preserve paleontological resources –H.R. 2974, 107th Cong., 1st Sess. (2002); S. 2727, 107th Cong., 2nd Sess. (2002).
[56] S. 546, 108th Cong., 1st Sess. (2003). Introduced by Sen. Akaka on March 6, 2003 and referred to the Committee on Energy and Natural Resources. The Subcommittee on National Parks held a hearing on June 10, 2003. The bill was reported out of committee on July 11, 2003 (S.Rept. 108-93). It passed the Senate with an amendment by unanimous consent on July 17, 2003. The bill was received in the House on July 28, 2003 and referred to the Committee on Resources and the Committee on Agriculture. No further action has been taken.
[57] Introduced by Rep. McGovern on June 11, 2003, and referred to the Committee on Resources. On June 19, 2003, it was referred to the Subcommittee on National Parks, Recreation and Public Lands, the Subcommittee on Forests and Forest Health, and the Subcommittee on Fisheries Conservation, Wildlife and Oceans. On June 19, 2003, the Subcommittees on Fisheries and Forest held a joint hearing. Also, on June 11, 2003, the bill was referred to the Agriculture Committee, and it was referred to the Subcommittee on Department Operations, Oversight, Nutrition and Forestry on June 24, 2003. No further action has been taken.

In: Public Lands: Use and Misuse
Editor: William E. Neeley, pp. 49-63

ISBN: 978-1-60021-352-6

Chapter 4

WILDERNESS: OVERVIEW AND STATISTICS*

Ross W. Gorte

SUMMARY

Congress enacted the Wilderness Act in 1964. This Act created the National Wilderness Preservation System, reserved to Congress the authority to designate wilderness areas, and directed the Secretaries of Agriculture and of the Interior to review certain lands for their wilderness potential. The Act also designated 54 wilderness areas with 9 million acres of federal land. Congress began expanding the Wilderness System in 1968, and today, there are 649 wilderness areas, totaling more than 105 million acres, in 44 states. Numerous bills to designate additional areas and to expand existing ones are introduced and considered in every Congress.

The Wilderness Act defined wilderness as an area of generally undisturbed federal land, but did not establish criteria or standards to determine whether an area should be designated, because of differing perceptions of wilderness and because of the varying purposes of wilderness. In general, wilderness areas are undeveloped, and commercial activities, motorized access, and roads, structures, and facilities are prohibited in wilderness areas. However, in response to conflicting demands, Congress has granted both general exemptions and specific exceptions to the general standards and prohibitions.

The federal government owns about 29% of the land in the United States, although the proportion in each state varies widely. Four federal agencies — the Bureau of Land Management, National Park Service, and Fish and Wildlife Service in the Department of the Interior and the Forest Service in the Department of Agriculture — manage most of the federal lands. These agencies manage the 106 million acres of designated wilderness, as well as many other lands. In addition, they have are protecting another 46 million acres as possible additions to the Wilderness System, and are reviewing the wilderness potential of additional lands.

In total, more than 23% of all federal land, and nearly 7% of all land in the United States, has been designated as wilderness or is being protected as possible wilderness. Alaska, because of its size and relatively pristine condition, dominates wilderness statistics — more than 54% of designated wilderness is in Alaska. In total, nearly 16% of all land (federal, state, private, and other) in Alaska has been designated as wilderness. In contrast, 4% of all land in the United States outside Alaska has been designated as wilderness.

* Excerpted from CRS Report RL31447, Updated March 18, 2005

In 1964, the Wilderness Act established a national system of congressionally designated areas to be preserved in a wilderness condition. The National Wilderness Preservation System was created with 9 million acres of Forest Service lands. Congress has since expanded the Wilderness System to more than 105 million acres (see **Table 1**) among some 620 million acres of land managed by the federal land management agencies — the Forest Service (FS) in the Department of Agriculture, and the National Park Service (NPS), Fish and Wildlife Service (FWS), and Bureau of Land Management (BLM) in the Department of the Interior. (See **Table 2**.) Federal agencies, Members of Congress, and interest groups have recommended more lands for inclusion in the System. Furthermore, at the direction of Congress, agencies have studied, or are studying, the wilderness potential of their lands. This report provides a brief history of wilderness, describes what wilderness is, identifies permitted and prohibited uses in wilderness areas, and provides data on wilderness designations and federal agency recommendations, as of December 31, 2004.

HISTORY OF WILDERNESS

The federal government acquired 1.8 billion acres of land through purchases, treaties, and other agreements. Initial federal policy was generally to transfer ownership to states and private ownership, but Congress has also provided for reserving certain lands for federal purposes, and over time has reserved or withdrawn increasing acreage for national parks, national forests, wildlife refuges, etc.[1] The general policy of federal lands disposal was changed to a general policy of retaining the remaining lands in the Federal Land Policy and Management Act of 1976.[2]

Beginning in 1897, management of the national forests emphasized conservation — protecting and developing the lands. It did not take long for some FS leaders to recognize the need to preserve some areas in a natural state. Acting at its own discretion, the FS created the first wilderness area in the Gila National Forest (NM) in 1924. In the succeeding decades, the agency's system of wilderness, wild, and primitive areas grew to 14.6 million acres. However, in the 1950s, increasing timber harvests and recreation use of the national forests led to public concerns about the permanence of this purely administrative system. The FS had relied on its administrative authority in making these designations; there was no law guaranteeing the future of wilderness.

In response to these concerns, Congress enacted the Wilderness Act[3] in 1964. The Act defines wilderness, and prohibits or restricts certain activities in wilderness areas, while permitting other activities to occur. The Act also reserves to Congress the authority to designate areas as part of the National Wilderness Preservation System.

The Wilderness System was initially endowed with the 9.1 million acres of national forest lands that had been identified administratively as wilderness areas or wild areas. The Wilderness Act also directed the Agriculture Secretary to review the agency's 5.5 million acres of primitive areas, and the Secretary of the Interior to evaluate the wilderness potential of National Park System and National Wildlife Refuge System lands. The Secretaries were to report their recommendations to the President and to Congress within 10 years (i.e., by 1974). Separate recommendations were made for each area; many areas recommended for wilderness have been designated, although some of the recommendations are still pending (and are included in **Table 3**). FLPMA directed the Secretary of the Interior to conduct a similar review of the public lands administered by the BLM within 15 years (i.e., by 1991).

The BLM submitted its recommendations to the President, and presidential recommendations have been submitted to Congress.

The 90th Congress began expanding the Wilderness System in 1968, as shown in **Table 1**. Five laws were enacted, creating five new wilderness areas with 795,000 acres in four states. Wilderness designations generally increased in each succeeding Congress, rising to a peak of 60.8 million acres designated during the 96th Congress (1979-1980). The largest was 56.4 million acres of wilderness designated in the Alaska National Interest Lands Conservation Act.[4]

In 1977, the FS began a review (RARE II[5]) of 62 million acres of national forest roadless areas, as an acceleration of part of the land management planning process mandated by the Forest and Rangeland Renewable Resources Planning Act of 1974 and the National Forest Management Act of 1976.[6] The RARE II Final Environmental Statement was issued in January 1979, recommending more than 15 million acres (24.3% of the study area) for addition to the Wilderness System. Nearly 11 million acres (17.4%) were to be studied further in the ongoing FS planning under process NFMA. The remaining 36 million acres (58.3% of the RARE II area) were to be available for other uses — such as logging, energy and mineral developments, and motorized recreation — which might be incompatible with preserving wilderness characteristics. In April 1979, President Jimmy Carter presented the recommendations to Congress with minor changes.

Table 1. Additions to the National Wilderness Preservation System

Congress	Number of Laws [a]	Number of States	Number of Areas New	(Additions)	Acres Designated [b]
88th	1	13	54	(0)	9,139,721
89th	0	0	0	(0)	0
90th	5	4	5	(1)	794,550
91st	3	12	25	(0)	305,619
92nd	9	7	8	(1)	912,439
93rd	5	22	35	(0)	1,264,594
94th	6	21	35	(0)	2,142,486
95th	7	18	28	(5)	4,555,496
96th	6	10	70	(11)	60,799,111
97th	5	5	7	(0)	83,261
98th	21	21	177	(49)	8,576,450
99th	4	4	11	(2)	97,393
100th	7	8	22	(4)	1,988,509
101st	5	5	68	(3)	1,759,479
102nd	2	2	6	(4)	424,590
103rd	2	2	79	(14)	8,272,699
104th	1	2	1	(2)	29,420
105th	1	1	0	(1)	160
106th	8	6	18	(1)	1,086,490
107th	5	5	18	(13)	441,520
108th	1	1	14	(0)	768,294
Total	104	44	681	(111)	106,255,809

[a] Excludes laws with minor boundary and acreage adjustments (less than 10 acres of net change).

[b] Column total differs from this figure, because of acreage revisions.

In 1980, the state of California successfully challenged the FS RARE II recommendations for 44 areas allocated to nonwilderness uses, with the court decision substantially upheld on appeal in 1982.[7] The Reagan Administration responded in 1983 by directing a re-evaluation of all RARE II recommendations, except in states with wilderness laws containing certain provisions known as *release language*.[8] Tensions between the Administration and Congress, and among interest groups, led to a particularly intense debate during the 98th Congress (1983-1984). A compromise version of release language, achieved in May 1984, led the 98th Congress to enact 21 wilderness laws designating 8.6 million acres of wilderness in 21 states — more laws and more acres (outside of Alaska) than any Congress since the Wilderness System was created.

Since the Wilderness Act created the National Wilderness Preservation System in 1964, Congress has enacted 103 additional laws designating new wilderness areas or adding to existing ones, as shown in **Table 1**. The Wilderness System now contains 681 wilderness areas with more than 106 million acres in 44 states, managed by the four federal land management agencies, as shown in **Table 3**. In addition, the agencies have recommended another 46.5 million acres in 32 states be added to the Wilderness System, as shown in **Table 4**; these lands are generally managed to protect their wilderness character while Congress considers adding them to the Wilderness System. Additional lands are being studied by the agencies, to determine if they should be added to the System, but comprehensive data on lands being reviewed for wilderness potential are not available.

Questions and discussions persist over the protection and management of areas that some believe should be designated as wilderness and others believe should be available for development. The Clinton Administration moved to protect many of the remaining national forest areas that could be designated as wilderness, initially in January 1998 with a temporary moratorium on road construction in roadless areas, and finally with a rule that prohibited most road construction and many other activities in *inventoried roadless areas* (i.e., the remaining undesignated RARE II areas).[9] The Clinton rule was twice enjoined, and the Bush Administration has proposed a new general rule [10] that would allow governors to petition the FS for separate statewide rules on roadless area management.[11]

Questions also persist over BLM *wilderness study areas*. These WSAs are the areas the BLM studied as potential wilderness under §603 of FLPMA. Under §603(b), the BLM is required to protect the wilderness characteristics of all WSAs (including areas not recommended for wilderness) "until Congress determines otherwise." Some BLM WSAs have been designated as wilderness by Congress (as reflected in **Table 3**), and generally in the same statutes, Congress has released the BLM from the requirement to protect the wilderness characteristics of certain other areas. However, release language in BLM wilderness statutes has generally been more controversial than for national forest areas.[12]

WHAT IS WILDERNESS?

The Wilderness Act defines wilderness as an area of generally undisturbed federal land. Specifically, §2(c) states:

> A wilderness, in contrast with those areas where man and his works dominate the landscape, is hereby recognized as an area where the earth and its community of life are untrammeled by

> man, where man himself is a visitor who does not remain. An area of wilderness is further defined to mean .... an area of undeveloped Federal land retaining its primeval character and influence, without permanent improvements or human habitation, which is protected and managed so as to preserve its natural conditions and which (1) generally appears to have been affected primarily by the forces of nature, with the imprint of man's work substantially unnoticeable; (2) has outstanding opportunities for solitude or a primitive and unconfined type of recreation; (3) has at least five thousand acres of land or is of sufficient size as to make practicable its preservation and use in an unimpaired condition; and (4) may also contain ecological, geological, or other features of scientific, educational, scenic, or historical value.

This definition provides some general guidelines for determining which areas should, or should not, be designated wilderness, but there are no specific criteria in the law. The phrases "untrammeled by man," "retaining its primeval character," and "man's work substantially unnoticeable" are far from precise. Even the numerical standard — 5,000 acres — is not absolute; smaller areas can be designated, if they can be protected, and the smallest wilderness area — Wisconsin Islands in the Green Bay National Wildlife Refuge — is only 2 acres.

One reason for the imprecise criteria for wilderness is differing perceptions of what constitutes *wilderness*. To some, a "wilderness" is an area where there is absolutely no sign of human presence: no traffic can be heard (including aircraft); no roads, structures, or litter can be seen. To others, sleeping in a van or camper in a 400-site campground in Yellowstone National Park is a "wilderness experience." Complicating these differing perceptions is the wide-ranging ability to "get away from it all" in various areas; in a densely wooded area, "getting away" might be measured in yards, while in mountainous or desert terrain, human developments can sometimes be seen for miles.

In an attempt to accommodate these contrasting views of wilderness, the Wilderness Act provided certain exemptions and delayed implementation of restrictions for wilderness areas, as will be discussed below. At times, Congress has also responded to the conflicting demands of various interest groups by allowing additional exemptions for certain uses (especially for existing activities) in particular wilderness designations. Ultimately, "wilderness areas" are whatever Congress designates as wilderness, regardless of developments or activities which some might argue conflict with the definition of wilderness.

PROHIBITED AND PERMITTED USES

In general, the Wilderness Act prohibits commercial activities, motorized access, and roads, structures, and facilities in wilderness areas. Specifically, §4(c) states:

> Except as specifically provided for in this Act, and subject to existing private rights, there shall be no commercial enterprise and no permanent road within any wilderness area designated by this Act and, except as necessary to meet minimum requirements for the administration of the area for the purpose of this Act (including measures required in emergencies involving the health and safety of persons within the area), there shall be no temporary road, no use of motor vehicles, motorized equipment or motorboats, no landing of aircraft, no other form of mechanical transport, and no structure or installation within any such area.

This section prohibits most commercial resource exploitation (such as timber harvesting) and motorized entry (via cars, trucks, off-road vehicles, aircraft, or motorboats) except in emergencies. However, §4(d) provides numerous exceptions, including (a) possible continued use of motorboats and aircraft; (b) fire, insect, and disease control measures; (c) mineral prospecting conducted "in a manner compatible with the preservation of the wilderness environment;" (d) water projects; (e) continued livestock grazing; and (f) commercial recreation activities.

In addition to these exemptions, the Wilderness Act extended the mining and mineral leasing laws for wilderness areas in national forests for 20 years, through 1983. New mining claims and mineral leases were permitted for many wilderness areas, and exploration and development were authorized "subject, however, to such reasonable regulations governing ingress and egress as may be prescribed by the Secretary of Agriculture."[13] Despite this authority, no permits for on-site exploration were considered until James Watt became the Secretary of the Interior in 1981.[14] Litigation halted a drilling application in Montana that year, and Congress enacted a moratorium on wilderness area leasing and exploration in the Department of the Interior appropriations laws for FY1983 and FY1984 (P.L. 97-394 and P.L. 98-146, respectively). However, mineral rights existing on or before December 31, 1983 (or before the area was designated), remain valid, and can be developed if the right-holder chooses, under "reasonable regulations" determined by the Secretary of Agriculture, and some mineral exploration has occurred in designated wilderness areas under such regulations.[15]

The Wilderness Act also directs that the Act not alter existing federal-state relationships with respect to state water laws or state fish and wildlife responsibilities. Specifically, §4(d) (as codified at 16 U.S.C. §1133) states:

> (7) Nothing in this Act shall constitute an express or implied claim or denial on the part of the Federal Government as to exemption from State water laws.
> (8) Nothing in this Act shall be construed as affecting the jurisdiction or responsibilities of the several States with respect to wildlife and fish in the national forests.

However, the extent and nature of federal water rights that might arise from wilderness designations continue to be an important issue for Congress.[16]

Finally, as noted above, Congress has also enacted numerous exemptions to the Wilderness Act's standard prohibitions on activities and developments.[17] These exemptions typically apply to one or a few areas and typically authorize a particular activity (that might not be permitted under the Wilderness Act's management guidance) to be allowed to continue in the area at the level or intensity that occurred prior to the area's designation as wilderness.

Statistics on Wilderness Designations and Recommendations, as of December 31, 2004

The following tables present data on the federal lands managed by the four principal federal land management agencies and on the acreage designated as wilderness and recommended by the agencies for wilderness. The data were gathered from several agency sources, as described below. This section describes the agency land data shown in **Table 2** and the wilderness data shown in **Tables 3**, **4**, and **5**.

Agency Land Data. Table 2 shows the area managed by the four major federal land management agencies.[18] The data are not directly comparable across agencies, however, because of differences in accounting practices. The agency data also differ from the data maintained by the U.S. General Services Administration (GSA).[19] Differences occur in part because official ownership status often differs from managerial responsibility; for example, the FS administers 462,678 acres in Oregon that are technically public (BLM) lands. Another complication is partial ownership, such as split estates, with the federal government owning only the surface (or the subsurface), and another owner for the subsurface (or surface) rights; similarly, some lands are managed by the federal government under easements and long-term leases, without federal ownership. Thus, the agency acreage statistics in **Table 2** may overstate actual federal land ownership.

The data in **Table 2** are from agency sources; agency data (rather than GSA data) were used because they most closely match the agency wilderness data. The acreage shown in **Table 2** is generally limited to the lands owned by the federal government (i.e., excluding easements and long-term leases) and administered by the agency or for which the agency has primary management responsibility. This list identifies the land area data source for each of the agencies.

U.S. Dept. of Agriculture, Forest Service, *Land Areas Report As of September 30, 2004*, at [http://www.fs.fed.us/land/staff/lar/LAR04/table4.htm], visited on March 16, 2005.

U.S. Dept. of the Interior, National Park Service, Land Resources Division, Public Use Statistics Office, *National Park System Listing of Acreage as of: 9/30/2004*, at [http://www2.nature.nps.gov/stats/acrebypark04fy.pdf], visited on March 16, 2005.

U.S. Dept. of the Interior, Fish and Wildlife Service, Division of Realty, *Annual Report of Lands Under Control of the U.S. Fish and Wildlife Service as of September 30, 2003*, Table 2, Summary by States, Associated Governments and Possessions, at [http://www.fws.gov/realty/PDF_Files/2003_lands.pdf], visited on March 16, 2005.

U.S. Dept. of the Interior, Bureau of Land Management, *Public Land Statistics 2003*, at [http://www.blm.gov/natacq/pls03/pls1-4_03.pdf], visited on March 16, 2005.

Wilderness Statistics: Data Description and Assumptions. The wilderness statistics presented in **Tables 3** and **4** are the current acreage estimates by the agencies. Acreages are estimates, since few (if any) of the areas have been precisely surveyed. **Table 3** is the acreage for areas that have been designated by Congress. **Table 4** identifies the acreage of areas being protected by the agencies for possible addition to the Wilderness System, but which have not yet been acted upon by Congress. In addition, the agencies continue to review the wilderness potential of other lands under their jurisdiction, both of congressionally designated wilderness study areas and under congressionally directed land management planning efforts. However, statistics on acreage being studied, particularly in the planning efforts, are unavailable.

For the FS, the same report as for general land statistics (listed above) provides designated wilderness data, at [http://www.fs.fed.us/land/staff/lar/ LAR04/table9. htm], visited on March 16, 2005. FS wilderness recommendations are from the *Roadless Area Conservation FEIS*,[20] with updated information for the agency.[21] The BLM's *Public Land Statistics, 2003* also shows designated wilderness and wilderness study areas, at [http://www.blm.gov/natacq/pls03/pls5-4_03.pdf] and [http://www.blm.gov/natacq/pls03/pls-5-5_03.pdf], respectively, visited on March 16, 2005.[22] NPS data on designated, recommended (by the Secretary or the President), and proposed (by the agency) wilderness areas are available on other NPS sites, respectively, at [http://wilderness.nps.gov/map locator.cfm?f=5], [http://wilderness.nps.gov/maplocator.cfm?f=3], and [http://wilderness. nps.gov/maplocator.cfm?f=4], visited on January 6, 2005. FWS designated wilderness data are in Table 8 of the agency's general lands report, listed above. Recommended FWS wilderness are from an unpublished 2000 FWS report, adjusted to reflect subsequent congressional designations.

Wilderness Statistics: Summary of Data. As of December 31, 2004, Congress had designated 106.3 million acres of federal land in units of the National Wilderness Preservation System, as shown in **Table 3**. More than 54% of this land — 57.5 million acres — is in Alaska, and includes most of the wilderness areas managed by the NPS (76%) and by the FWS (90%). Nearly a third of the Wilderness System is managed by the FS, but 83% of FS wilderness area is outside Alaska.

Another 46.5 million acres are being protected by various agencies as possible additions to the Wilderness System, as shown in **Table 4**. More than half of these are pending recommendations in the National Park System, and include several large, well-known areas, such as Yellowstone, Big Bend, Glacier, and Great Smoky Mountains National Parks. For the FS, Congress has not acted on RARE II recommendations for Idaho and Montana; the FS data shown in **Table 4** are largely the result of the agency's land management planning process. The BLM submitted its recommendations to the President by 1991, as required by FLPMA, and Presidents Bush and Clinton sent recommendations for BLM wilderness to Congress. The 14.6 million acres of BLM WSAs account for nearly a third of the possible wilderness.

In total, 152.8 million acres, of a total U.S. landmass of 2.27 billion acres, have been designated as wilderness or are being protected as possible wilderness. Nearly half of this — 76.0 million acres — is in Alaska, and accounts for 16% of all land in the state. The remaining 76.8 million acres are distributed among 45 other states; only Connecticut, Iowa, Kansas, and Rhode Island have no federal lands designated as wilderness or protected as possible wilderness. Total land designated as or recommended for wilderness accounts for less than 7% of all land in the United States, and more than 23% of all federal land.

Table 2. Total Area Managed by Federal Land Management Agencies (in acres)

	USDA Forest Service	National Park Service	Fish & Wildlife Service	Bureau of Land Management
Alabama	667,314	16,715	30,042	111,369
Alaska	21,973,662	51,078,663	76,567,246	85,652,163
Arizona	11,262,527	2,602,990	1,677,951	12,228,398
Arkansas	2,593,028	98,374	360,803	295,185
California	20,769,716	7,554,824	281,258	15,198,670
Colorado	14,498,801	604,333	70,042	8,368,106
Connecticut	24	5,719	899	0
Delaware	0	0	25,173	0
Florida	1,156,827	2,435,335	288,996	26,899
Georgia	865,205	39,575	473,318	0
Hawaii	1	353,405	298,374	0
Idaho	20,715,568	96,268	48,563	11,993,499

Table 2. Continued.

	USDA Forest Service	National Park Service	Fish & Wildlife Service	Bureau of Land Management
Illinois	293,101	12	82,407	224
Indiana	200,935	10,379	13,693	0
Iowa	0	2,708	65,202	378
Kansas	108,175	461	29,447	0
Kentucky	811,042	94,033	9,526	0
Louisiana	604,373	14,540	535,882	321,734
Maine	53,040	66,706	61,054	0
Maryland	0	39,848	45,448	0
Massachusetts	0	32,947	16,893	0
Michigan	2,868,468	631,590	113,282	74,807
Minnesota	2,840,385	139,508	460,867	146,658
Mississippi	1,171,158	103,155	208,833	56,212
Missouri	1,489,327	54,173	58,804	2,094
Montana	16,923,859	1,214,234	627,548	7,964,028
Nebraska	352,252	5,434	172,333	6,354
Nevada	5,836,348	774,509	2,333,538	47,860,756
New Hampshire	732,413	8,072	18,832	0
New Jersey	0	35,216	69,068	0
New Mexico	9,419,498	376,527	326,664	13,371,431
New York	16,211	33,130	27,134	0
North Carolina	1,254,876	362,592	435,782	0
North Dakota	1,105,977	71,241	480,264	59,482
Ohio	236,638	19,238	8,277	0
Oklahoma	400,172	9,998	105,036	2,136
Oregon	15,667,116	190,955	557,686	16,135,906
Pennsylvania	513,427	48,411	10,003	0
Rhode Island	0	5	2,210	0
South Carolina	623,724	27,687	121,732	0
South Dakota	2,014,005	141,317	203,444	274,450
Tennessee	700,974	351,108	48,850	0
Texas	755,389	1,183,236	493,941	11,833
Utah	8,193,568	2,094,161	107,227	22,867,662
Vermont	393,868	8,830	33,144	0
Virginia	1,664,071	305,448	129,080	805
Washington	9,276,203	1,832,050	146,771	403,316
West Virginia	1,041,094	62,537	18,572	0
Wisconsin	1,527,336	61,731	196,940	159,982
Wyoming	9,238,063	2,343,693	70,674	18,355,293
Territories	28,149	21,764	1,720,487	0
U.S. Total	192,857,908	77,659,476	90,269,238	261,950,378

Table 3. Federal Designated Wilderness Acreage, by State and by Agency

	USDA Forest Service		National Park Service		U.S. Fish and Wildlife Service		Bureau of Land Management		Total Designated Area		Share of NWPS
Alabama	41,367	6.2%	0	0.0%	0	0.0%	0	0.0%	41,367	3.4%	0.04%
Alaska	5,753,448	26.2%	33,079,611	64.8%	18,689,349	24.4%	0	0.0%	57,522,408	23.6%	54.14%
Arizona	1,345,008	11.9%	444,055	17.1%	1,343,444	80.1%	1,396,466	11.4%	4,528,973	12.4%	4.26%
Arkansas	116,578	4.5%	34,933	35.5%	2,144	0.6%	0	0.0%	153,655	3.9%	0.14%
California	4,430,849	21.3%	5,997,045	79.4%	9,172	3.3%	3,621,312	23.8%	14,058,378	29.9%	13.23%
Colorado	3,146,150	21.7%	60,466	10.0%	2,560	3.7%	139,524	1.7%	3,348,700	14.5%	3.15%
Connecticut	0	0.0%	0	0.0%	0	0.0%	0	n.r	0	0.0%	0.00%
Delaware	0	n.r	0	n.r	0	0.0%	0	n.r	0	0.0%	0.00%
Florida	74,495	6.4%	1,296,500	53.2%	51,252	17.7%	0	0.0%	1,422,247	30.9%	1.34%
Georgia	114,537	13.2%	8,840	22.3%	362,107	76.5%	0	n.r	485,484	21.0%	0.46%
Hawaii	0	0.0%	155,509	44.0%	0	0.0%	0	n.r	155,509	23.2%	0.15%
Idaho	3,961,667	19.1%	43,243	44.9%	0	0.0%	802	0.01%	4,005,712	11.4%	3.77%
Illinois	28,732	9.8%	0	0.0%	4,050	4.9%	0	0.0%	32,782	5.0%	0.03%
Indiana	12,945	6.4%	0	0.0%	0	0.0%	0	n.r	12,945	2.4%	0.01%
Iowa	0	n.r	0	0.0%	0	0.0%	0	0.0%	0	0.0%	0.00%
Kansas	0	0.0%	0	0.0%	0	0.0%	0	n.r	0	0.0%	0.00%
Kentucky	18,097	2.2%	0	0.0%	0	0.0%	0	n.r	18,097	1.1%	0.02%
Louisiana	8,679	1.4%	0	0.0%	8,346	1.6%	0	0.0%	17,025	1.1%	0.02%
Maine	12,000	22.6%	0	0.0%	7,392	12.1%	0	n.r	19,392	11.8%	0.02%
Maryland	0	n.r	0	0.0%	0	0.0%	0	n.r	0	0.0%	0.00%
Massachusetts	0	n.r	0	0.0%	2,420	14.3%	0	n.r	2,420	2.3%	0.00%
Michigan	91,891	3.2%	132,018	20.9%	25,310	22.3%	0	0.0%	249,219	6.8%	0.23%
Minnesota	809,772	28.5%	0	0.0%	6,180	1.3%	0	0.0%	815,952	23.1%	0.77%
Mississippi	6,046	0.5%	4,080	4.0%	0	0.0%	0	0.0%	10,126	0.5%	0.01%
Missouri	63,383	4.3%	0	0.0%	7,730	13.1%	0	0.0%	71,113	3.2%	0.07%
Montana	3,372,503	19.9%	0	0.0%	64,535	10.3%	6,000	0.1%	3,443,038	11.8%	3.24%

Table 3. (Continued)

	USDA Forest Service		National Park Service		U.S. Fish and Wildlife Service		Bureau of Land Management		Total Designated Area		Share of NWPS
Nebraska	7,794	2.2%	0	0.0%	4,635	2.7%	0	0.0%	12,429	0.9%	0.01%
Nevada	870,567	14.9%	125,000	16.1%	0	0.0%	1,758,613	3.7%	2,754,180	4.3%	2.59%
New Hampshire	102,932	14.1%	0	0.0%	0	0.0%	0	n.r	102,932	12.4%	0.10%
New Jersey	0	n.r	0	0.0%	10,341	15.0%	0	n.r	10,341	5.7%	0.01%
New Mexico	1,388,262	14.7%	56,392	15.0%	39,908	12.2%	139,281	1.0%	1,623,843	6.1%	1.53%
New York	0	0.0%	1,363	4.1%	0	0.0%	0	n.r	1,363	0.6%	0.00%
North Carolina	102,634	8.2%	0	0.0%	8,785	2.0%	0	n.r	111,419	3.1%	0.10%
North Dakota	0	0.0%	29,920	42.0%	9,732	2.0%	0	0.0%	39,652	3.0%	0.04%
Ohio	0	0.0%	0	0.0%	77	0.9%	0	n.r	77	0.02%	0.00%
Oklahoma	14,543	3.6%	0	0.0%	8,570	8.2%	0	0.0%	23,113	1.7%	0.02%
Oregon	2,086,504	13.3%	0	0.0%	940	0.2%	186,723	1.2%	2,274,167	7.4%	2.14%
Pennsylvania	9,031	1.8%	0	0.0%	0	0.0%	0	n.r	9,031	1.2%	0.01%
Rhode Island	0	n.r	0	0.0%	0	0.0%	0	n.r	0	0.0%	0.00%
South Carolina	16,671	2.7%	15,010	54.2%	29,000	23.8%	0	n.r	60,681	4.9%	0.06%
South Dakota	13,426	0.7%	64,144	45.4%	0	0.0%	0	0.0%	77,570	3.4%	0.07%
Tennessee	66,349	9.5%	0	0.0%	0	0.0%	0	n.r	66,349	3.3%	0.06%
Texas	38,483	5.1%	46,850	4.0%	0	0.0%	0	n.r	85,333	2.7%	0.08%
Utah	772,894	9.4%	0	0.0%	0	0.0%	27,720	0.1%	800,614	2.3%	0.75%
Vermont	59,421	15.1%	0	0.0%	0	0.0%	0	n.r	59,421	13.2%	0.06%
Virginia	97,635	5.9%	79,579	26.1%	0	0.0%	0	n.r	177,214	6.8%	0.17%
Washington	2,569,391	27.7%	1,739,763	95.0%	839	0.6%	7,140	1.8%	4,317,133	32.6%	4.06%
West Virginia	80,852	7.8%	0	0.0%	0	0.0%	0	n.r	80,852	6.4%	0.08%
Wisconsin	42,294	2.8%	0	0.0%	29	0.01%	0	0.0%	42,323	2.1%	0.04%
Wyoming	3,111,232	33.7%	0	0.0%	0	0.0%	0	0.0%	3,111,232	9.9%	2.93%
Territories	0	0.0%	0	0.0%	0	0.0%	0	n.r	0	0.0%	0.00%
U.S. Total	34,859,062	17.9%	43,414,321	55.9%	20,698,845	22.9%	7,283,581	2.8%	106,255,809	15.8%	100.0%
Share of NWPS		32.8%		40.9%		19.5%		6.9%		100.0%	

n.r = not relevant; the agency owns no land within the state.

Table 4. Additional Acreage Protected as Potential Wilderness, by State and by Agency (in acres and percentage of agency/federal land)

	USDA Forest Service [a]		National Park Service		U.S. Fish and Wildlife Service		Bureau of Land Management		Total Recommended Area		Share of Recom.
Alabama	1,000	0.1%	0	0.0%	0	0.0%	0	0.0%	1,000	0.1%	0.00%
Alaska	1,412,000	6.4%	16,143,800	31.6%	0	0.0%	784,238	0.9%	18,430,038	7.8%	39.66%
Arizona	61,000	0.5%	1,973,716	75.8%	0	0.0%	63,930	0.5%	2,098,646	7.6%	4.52%
Arkansas	0	0.0%	0	0.0%	975	0.3%	0	0.0%	975	0.03%	0.00%
California	164,000	0.8%	0	0.0%	0	0.0%	974,769	6.4%	1,138,769	2.6%	2.45%
Colorado	93,000	0.6%	414,545	68.6%	0	0.0%	621,737	7.4%	1,129,282	4.8%	2.43%
Connecticut	0	0.0%	0	0.0%	0	0.0%	0	n.r	0	0.0%	0.0%
Delaware	0	n.r	0	n.r	2,000	8.0%	0	n.r	2,000	8.0%	0.00%
Florida	6,000	0.5%	0	0.0%	0	0.0%	0	0.0%	6,000	0.2%	0.01%
Georgia	8,000	0.9%	0	0.0%	0	0.0%	0	n.r	8,000	0.6%	0.02%
Hawaii	0	0.0%	0	0.0%	1,742	0.6%	0	n.r	1,742	0.3%	0.00%
Idaho	1,406,000	6.8%	[b] 9,400	9.8%	0	0.0%	1,341,709	11.2%	2,757,109	8.4%	5.93%
Illinois	0	0.0%	0	0.0%	0	0.0%	0	0.0%	0	0.0%	0.0%
Indiana	0	0.0%	0	0.0%	0	0.0%	0	n.r	0	0.0%	0.0%
Iowa	0	n.r	0	0.0%	0	0.0%	0	0.0%	0	0.0%	0.0%
Kansas	0	0.0%	0	0.0%	0	0.0%	0	0.0%	0	0.0%	0.0%
Kentucky	0	0.0%	7,398	7.9%	0	0.0%	0	n.r	7,398	0.8%	0.02%
Louisiana	0	0.0%	0	0.0%	0	0.0%	0	0.0%	0	0.0%	0.0%
Maine	0	0.0%	0	0.0%	0	0.0%	0	n.r	0	0.0%	0.0%
Maryland	0	n.r	440	1.1%	418	0.9%	0	n.r	858	1.0%	0.00%
Massachusetts	0	n.r	0	0.0%	3,110	21.9%	0	n.r	3,110	6.2%	0.01%
Michigan	0	0.0%	7,128	1.1%	0	0.0%	0	0.0%	7,128	0.2%	0.02%
Minnesota	0	0.0%	127,436	91.3%	1,406	0.3%	0	0.0%	128,842	3.6%	0.28%
Mississippi	0	0.0%	0	0.0%	1,200	0.6%	0	0.0%	1,200	0.1%	0.00%
Missouri	0	0.0%	0	0.0%	0	0.0%	0	0.0%	0	0.0%	0.0%

Table 4. (Continued)

	USDA Forest Service		National Park Service		U.S. Fish and Wildlife Service		Bureau of Land Management		Total Recommended Area		Share of Recom.
Montana	812,000	4.8%	1,090,208	89.8%	161,580	25.98%	450,823	5.7%	2,514,611	9.4%	5.41%
Nebraska	39,000	11.1%	0	0.0%	40,819	23.8%	0	0.0%	79,819	14.9%	0.17%
Nevada	0	0.0%	659,950	85.2%	1,675,148	72.7%	2,877,917	6.0%	5,213,015	9.2%	11.22%
New Hampshire	0	0.0%	0	0.0%	0	0.0%	0	n.r	0	0.0%	0.0%
New Jersey	0	n.r	0	0.0%	0	0.0%	0	n.r	0	0.0%	0.0%
New Mexico	66,000	0.7%	97,428	25.9%	0	0.0%	970,532	7.3%	1,133,960	4.8%	2.44%
New York	0	0.0%	0	0.0%	0	0.0%	0	n.r	0	0.0%	0.0%
North Carolina	15,000	1.2%	219,100	60.4%	950	0.2%	0	n.r	235,050	11.4%	0.51%
North Dakota	0	0.0%	0	0.0%	0	0.0%	0	0.0%	0	0.0%	0.0%
Ohio	0	0.0%	0	0.0%	0	0.0%	0	n.r	0	0.0%	0.0%
Oklahoma	0	0.0%	0	0.0%	0	0.0%	0	0.0%	0	0.0%	0.0%
Oregon	0	0.0%	127,058	66.5%	50,390	9.1%	2,701,190	16.7%	2,878,638	8.8%	6.19%
Pennsylvania	0	0.0%	0	0.0%	0	0.0%	0	n.r	0	0.0%	0.0%
Rhode Island	0	n.r	0	0.0%	0	0.0%	0	n.r	0	0.0%	0.0%
South Carolina	2,000	0.3%	0	0.0%	163	0.2%	0	n.r	2,163	0.3%	0.00%
South Dakota	0	0.0%	0	0.0%	0	0.0%	0	0.0%	0	0.0%	0.0%
Tennessee	20,000	2.9%	199,800	56.9%	0	0.0%	0	n.r	219,800	20.0%	0.47%
Texas	0	0.0%	538,250	45.5%	0	0.0%	0	n.r	538,250	22.0%	1.16%
Utah	83,000	1.0%	1,852,852	88.5%	0	0.0%	3,255,490	14.2%	5,191,342	15.6%	11.17%
Vermont	0	0.0%	0	0.0%	620	1.9%	0	n.r	620	0.1%	0.00%
Virginia	37,000	2.2%	0	0.0%	3,047	2.4%	0	n.r	40,047	1.9%	0.09%
Washington	15,000	0.2%	0	0.0%	0	0.0%	5,518	1.4%	20,518	0.2%	0.04%
West Virginia	0	0.0%	0	0.0%	0	0.0%	0	n.r	0	0.0%	0.0%
Wisconsin	16,000	1.0%	0	0.0%	0	0.0%	0	0.0%	16,000	0.8%	0.03%
Wyoming	45,000	0.5%	2,080,088	88.8%	0	0.0%	575,841	3.1%	2,700,929	0.9%	5.81%
Territories	10,000	35.5%	0	0.0%	0	0.0%	0	n.r	10,000	0.6%	0.02%
U.S. Total	4,312,000	2.2%	25,593,588	33.0%	1,944,008	2.2%	14,623,694	5.6%	46,473,290	7.5 %	100.0%
Share of Recommended		9.3%		55.1%		4.2%		31.5%		100.0%	

[a] FS data are rounded to the nearest 1,000 acres.

[b] This excludes 396,696 acres of recommended wilderness within Craters of the Moon National Monument, that are administered by the BLM, and are included in the BLM's recommended wilderness in Idaho.

n.r = not relevant; the agency owns no land within the state.

REFERENCES

[1] See CRS Report RL30126, Federal Land Ownership: Constitutional Authority; the History of Acquisition, Disposal, and Retention; and Current Acquisition and Disposal Authorities, by Ross W. Gorte and Pamela Baldwin (archived, available from the authors).
[2] FLPMA, Act of Oct. 21, 1976; P.L. 94-579, 90 Stat. 2743. 43 U.S.C. §§1701-1719, et al.
[3] Act of Sept. 3, 1964; P.L. 88-577, 78 Stat. 890. 16 U.S.C. §§1131-1136.
[4] ANILCA, Act of Dec. 2, 1980; P.L. 96-487, 94 Stat. 2371.
[5] The first Roadless Area Review and Evaluation (RARE) was begun under the agency's administrative authority in 1970, but was abandoned in 1972 because of a lawsuit asserting the review had been restricted in ways that violated the National Environmental Policy Act of 1969 (NEPA, Act of Jan. 1, 1970; P.L. 91-190, 83 Stat. 852; 42 U.S.C. §§4321-4347).
[6] Respectively: RPA, Act of Aug. 17, 1974; P.L. 93-378, 88 Stat. 476; and NFMA, Act of Oct. 22, 1976; P.L. 94-588, 90 Stat. 2949. 16 U.S.C. §§1600-1614, et al.
[7] California v. Bergland, 483 F. Supp. 465 (E.D.Cal. 1980), aff'd in part, rev'd in part, 690 F.2d 753 (9th Cir. 1982).
[8] Release language provides direction on the timing of future wilderness review and of the management of areas not designated as wilderness until the next review. For a history of the debate over release language provisions, see CRS Report 93-280 ENR, Wilderness Legislation: History of Release Language, 1979-1992, by Ross W. Gorte and Pamela Baldwin (archived, available from the authors).
[9] 66 Fed. Reg. 3244 (Jan. 12, 2001).
[10] 69 Fed. Reg. 42636, July 16, 2004.
[11] For more background information on and the current status of these rules, see CRS Report RL30647, The National Forest System Roadless Areas Initiative, by Pamela Baldwin.
[12] See CRS Report RS21917, Bureau of Land Management (BLM) Wilderness Review Issues, by Ross W. Gorte and Pamela Baldwin.
[13] Most lands in the National Park System and the National Wildlife Refuge System have been withdrawn from access under the mining and mineral leasing laws, while extensive BLM wilderness designations were apparently not contemplated until FLPMA was enacted in 1976. Thus, the Wilderness Act addressed mining and mineral leasing only in the national forests.
[14] Although national forests are managed by the FS in the Department of Agriculture, mining claims and mineral leases on most federal lands, including the national forests, are administered by the BLM in the Department of the Interior.
[15] Olen Paul Mathews, Amy Haak, and Kathryn Toffenetti, "Mining and Wilderness: Incompatible Uses or Justifiable Compromise?" Environment, v. 27 (April 1985): 12-17, 30-36.
[16] For a more thorough discussion of this issue, see CRS Report 89-11 A, Wilderness Areas and Federal Water Rights, by Pamela Baldwin.

[17] See CRS Report RS22025, Wilderness Laws: Prohibited and Permitted Uses, by Ross W. Gorte.

[18] Other federal agencies, such as the Department of Defense, control some federal land, but land and resource management is not their primary mission.

[19] U.S. General Services Administration, Office of Government wide Policy, Overview of the United States Government's Owned and Leased Real Property: Federal Real Property Profile as of September 30, 2003, at [http://www.gsa.gov/gsa/cm_attachments/GSA_DOCUMENT/Annual%20Report%20%20FY2003-R4_R2M-n11_0Z5RDZ-i34-pR.pdf], visited on March 18, 2005.

[20] U.S. Dept. of Agriculture, Forest Service, Roadless Area Conservation Final Environmental Impact Statement, Volume 1 (Washington, DC: Nov. 2000), Appendix A, pages A-5 — A-11.

[21] Personal communication with Gary Yeck, Office of Legislative Affairs, USDA Forest Service, Washington, DC, on Jan. 31, 2005.

[22] The data in **Table 4** are actually the preliminary data from Public Land Statistics, 2004, which is not yet published, but which corrects the 2003 data for wilderness designated in P.L. 108-424.

In: Public Lands: Use and Misuse
Editor: William E. Neeley, pp. 65-79
ISBN: 978-1-60021-352-6

Chapter 5

SNOWMOBILES: ENVIRONMENTAL STANDARDS AND ACCESS TO NATIONAL PARKS*

James E. McCarthy

SUMMARY

The use of snowmobiles in national parks has been controversial because of their potential impacts on wildlife and the absence of standards for their emissions and noise. This report focuses on the latter set of issues.

Congress has addressed snowmobile issues primarily through provisions in appropriations bills. On November 20, 2004, the House and Senate approved the conference report on H.R. 4818, the Consolidated Appropriations Act, 2005 (P.L. 108-447). Among its many provisions, the bill establishes winter use rules for Yellowstone and Grand Teton National Parks, allowing up to 720 snowmobiles daily in Yellowstone and 140 in Grand Teton, during the 2004-2005 winter season. Earlier the House voted twice against amendments to Interior Department appropriation bills that would have prohibited recreational snowmobiling in the two parks.

Most current model snowmobiles emit significant quantities of pollution. In one hour, a typical snowmobile emits as much hydrocarbon as a 2001 model auto emits in about two years (24,300 miles) of driving. On November 8, 2002, the Environmental Protection Agency (EPA) promulgated regulations limiting air emissions from snowmobiles. These regulations would require a 30% reduction in emissions beginning in 2006, with more stringent standards (requiring 50% reductions) effective in 2010 and 2012. The standards were challenged in court by both the snowmobile manufacturers and environmental groups and were vacated in part and remanded to EPA in part by the Court of Appeals for the D.C. Circuit, June 1, 2004. EPA has not promulgated any standards for snowmobile noise.

Regarding national parks, the National Park Service has allowed snowmobile use in 43 units of the park system, in many cases in apparent violation of Executive Orders from the Nixon and Carter years. Outside of Alaska (where snowmobiles are permitted in most national parks by law), the most popular national park for snowmobiling has been Yellowstone, which saw more than 76,000 snowmobile visits in the 1999-2000 winter season. Under the Clinton Administration, the National Park Service decided that the emissions and noise from snowmobiling were incompatible with protecting the park, and promulgated rules that would have phased out snowmobiles from Yellowstone, with a complete ban beginning in the winter

* Excerpted from CRS Report RL31149, Updated December 9, 2004

of 2003-2004. The Bush Administration revisited these rules in settlement of a lawsuit, and announced modifications in March 2003. The modifications would have allowed 950 cleaner, quieter snowmobiles to enter Yellowstone Park per day. These rules and the Clinton Administration action have been the subject of conflicting court rulings: a federal court in Wyoming has vacated and remanded the Clinton Administration's phase-out, while a federal court in the District of Columbia has vacated and remanded the Bush Administration rules.

Efforts to reduce snowmobile emissions and noise remain contentious. This report discusses snowmobile access to the parks, snowmobile emissions, and the new EPA standards, and concludes with a discussion of legislative proposals in the 107th and 108th Congresses. It will be updated as events warrant.

Proposals by the National Park Service to enforce long-standing policy that regulates the use of snowmobiles in national parks have raised a number of questions regarding the current and potential regulation of such vehicles. National Park System units account for only about 3% of the land mass of the United States and possess few trails and roads suitable for snowmobiles, compared to areas available on other federal lands; but — for both proponents and opponents — the question of snowmobile access to the parks has taken on a far greater importance. To the snowmobile industry and to many in communities neighboring national parks, "Snowmobiling is an important part of the economic engine that supports northern communities, winter tourism."[1] To environmental groups, snowmobiling "is one of the most environmentally devastating recreational activities permitted by the Park Service .... resulting in adverse impacts to Park wildlife, air and water quality, vegetation, Park ecology, and Park users."[2] Underlying the debate are broader questions concerning regulation of emissions and noise from the vehicles and the degree to which restrictions may serve as a precedent or stigma affecting snowmobile and motorized recreation[3] use more generally.

SNOWMOBILE USE IN NATIONAL PARKS

In recent years, snowmobiles have been allowed access to 43 units of the National Park System, including such major parks as Yellowstone, Grand Teton, Rocky Mountain, Acadia, Zion, Mount Rainier, and Sequoia. While numerous park units have allowed such access, recreational use of snowmobiles is not widespread in the park system as a whole. The National Park Service (NPS) administers 388 units (parks, seashores, monuments, etc.). Of these, 345 (89%) have not been open to snowmobiles. Many units are located in climates unsuitable for them or are too small to be used for such recreation. Others (e.g., Glacier National Park and Yosemite) have banned snowmobiles since the 1970s. According to the National Park Service, use of snowmobiles outside of Alaska is mostly concentrated in five units of the park system: Yellowstone National Park, Voyageurs National Park, Rocky Mountain National Park, Pictured Rocks National Lakeshore, and the John D. Rockefeller **Memorial Parkway (see Table 1).**

Table 1. National Park Use by Snowmobiles, Winter 1999-2000

Park Service Unit	Location	Number of Snowmobiles Entering the Park
Yellowstone National Park	Wyoming	76,571
Voyageurs National Park	Minnesota	35,000
Rocky Mountain National Park	Colorado	27,000
Pictured Rocks National Lakeshore	Michigan	26,000
John D. Rockefeller Memorial Parkway	Wyoming	23,399

Sources: National Park Service, National Parks Conservation Association.

PARK SERVICE POLICY ON SNOWMOBILE ACCESS

Although recreational access by snowmobiles has been permitted in these units of the park system, the Park Service in recent years has concluded that such use has generally been in violation of Executive Orders 11644 and 11989, issued by Presidents Nixon and Carter respectively. The Nixon Order directed that use of off-road vehicles on public lands "be controlled and directed so as to protect the resources of those lands, to promote the safety of all users of those lands, and to minimize conflicts among the various uses of those lands."[4] It specified that off-road vehicle "areas and trails shall be located in areas of the National Park system ... only if the respective agency head determines that off-road vehicle use in such locations will not adversely affect their natural, aesthetic, or scenic values," and it directed the Park Service to "monitor the effects of the use of off-road vehicles" and to rescind or limit this use "as necessary to further the policy of this order."

In January 1999, the Park Service received a rulemaking petition from the Bluewater Network and 60 other environmental organizations seeking a ban on snowmobiles from all units of the National Park Service. In response, the Service surveyed units of the System to assess the extent to which they were complying with the Executive Orders. According to Interior Department testimony: "The results graphically demonstrated that the National Park Service was not complying with its statutory and regulatory mandates.... Consequently, maintaining the status quo with regard to snowmobiling was simply not an option."[5] On April 27, 2000, the Department of the Interior and the National Park Service announced that "snowmobiling for general recreational purposes will be prohibited throughout the Park System, with a limited number of narrow exceptions."[6] By July 2000, the Department had backed away from its strict enforcement stance with a clarification: there would be no snowmobile ban in park units pending a formal rulemaking and public comment period, and snowmobile practices prior to the April 2000 announcement (i.e., access to more than 40 parks) would continue in place through the 2000-2001 winter season.[7] NPS has taken no further action to enunciate a general policy.

Since the summer of 2000, the focus has been on Denali National Park in Alaska and the Yellowstone/Grand Teton area. Both of these areas had been considered exceptions subject to special consideration even under the April 2000 policy announced by the Park Service. Whether snowmobile access to these parks will be allowed to continue has generated substantial public interest.

Denali National Park. In Alaska, vast distances, lack of roads, abundant snow cover, and small dispersed populations make snow machine use ubiquitous. In general, national parks in Alaska allow snowmobile access under the provisions of the Alaska National Interest Lands Conservation Act (ANILCA, P.L. 96-487). However, access to the 2 million acres formerly known as Mt. McKinley National Park (now the core of Denali National Park) has been an issue. Prior to passage of ANILCA (1980), snowmobiles had been banned from this park. In 1999, the Park Service reinstated this policy, banning snowmobiles first on a temporary and later on a permanent basis.[8] Litigation regarding access to Denali was initiated by snowmobile user groups, but was withdrawn in June 2001, on the assumption that legislation would be introduced to address the issue. Legislation (H.R. 4677 / S. 2589, 107th Congress) was introduced in the spring of 2002 that would have allowed access to some portions of the old Park, while continuing the ban elsewhere. No action was taken on these bills, however, and similar legislation was not introduced in the 108th Congress.

Yellowstone/Grand Teton. The other exception to the National Park Service's general policy was the Yellowstone/Grand Teton National Park area. The NPS had been sued in May 1997 by groups who alleged that the Service was violating the National Environmental Policy Act, the Endangered Species Act, the National Park Service Organic Act, and the Yellowstone Act in allowing use of snowmobiles in the two parks and on the Rockefeller Memorial Parkway (which links them). The lawsuit was settled within months when the NPS agreed to conduct an Environmental Impact Study (EIS) of winter use of the parks. Upon completion of the study, the Clinton Administration promulgated a final rule in January 2001, banning snowmobiles from Yellowstone, Grand Teton, and the Rockefeller Parkway beginning in the winter of 2003-2004, but allowing continued visitor access through the use of "snowcoaches" — guided tour-vans that run on rubber treads.[9]

Snowmobile manufacturers, represented by the International Snowmobile Manufacturers Association (ISMA), have suggested that "cleaner, quieter" snowmobiles — a phrase not initially defined — be allowed continued access to the parks. Their suggestion found a receptive audience in the Bush Administration. On June 29, 2001, the Administration responded to a suit filed by ISMA and the State of Wyoming by agreeing to reopen the decision to ban the vehicles from the three Yellowstone area units. The Park Service agreed to prepare a Supplemental EIS and reach a new Record of Decision by November 15, 2002 (a deadline subsequently extended to March 15, 2003).

The Record of Decision was signed March 25, 2003, and a final rule implementing it was promulgated December 11, 2003.[10] Despite receiving 104,802 comments on the final proposal, 91% of which "believed the proposed regulation does not adequately protect park resources due to the presence of snowmobiles,"[11] the Park Service reversed the ban in favor of daily limits on entrants, emission standards for the snowmobiles, other access requirements, and an "adaptive management strategy," allowing park managers to take remedial action if monitoring indicates unacceptable impacts from implementation. In explaining its position, the NPS stated: "We are trying to provide a range of appropriate activities in the parks, while protecting park resources and values."[12]

The new rule would set a daily limit of 950 snowmobile entrance passes for Yellowstone Park, 115 in Grand Teton National Park, and 400 on Rockefeller Memorial Parkway.[13] On most days, this limit would result in no reduction of snowmobile users; but on weekends and holidays, when as many as 1,700 snowmobiles have entered the three park units, it could limit the number of entrants.

Snowmobile users would generally be required to be accompanied by trained guides (although the regulations would allow group members to be as much as 1/3 of a mile from the guide, and the rule preamble concedes, given the noise of a snowmobile, that communication is difficult if not impossible even between passengers on the same machine). To discourage irresponsible behavior, alcohol use by snowmobile users would be strictly limited.

The machines themselves would be required to achieve a 90% reduction in hydrocarbon emissions and a 70% reduction in carbon monoxide under the Bush Administration rules. Noise emissions would be limited to 73 dB(A), which the NPS estimates is about a 50% reduction compared to conventional snowmobiles. To implement these provisions, the Yellowstone Park Superintendent released a list of 10 snowmobile models approved for use during the 2003-2004 winter season, on September 16, 2003.[14] (The list was updated on October 6, 2004, and now contains 16 models.[15])

A hearing on the new rules was held in the U.S. District Court for the District of Columbia on December 15, 2003. The rules were vacated and remanded to the National Park Service by Judge Emmett Sullivan on December 16. The judge held that there was no evidence in the record to support the Bush Administration reversal of the previous agency position and that the decision, therefore, was "arbitrary and capricious." The court also held that the Supplemental EIS accompanying the changes was "flatly inadequate" under NEPA and that the snowmobile decision was "completely politically driven and result oriented."[16] The judge also ordered NPS to respond to Bluewater Network's 1999 rulemaking petition (seeking a ban on snowmobiles in all National Park System units) by February 17, 2004.[17] Judge Sullivan's decision reinstated the Clinton Administration rule and cut the number of snowmobiles entering the three Yellowstone area park units in half for the 2003-2004 winter season in preparation for a complete ban in 2004-5.

Both ISMA and the State of Wyoming appealed the court's ruling. Their request for a stay of the Clinton-era rules pending resolution of their appeal was denied by Judge Sullivan in late December 2003 and by a three-judge panel of the Court of Appeals January 13, 2004. Meanwhile, however, the same groups petitioned the Federal District Court for Wyoming to overturn the Clinton-era rules. That court responded February 10, 2004, when Judge Clarence Brimmer issued a temporary restraining order against the Clinton rules and ordered the National Park Service to develop temporary rules for the remainder of the 2004 winter season. On February 11, the Park Service issued such rules, allowing 780 snowmobiles to enter Yellowstone Park each day, an increase of 287 machines. Grand Teton Park and the Rockefeller Parkway were allowed 140 snowmobiles, an increase of 90. An appeal of Judge Brimmer's order was denied by the 10th Circuit Court in Denver on March 10. (The Wyoming court vacated and remanded the Clinton rules on October 14, 2004.)

As a result of the court decisions, snowmobile use in the three parks was substantially reduced during the 2003-2004 winter season. According to NPS, an average of 258 snowmobiles entered Yellowstone in January and February 2004, a reduction of two-thirds from the historic average. In Grand Teton and the Rockefeller Parkway, the reduction was almost total: through February 10, only about 5 snowmobiles a day entered the two parks. After the February 10 court decision, this number increased to about 20.[18]

Another result of the court decisions was that the Park Service began additional studies to develop new winter use plans. On June 2, 2004, the National Park Service began additional studies to establish a Temporary Winter Use Plan for 2004-2005 and up to two additional winter seasons.[19] During this three-year period, NPS expects to complete a long-term analysis of the environmental impacts of winter use, culminating in a permanent decision about snowmobile access. An Environmental Assessment and proposed Temporary Winter Use Plan were made available for public review September 7, 2004,[20] and final regulations were published November 10, 2004.[21]

The Temporary Plan would allow 720 snowmobiles per day in Yellowstone, all commercially guided, and 140 snowmobiles in Grand Teton National Park and the John D. Rockefeller, Jr., Memorial Parkway. With minor exceptions, all of the snowmobiles would be required to meet NPS best available technology (BAT) requirements shown below in Table 2.[22] Snowcoaches would also be allowed. NPS says the combination of snowmobiles and snowcoaches "should provide a viable program for winter access to the parks, and ... the opportunity for achieving historic visitor use levels."[23]

Further developments in both the Wyoming and D.C. court cases are expected, but Congress has insured that any such decisions will not affect the rules for the 2004-2005 winter season. On November 20, 2004, both the House and Senate approved language, in Section 146 of Title I of Division E of the Consolidated Appropriations Act, 2005 (H.R. 4818, H.Rept. 108-792), providing that the Temporary Winter Use Rules described above "shall be in force and effect for the winter use season of 2004-2005." The President signed the bill December 8 (P.L. 108-447).

Clean Air Act and Noise Control Act Regulation

In reversing the Clinton Administration rules on Yellowstone access, the National Park Service set limits on emissions and noise from the snowmobiles that would be allowed in the three Yellowstone area park units. Simultaneously, EPA has developed emission limits applicable to all new snowmobiles beginning in 2006. The following sections of this report describe the EPA proposals and look at the broader issue of snowmobile emissions.

The Clean Air Act gives EPA authority to regulate emissions from mobile sources of pollution, including off-road sources such as snowmobiles; but snowmobiles, until now, have not been subject to any federal or state emission regulations. Nor have they ever been subject to noise regulations. EPA has authority under Section 6 of the Noise Control Act of 1972 to regulate noise from "transportation equipment (including recreational vehicles and related equipment)." But the Agency's Office of Noise Abatement and Control was disbanded in 1982, and EPA has not issued any regulations under the statute in the 22 years since then.

Snowmobile Emissions

Snowmobiles generally run on two-stroke engines — the type of engine that traditionally has powered outboard motors and lawnmowers. In a two-stroke engine, fuel enters the combustion chamber at the same time that exhaust gases are expelled from it. As a result, as much as one-third of the fuel passes through the engine without being combusted.[24] This causes poor fuel economy and high levels of emissions, particularly hydrocarbons and carbon monoxide. In one hour, a typical snowmobile emits as much hydrocarbon as a 2001 model automobile emits in 24,300 miles of driving.[25] In a day of use, a snowmobile may emit as much hydrocarbon as an automobile emits in 8-10 years of operation. Snowmobiles also emit as much carbon monoxide in an hour as a 2001 model auto does in 1,520 miles of driving. The impact of these emissions on ambient air quality (as described below) is of at least equal concern as that of hydrocarbons because of the tendency for atmospheric accumulation of CO in winter.

The hydrocarbons (gasoline) emitted by snowmobiles contain benzene, formaldehyde, and at least three other substances that are known or suspected human carcinogens. Carbon monoxide, on the other hand, is a poisonous gas that, at low levels, can affect those who suffer from cardiovascular disease, such as angina.

In preparing the 2000 Environmental Impact Statement for the decision on snowmobile access to Yellowstone, the National Park Service measured emissions from snowmobiles and compared them to other emission sources in the park. The Service also estimated the concentrations (ambient levels) of carbon monoxide (CO) and particulate matter (PM) present in the air and compared these concentrations to air quality standards. The EIS concluded that the 8-hour maximum concentration of carbon monoxide at the West Yellowstone entrance to the park exceeded the National Ambient Air Quality Standard for CO by nearly 70% (a concentration of 15.15 parts per million vs. the standard of 9).[26] The analysis also concluded that snowmobiles accounted for 97.9% of the CO at West Yellowstone during winter months.

Noise has also been an issue. Opponents of allowing snowmobiles in Yellowstone and other units of the national park system argue that the parks are special places whose remoteness, beauty, and quiet inspire reflection and awe. The noise of engines is incompatible with this atmosphere, they argue. Snowmobile enthusiasts counter that the parks cover vast areas and that snowmobiles are restricted to a few roads — the same roads traversed by cars, recreational vehicles, and buses in summer. They also assert that snowmobile use is compatible with the NPS responsibility to promote visitor use and enjoyment of park resources. Park Service studies indicate that the sound of snowmobiles can be heard for significantly greater distances than that of automobiles, however, and is essentially continuous during the winter at key locations in Yellowstone: snowmobile noise can be heard 95% of the time by visitors at Old Faithful and 87% of the time at the Grand Canyon of the Yellowstone.[27]

EPA's New Regulations

Regulations for snowmobile and other non-road engine emissions were signed by EPA Administrator Whitman September 13, 2002 and appeared in the Federal Register November 8, 2002.[28] As shown in Table 2, the regulations would reduce both carbon monoxide and hydrocarbon emissions from new snowmobiles a little more than 30% starting in 2006 and an average of 50% by 2012, with an intermediate step in 2010. (The regulations do not require any controls on snowmobiles sold before 2006.) For comparison, Table 2 also shows the Yellowstone-specific standards that have been imposed by the National Park Service.

According to EPA, the 2006/2007 reductions can be achieved without major changes in technology, in part because they apply to the average of a manufacturer's fleet emissions, rather than to individual machines. This will allow manufacturers to provide a range of models, some with advanced emission controls and others without: "While some advanced technologies such as two-stroke direct injection and four-stroke engines, would be found in some models, many models would still be equipped with two-stroke engines with relatively minor engine modifications resulting in minimum emission reductions, while some models may not even have any emission controls."[29] EPA estimates the cost of these Phase 1 controls at $73 per snowmobile. Vehicles meeting the standards will be more fuel-efficient, resulting in an average reduction in operating cost of $57, thus offsetting most of the initial cost increase.

The 2010 and 2012 standards, which also are fleet averages, can also be met without eliminating two-stroke engines, according to the Agency. Because two-stroke engines produce more power than similar size four-strokes and are easy to start in cold weather, the Agency expects the industry to continue to manufacture mostly two-stroke engines even in 2012, although many would be modified with direct injection technology to reduce emissions. According to the Agency, "A potential scenario for meeting these standards could be a mixture of 50 percent direct injection, 20 percent four-stroke engines, and 30 percent with engine modifications."[30] The cost of these changes would average an additional $131 per snowmobile in 2010, according to EPA, but the costs would be offset by $286 in fuel savings and improved performance, so that lifetime costs would actually be $155 lower. The same is true of the 2012 standards: the added cost of $89 per snowmobile is offset by $191 in fuel savings and improved performance, according to EPA, for a net savings of $102 per vehicle.[31]

Table 2. EPA and NPS Snowmobile Emission Limits

Year	Carbon Monoxide (CO)	% Reduction	Hydrocarbons (HC)	% Reduction
current average	397 g/kW-hr		150 g/kW-hr	
2006/2007*	275 g/kW-hr	30.7%	100 g/kW-hr	33.3%
2010	275 g/kW-hr	30.7%	75 g/kW-hr	50%
2012**	200 g/kW-hr*	49.6%	75 g/kW-hr*	50%
Yellowstone/2003 (NPS)	120 g/kW-hr	70%	15 g/kW-hr	90%

g/kW-hr = grams per kilowatt-hour.

* Half of snowmobiles sold in 2006 must comply with the EPA standards. With a few exceptions, all snowmobiles sold in 2007 must comply.

** EPA's 2012 standards allow manufacturers to trade additional reductions in HC for increases in CO emissions, provided that CO emissions are reduced at least 30%, HC emissions are reduced at least 50%, and the total of HC+CO emissions sums to 100%. Thus, for example, HC reductions of 60% and CO reductions of 40% would satisfy the requirement, as would HC reductions of 70% and CO reductions of 30%.

The costs of each of the three phases are incremental. Thus, when fully implemented, the standards would cost an additional $293 per snowmobile, according to the Agency; lifetime operating costs, however, would decline by $534. Combining these two factors, the standards would decrease total costs by $241 per snowmobile when fully implemented.

As compared to the standards EPA proposed in 2001, the final standards were weakened or made more flexible in three respects, and strengthened in two. First, the 2006 standards are to be phased in, with only 50% of 2006 model snowmobiles required to meet the standard, and full compliance delayed until the 2007 model year. Second, the 2010 standard for carbon monoxide remains at the 2006 level of 275 grams per kilowatt-hour; in EPA's original proposal, it would have been reduced to 200. Third, in 2012, manufacturers will have to meet the standards originally proposed for 2010, but, within limits, they will be allowed to trade reductions in CO for additional reductions in hydrocarbons. Thus, reductions of CO may not reach the 50% level originally proposed; if they don't, however, the extra CO emissions would be offset by additional reductions in hydrocarbons.

The standards were strengthened in two respects. First, EPA added a permeation emission standard for fuel tanks and hoses. Fuel evaporates through hoses and through the walls of plastic containers (such as those used as fuel tanks on snowmobiles). The tank and hose standards require an 85% reduction in plastic fuel tank permeation emissions and a 95% reduction in fuel system hose permeation beginning in 2008, in order to lower hydrocarbon emissions from evaporation. The cost of this standard is estimated at $7 per vehicle, with cost savings of $11.[32] The second, relatively minor, strengthening was the addition of a cap on emissions of nitrogen oxides (NOx) in 2012. The NOx cap was set at approximately the current level of emissions. It was added because some of the technologies that might be used to lower HC and CO could simultaneously increase NOx. To prevent that, the Agency added a cap at current levels.[33]

The standards do not include noise limits. While acknowledging that the Agency has the authority to set noise standards, the proposal stated that "at this time we do not have funding to pursue noise standards for nonroad equipment that does not have an existing noise requirement."[34] An Agency source confirmed that the proposed standards would have essentially no impact on noise.[35] Despite receiving comments from a number of organizations that the standards should address noise, the Agency restated in its response to public comments that it would not address the issue, adding that Congress would need to provide appropriations for the Agency to begin any noise control initiative.[36] (As noted, the National Park Service promulgated noise standards applicable to snowmobiles entering its three Yellowstone area park units beginning December 17, 2003, under the winter use rule that was vacated; it restated these standards in its Temporary Winter Use Plan in effect for the 2004-2005 season.[37] According to Park Service estimates, these standards would require a reduction of about 50% in noise emitted by the affected snowmobiles, compared to conventional uncontrolled snowmobiles.)

REACTION TO THE EPA STANDARDS

Both the snowmobile industry and environmentalists have challenged EPA's standards in court. On June 1, 2004, the U.S. Court of Appeals for the D.C. Circuit vacated the standard for nitrogen oxides and remanded the standards for hydrocarbons and carbon monoxide. The court directed EPA "to clarify (1) the statutory and evidentiary basis of the Agency's assumption that the standards must be sufficiently lenient to permit the continued production of all existing snowmobile models, and (2) the analysis and evidence underlying the Agency's conclusion that advanced technologies can be applied to no more than 70% of new snowmobiles by 2012."[38]

The International Snowmobile Manufacturers Association (ISMA) has argued that EPA grossly underestimated the costs of compliance, and that the standards would lead to the elimination of entry-level snowmobiles from the market. Cleaner, quieter machines can be made, according to ISMA, but they cost more, are heavier, and can only be ridden on groomed roads. ISMA estimates that the cleanest four-stroke engines cost an additional $1,700 (about 30% more than current average prices). Even modest improvements to two-stroke engines will cost $350-$400 per machine, according to the Association.[39]

Bluewater Network, on the other hand — the environmental group most identified with snowmobile issues — feels the rules should be much stronger.[40] In comments submitted to EPA, Bluewater encouraged the Agency to set standards "that can only be met using the best available technology, which we believe to be four-stroke engines with particle traps and three-way catalysts."[41] They also want mandatory emission labels for the machines, and are disappointed that the Agency chose not to set noise standards.

Bluewater points to the Clean Snowmobile Challenge, an annual design contest open to college engineering students and sponsored by the Society of Automotive Engineers, as demonstrating that machines far cleaner than EPA's proposed standards are feasible. The winning entry in the 2001 Challenge reduced CO 78.8% and unburned hydrocarbons 97.6% and significantly reduced noise, at a cost of $600.[42] "If college students are able to build cleaner and quieter machines, surely the billion-dollar snowmobile industry can do as well," says Bluewater Public Land Director Sean Smith.[43]

Both Bluewater and the snowmobile manufacturers argue that EPA has misinterpreted the legal authority on which the new standards rely. Bluewater (as well as other environmental groups and STAPPA, the association representing state air pollution program administrators) argues that EPA is promulgating standards that are less stringent than the law requires. Section 213(a)(3) of the Clean Air Act requires the Agency to promulgate standards that "achieve the greatest degree of emission reduction achievable ... giving appropriate consideration to the cost ... and to noise, energy, and safety factors...." Four-stroke engine technology, achieving greater emission reductions than the Agency proposed, is already available, they note — machines using this technology are on the market. Cost, noise, and energy factors cannot be used as arguments against adoption of this technology: the lifetime cost of such engines would be lower than that of current engines, according to the Agency's own analysis; the technology uses far less energy, and could be substantially quieter than current engines. Thus, according to these groups, the Agency's standards do not meet the requirements of the act.

Snowmobile and other nonroad-vehicle manufacturers, on the other hand, focus on Section 213(a)(2) of the act, which ties the Agency's authority to regulate nonroad engines to a finding by the Administrator that emissions from such engines or vehicles "are significant contributors to ozone or carbon monoxide concentrations in more than 1 area which has failed to attain the national ambient air quality standards for ozone or carbon monoxide." EPA addressed this issue before beginning the process of developing regulations: on June 17, 1994, the Agency made an affirmative determination that emissions from nonroad engines and vehicles are significant contributors to ozone, CO, and particulate matter in more than one nonattainment area.[44] On December 7, 2000, the Agency issued a finding that recreational vehicles (including snowmobiles) are among the specific categories of nonroad vehicles that contribute to such pollution.[45] In its October 5, 2001 Federal Register notice, which proposed the snowmobile standards, the Agency identified 7 areas in Alaska, Washington, Colorado, Oregon, and Montana that have significant populations of snowmobiles and have failed to attain the air quality standard for CO.[46]

Manufacturers of snowmobiles and other nonroad vehicles note, however, that carbon monoxide concentrations have declined [chiefly as a result of auto emission standards] and that none of the 7 areas identified by the Agency has exceeded the CO standard in recent years, even if they are still formally classified as nonattainment. CO nonattainment today is essentially a problem in urban "hot spots," according to manufacturers, and snowmobiles make no contribution to that problem.[47]

LEGISLATIVE ISSUES

Members of Congress, both from western and other states, have expressed an interest in whether there will be continued snowmobile access to national parks. Four hearings have been held on these issues since the 106th Congress. In November 2004, Congress approved language in the Consolidated Appropriations Act, 2005 (H.R. 4818, H.Rept. 108-792), providing that the Temporary Winter Use Rules permitting snowmobiles in Yellowstone and Grand Teton National Parks and the Rockefeller Memorial Parkway "shall be in force and effect for the winter use season of 2004-2005."[48] Previously, a provision was attached to the FY2001 Consolidated Appropriations Act (P.L. 106-554) to block the National Park Service from reducing snowmobile use in any units of the National Park System during the 2000-2001 or 2001-2002 winter seasons.[49]

In the 108th Congress, Representative Holt has twice attempted to amend Interior Department Appropriation bills to prohibit spending to manage recreational snowmobile use in the three Yellowstone area park units except in accordance with the Clinton Administration rule phasing out snowmobiles. The first such amendment (H.Amdt. 266 to H.R. 2691) was defeated on a tie vote, 210-210, July 17, 2003. The second attempt (H.Amdt. 563 to H.R. 4568) was defeated on June 17, 2004, by a vote of 224-198.

Other legislation has been introduced, but not acted on. In the first session of the 107th Congress, two bills addressing snowmobile use were introduced: S. 365, introduced by Senator Thomas, to require the National Park Service to allow continued access to snowmobiles; and H.R. 1465, introduced by Representative Holt, with the opposite intention — to codify proposed NPS restrictions. The Holt bill would have set forth a general prohibition on snowmobile access to national parks, with a limited number of exceptions — for parks in Alaska, for Voyageurs National Park, for access to private inholdings for owners and their guests, and for designated routes that provide direct access to public lands open to public snowmobile use in the vicinity of a park. These restrictions would have applied to all snowmobiles irrespective of their emission or noise levels. S. 365, on the other hand, assumed that EPA regulations would result in cleaner, quieter machines. The bill would have preserved access to the parks for current unregulated snowmobiles for a period of at least five years after the date of enactment, and would have directed the National Park Service, at the completion of that period, to propose noise standards for snowmobile use in national parks "taking into account noise reductions achieved in conjunction with" EPA's emission standards. Neither of these bills was reintroduced in the 108th Congress.

Bills addressing snowmobile issues were also introduced in the second session of the 107th Congress. In response to the draft Supplemental EIS on access to Grand Teton, Yellowstone, and the Rockefeller Parkway and the NPS plan to allow snowmobiles access, H.R. 5044 was introduced. This bill, introduced by Representative Holt, would have banned snowmobile access to the three areas. An identical bill, S. 2697, was introduced in the Senate by Senator Reid. Bills similar to these (H.R. 1130 and S. 965) were reintroduced in the 108th Congress by the same sponsors, but no action was taken on them.

Finally, two bills were introduced during the second session of the 107th Congress in response to the closure to snowmobiles of a portion of Denali National Park, discussed previously. Representative Don Young's H.R. 4677 would have opened portions of the closed sections of Denali to snowmobiles, but continued to prohibit use in other portions of the closed sections; a similar bill, S. 2589, was introduced in the Senate by Senator Murkowski. These bills were not acted on, and have not been reintroduced.

CONCLUSIONS

Despite actions by Congress, EPA, NPS, and the courts, snowmobile issues remain far from resolved. Congress has provided a temporary resolution of the Yellowstone access issue, but since it affects only the current winter season, the issue is likely to return in the 109th Congress. EPA and the National Park Service have been charged by the courts with revising emission standards and developing snowmobile access requirements, respectively. Their actions will provide further opportunities for public and congressional involvement. The courts will also continue to be involved in these issues, with the continuing legal proceedings over Yellowstone access, as well as the suits filed regarding emission standards for snowmobiles.

Public interest in snowmobile issues remains significant: the reopening of the Yellowstone area Winter Use Plan in early 2003, for example, generated 350,000 public comments. Thus, Congress can be expected to retain an interest in the resolution of these issues.

REFERENCES

[1] Statement of Ed Klim, President, International Snowmobile Manufacturers Association, at U.S. EPA Public Hearing, Washington, D.C., October 24, 2001.

[2] Petition to Prohibit Snowmobiling and Road Grooming in National Parks, submitted to the National Park Service, January 21, 1999, by Bluewater Network and 60 other environmental groups. A copy of the petition is attached to the testimony of Sean Smith, Public Lands Director, Bluewater Network, submitted to the Subcommittee on National Parks, Historic Preservation and Recreation, Senate Energy and Natural Resources Committee, May 25, 2000.

[3] Motorized recreation includes all-terrain vehicles, off-road motorcycles, and personal water craft, in addition to snowmobiles.

[4] Executive Order 11644, "Use of Off-Road Vehicles on the Public Lands," 37 Federal Register 2877, February 9, 1972.

[5] Statement of Donald J. Barry, Assistant Secretary for Fish and Wildlife and Parks, U.S. Department of the Interior, before the House Committee on Resources, Subcommittee on National Parks and Public Lands, and the Senate Committee on Energy and Natural Resources, Subcommittee on National Parks, Historic Preservation, and Recreation, May 25, 2000.

[6] U.S. Department of the Interior, Office of the Assistant Secretary, "National Park Service Puts the Brakes on Escalating Snowmobile Use in the National Park System," Press Release, April 27, 2000, p. 2. In addition to Alaska parks and the three Yellowstone area units discussed below, Voyageurs National Park in Minnesota was also exempted because of the express authorization of snowmobiles in its enabling legislation.

[7] Statement of Denis P. Galvin, Deputy Director, National Park Service before the Subcommittee on National Parks and Public Lands, House Committee on Resources, Oversight Hearing on General Issues Involving Access to National Parks, July 20, 2000, p. 2.
[8] The temporary closure was instituted on February 3, 1999. The permanent closure was finalized June 19, 2000, at 65 Federal Register 37863.
[9] Special Regulations, Areas of the National Park System, 66 Federal Register 7260, January 22, 2001.
[10] Special Regulations, Areas of the National Park System, 68 Federal Register 69268, December 11, 2003.
[11] Ibid., p. 69269.
[12] Ibid.
[13] Seventy-five of the passes are for the Continental Divide Snowmobile Trail, which lies in both Grand Teton National Park and the Parkway. These are counted in each unit's total.
[14] [http://www.nps.gov/yell/press/03115.htm].
[15] [http://www.nps.gov/yell/planvisit/todo/winter/batlist_current.htm].
[16] Fund for Animals v. Norton, 2003 U.S. Dist. LEXIS 22557 (D. D.C. December 16, 2003).
[17] NPS denied the petition February 17, 2004, stating that given the differences among parks, "a service-wide directive to prohibit all forms of recreational snowmobile use in the National Park System is no longer warranted and ... with requirements for monitoring and increased use of newer technology snowmobiles, recreational uses can continue to be a part of the NPS winter experience. This will allow decisions to be made on a park-by-park basis, relying on the professional judgment of each park's staff. They will be able to consider the lessons from Yellowstone, such as the use of Best Available Technology requirements, guiding requirements, and adaptive management, as well as overall technological improvements and any other new information, and will then be able to determine whether any review or revision of their special regulations is needed." See "Snowmobile Use in the National Park System," Memorandum from Assistant Secretary for Fish and Wildlife and Parks to the Director, National Park Service, February 17, 2004, pp. 4-5.
[18] Yellowstone National Park, "Winter Use Plans Environmental Assessment and Proposed Rule," December 6, 2004, p. 2 at [http://www.nps.gov/yell/planvisit/winteruse/].
[19] See [http://www.nps.gov/yell/press/0448.htm].
[20] 69 Federal Register 54072.
[21] Department of the Interior, National Park Service, "Special Regulations; Areas of the National Park System; Final Rule," 69 Federal Register 65347, November 10, 2004. Hereafter, "November 2004 Regulations."
[22] The exceptions are primarily for snowmobiles accessing other public lands or private property by way of specific road or trail segments. See November 2004 Regulations, p. 65351.
[23] November 2004 Regulations, p. 65350.
[24] In a four-stroke engine (used in automobiles and some newer outboard motors and lawn mowers, but not generally used in snowmobiles) the combustion chamber takes in fuel,

compresses it, ignites it, and exhausts it in separate cycles, leading to far more complete combustion and lower emissions, even without the application of emission controls.

[25] U.S. EPA, Office of Air and Radiation, *Draft Regulatory Support Document: Control of Emissions from Unregulated Nonroad Engines*, September 2001, p. I-25, available at [http://www.epa.gov/otaq/regs/ nonroad/proposal/cleanrec.htm#rsd].

[26] U.S. Department of the Interior, National Park Service, *Winter Use Plans, Final Environmental Impact Statement for the Yellowstone and Grand Teton National Parks and John D. Rockefeller, Jr., Memorial Parkway,* Volume 1, Chapter 4, p. 224, available at [http://www.planning.nps.gov/document/ yellwinterusevol1.pdf]. Ambient air quality standards were not exceeded elsewhere in the park.

[27] National Park Service, Proposed Rule, Special Regulations, Areas of the National Park System, 65 Federal Register 79026, December 18, 2000.

[28] U.S.EPA, Control of Emissions from Nonroad Large Spark-Ignition Engines, and Recreational Engines (Marine and Land-Based), Final Rule, 67 Federal Register 68241, available at [http://www.epa.gov/fedrgstr/EPA-AIR/2002/November/Day-08/a23801.htm].

[29] Notice of Proposed Rulemaking: Control of Emissions from Nonroad Large Spark Ignition Engines and Recreational Engines (Marine and Land-based), Preamble, 66 Federal Register 51154, October 5, 2001. Further discussion, including the cost estimates, is found on pp. 51169-51170. The preamble to the final standards says that one scenario for meeting the 2006/2007 standards would be 15% four-stroke engines, 15% direct injection two-strokes, 60% conventional two-strokes with improved carburetion, enleanment strategies, and engine modifications; presumably, the other 10% would have no modifications at all. Control of Emissions from Nonroad Large Spark-ignition Engines, and Recreational Engines (Marine and Land-based), Final Rule, as signed September 13, 2002, Preamble, p. 93, available at [http://www.epa.gov/otaq/regs/nonroad/2002/preamble.pdf].

[30] Preamble to the Final Rule, ibid., p. 94.

[31] Ibid., Table IX.B-1, p. 179.

[32] Ibid.

[33] Ibid., p. 73.

[34] Ibid., p. 135.

[35] Personal communication, John Mueller, U.S. EPA Office of Transportation and Air Quality, September 28, 2001.

[36] U.S. EPA, Office of Air and Radiation, *Summary and Analysis of Comments: Control of Emissions from Unregulated Nonroad Engines*, September 2002, p.II-78, available at [http://www.epa.gov/otaq/regs/ nonroad/2002/r02023.pdf].

[37] 36 CFR 7.13(a)(6)(C)(ii), November 2004 Regulations, p. 65361.

[38] Bluewater Network v. EPA, D.D.C., No. 03-1003, June 1, 2004, p. 4.

[39] Personal communication, Ed Klim, President, ISMA, September 27, 2001.

[40] Personal communication, Sean Smith, Bluewater Network, September 27, 2001. Also see "Bush Administration Fails to Protect Public Health, Folds to Industry Interests," Press Release, September 13, 2002, available at [http://www.bluewaternetwork.org/press_releases/ pr2002sep13_pl_eparule.pdf].

[41] Bluewater Network, "Comments on the Environmental Protection Agency's Advanced Notice of Proposed Rulemaking, Docket A-2000-01," p. 2.

[42] See " 'Clean' Snowmobile Produces Lower Emissions than the Average Car at SAE Clean Snowmobile Challenge 2001," Press Release, April 10, 2001.
[43] Personal communication, Sean Smith, Bluewater Network, September 27, 2001.
[44] 59 Federal Register 31306, June 17, 1994.
[45] 65 Federal Register 76790, December 7, 2000.
[46] 66 Federal Register 51105-51107, October 5, 2001. The Preamble to the final rule revised the list of 7 areas, identifying 6 nonattainment areas in which the Agency believes snowmobiles are significant contributors to CO concentrations; the Agency added that there are 6 additional areas that have not been classified nonattainment, but where air quality monitoring indicates a need for CO control. See Preamble to the Final Rule, previously cited, p. 18.
[47] Statement of Ed Klim, President, ISMA, at EPA Public Hearing, Washington, D.C., October 24, 2001.
[48] Section 146 of Title I of Division E of the Consolidated Appropriations Act, 2005 (H.R.4818, H.Rept. 108-792).
[49] The text of the snowmobile provision can be found in the conference report, H.Rept. 106-1033, which contains the text of nine bills incorporated by reference in the act.

In: Public Lands: Use and Misuse
Editor: William E. Neeley, pp. 81-97
ISBN: 978-1-60021-352-6

Chapter 6

RECREATION ON FEDERAL LANDS*

Kori Calvert, Sandra L. Johnson, Carol Hardy Vincent, Ross W. Gorte, Nicole T. Carter, Nic Lane, David L. Whiteman and M. Lynne Corn

SUMMARY

The growing and diverse nature of recreation on federal lands has increased the challenge of balancing recreation with other land uses, and balancing different types of recreation. Motorized recreation has been particularly controversial, with issues centering on access and environmental impacts. The 109th Congress is considering legislation and conducting oversight on issues involving recreation on federal lands, including traditional recreational pursuits and newer forms of motorized recreation. The Administration is addressing these issues through budgetary, regulatory, and other actions. Several prominent issues are covered in this report.

Motorized Recreation in the National Forests and on BLM Land. The use of off-highway vehicles (OHVs) on Forest Service (FS) and Bureau of Land Management (BLM) lands has been particularly controversial. Both agencies decide the extent of allowed OHV use through their planning processes. The FS finalized new regulations (Nov. 9, 2005) governing OHV use that require designating roads, trails, and areas open for OHV use and prohibit OHV use outside the designated system. The BLM is addressing transportation issues through national strategies and other guidance. A July 13, 2005, House Resources joint subcommittee hearing examined motorized recreation use on federal lands. The FY2007 Administration budget request would cut FS recreation management by 3% and trails funding by 19%, and BLM recreation management by 2%. The House-passed Interior appropriations bill restored or increased funding for these accounts.

Personal Watercraft and Snowmobiles. Personal watercraft (PWC) and snowmobile use in National Park Service (NPS) units has fueled debate over the balance between recreation on, and protection of, park lands and waters. Regulatory actions restricting use of these vehicles have been especially controversial. The NPS currently is evaluating PWC and snowmobile use in several areas. Service-wide management policies encompassing motorized and non-motorized recreation are being reviewed.

Aircraft Overflights. Grand Canyon National Park is at the center of a conflict over whether to limit air tours over national parks to reduce noise. The NPS and the Federal

* Excerpted from CRS Report IB10141, Updated June 8, 2006

Aviation Administration (FAA) continue to work to implement a 1987 law that sought to reduce noise at Grand Canyon, and a 2000 law that regulates overflights at other park units. Recent regulations require air tour operators to seek authority to fly over park units; the agencies then must develop Air Tour Management Plans at those park units. Further, the FAA is developing final safety regulations for commercial air tours nationally.

The National Trails System. While designation of trails is often popular, issues remain regarding funding, expansion, and quality of trails. The 109th Congress is considering a variety of trail measures, including adding routes to the National Trail System, authorizing studies of routes for possible additions to the system, and authorizing land acquisitions from willing sellers. Legislation has been introduced to create a new category of trails, called National Discovery Trails.

Other Issues. Other federal land recreation issues of interest to the 109th Congress include recreational uses within the National Wildlife Refuge System, recreation at federal water sites (Army Corps of Engineers and Bureau of Reclamation), recreation fees, and Grand Canyon Colorado River management.

Most Recent Developments

- In H.R. 5386, the House approved $67.0 million for BLM recreation management in FY2007, a 3% increase over the FY2006 appropriation.
- The House approved $264.0 million for FS recreation management, 1% above FY2006 and 4% above the request, and $73.4 million for trails, 1% below FY2006 and 22% above the request.
- On May 10, 2006, the House Appropriations Committee adopted an amendment to the FY2007 Interior appropriations bill (H.R. 5386, H.Rept. 109-465) urging NPS to complete PWC rulemakings "in an efficient and timely manner."
- On May 4, 2006, NPS issued final rules to allow PWC use within designated areas of Gulf Islands National Seashore.
- The House passed H.R. 5386 on May 18, 2006, with a provision (Sec. 124) to ensure that the rule allowing snowmobiles in three Yellowstone area parks will remain in effect throughout the 2006-2007 winter use season.
- On June 1, 2006, the Secretary of the Interior announced the designation of 36 new National Recreation Trails (NRTs), totaling more than 800 miles.

Background and Analysis

Introduction

Four federal agencies administer about 94% of the approximately 672 million acres of federally owned land in the United States: the National Park Service (NPS), the Fish and Wildlife Service (FWS), and the Bureau of Land Management (BLM) in the Department of the Interior (DOI), and the Forest Service (FS) in the Department of Agriculture. The lands these agencies administer are managed for a variety of purposes relating to the preservation, development, and use of the lands and natural resources. The NPS administers the Park System for recreational use of parklands and preservation of park resources, a mission that can be contradictory. The FWS manages wildlife refuges primarily for protecting and improving fish and wildlife habitats. The BLM manages public lands and the FS manages national forests for similar multiple uses — grazing, recreation, timber, water, and fish and wildlife. Most forests and public lands also are available for mineral exploration and development. The National Trails System, administered by the FS, NPS, and BLM, often in cooperation with state and local authorities, permits most recreation uses, but motorized vehicles generally are prohibited. This preservation/use dichotomy, while varying among agencies, is a focal point for debate over recreation on federal lands. Increased recreational use, and charges of overuse in some areas, contribute to disagreement on issues of access, regulation, integrity of natural and cultural resources, and motorized versus non-motorized recreational activities. Recreation debates also arise in areas managed by other federal agencies, such as reservoirs and rivers managed by the Army Corps of Engineers (in the Department of Defense) and the DOI's Bureau of Reclamation, where decisions on water releases may affect recreation.

The growth and development of western states, proximity of many urban areas to public lands, and growing popularity of outdoor recreation have translated into high demand for a variety of recreational opportunities on federal lands and waters. Agency figures indicate an overall increase in recreational visits to federal lands in recent decades. In 2005, DOI experienced 461 million recreation visits: 58 million visits to 3,496 BLM recreational sites; 273 million recreation visits to NPS units (then 388, now 390 units); 40 million visits to 545 FWS wildlife refuges; and 90 million visits to 308 Bureau of Reclamation recreation sites. (See [http://www.doi.gov/budget/2007/07Hilites/DH53.pdf].) The Forest Service reports 211 million recreation visits to its national forests and grasslands, and the Corps 400 million visits for the most recent year available.

Motorized Recreation

Over the last 40 years, new forms of motorized recreation — snowmobiles, personal watercraft, other off-highway vehicles — and non-motorized vehicles, such as mountain bikes, have gained in popularity. For instance, there were roughly 8.6 million visitor days of motorized recreation on BLM lands during FY2004. This figure includes off-highway vehicle (OHV) use of all- terrain vehicles, dune buggies, motorcycles, cars, trucks, and SUVs as well as recreation involving powerboats, personal watercraft, and snowmobiles. In 2004, OHV users accounted for between 11 and 12 million recreation visits to national forests and grasslands. These new forms intersect with the many popular traditional forms of recreation. These include water-based activities — fishing, canoeing, kayaking, rafting, etc. — and a variety of land-based pursuits — bird watching, camping, hiking, hunting, horseback riding, rock climbing, skiing, etc. The use of motorized OHVs on federal lands and waters has been particularly contentious, and lawsuits have challenged OHV management. OHV supporters argue that these vehicles provide outdoor recreation opportunities for the disabled, senior citizens, and others with mobility limitations; visitor access to hard-to-reach natural areas; economic benefits to communities serving riders; and, for snowmobiles, increased access to sites during the winter season. They believe technological advances do and will continue to limit noise and pollution. Critics of OHVs raise environmental concerns, including the potential for damage to land and water ecosystems and wildlife habitat; noise, air, and water pollution; and a diminished experience for recreationists seeking quiet and solitude.

Two executive orders define and generally guide administering OHV use on federal lands. The first (E.O. 11644, Feb. 8, 1972) defines an off-road vehicle, now commonly referred to as an off-highway vehicle, as "any motorized vehicle designed for or capable of cross country travel on or immediately over land, water, sand, snow, ice, marsh, swampland, or other natural terrain," with exceptions for any registered motorboat or authorized or emergency vehicles. It was issued to "establish policies and provide for procedures that will ensure that the use of off-road vehicles on public lands will be controlled and directed so as to protect the resources of those lands, to promote the safety of all users of those lands, and to minimize conflicts among the various uses of those lands." The order directed each agency head to develop and issue regulations to carry out this purpose and to provide for the designation of areas and trails on which OHVs may be permitted, and areas in which such vehicles would not be permitted. Agency heads were to monitor the effects of OHV use and amend or rescind designations of areas or other actions taken pursuant to this order as needed to further the policy of the executive order.

A subsequent executive order (E.O. 11989, May 24, 1977) amended the 1972 order to exclude military, emergency, and law enforcement vehicles from the definition of off-road vehicles (to which restrictions would apply). It provided authority to immediately close areas or trails if OHVs were causing or would cause considerable adverse effects on the soil, vegetation, wildlife, wildlife habitat, or cultural or historic resources of particular areas or trails. Areas could remain closed until the manager determined that "the adverse effects have been eliminated and that measures have been implemented to prevent future recurrence." Also, each agency head was authorized to adopt the policy that areas could be closed to OHV use except for those areas or trails that are specifically designated as open to such use. This meant that only open areas would have to be marked, a lesser burden on the agencies.

Overview of Issues

Federal land managers face a difficult task in managing lands to achieve multiple purposes: to provide recreational opportunities for popular, but often conflicting, motorized and non-motorized recreational uses; to protect resources for future generations; and to determine which lands should be open for development (e.g., timber harvesting, livestock grazing, and energy development). BLM and FS managers formulate guidance on the nature and extent of land uses, including OHV use, through regulations, national policies, land and resource management plans, and area-specific decisions. In 2004, the NPS conducted an internal survey of current OHV use, authorized and unauthorized, and the extent of OHV damage (if any) at NPS units to respond to concerns raised by Bluewater Network. Currently, NPS is developing regulatory guidance and planning documents for individual park units, and considering what elements of OHV management may best fit under a national OHV management strategy. Meanwhile, on November 29, 2005, Bluewater Network and two other conservation groups sued DOI and NPS over alleged OHV damage to park resources.

The NPS also released draft Management Policies for public review through February 18, 2006 (70 *Fed. Reg.* 60852, Oct. 19, 2005; 70 *Fed. Reg.* 71557, Nov. 29, 2005), part of ongoing efforts to review and revise policies guiding management throughout the national park system, including changing recreational uses and evolving technologies. (See [http://parkplanning.nps.gov/ document.cfm?projectId=13746&documentID=12825] for the proposed Management Policies and an annotated comparison between the 2001 document and current draft proposal.) The draft language requires "balance" between "conservation and enjoyment," whereas current policy states that "conservation is to be predominant" in conservation/enjoyment conflicts (sec. 1.4.3). The draft defines key concepts ("conserve, preserve, protect," "impairment," "appropriate use," and "unacceptable impacts"). The proposed policies also revise language pertaining to soundscape management (sec. 4.9), use of motorized equipment (sec. 8.2), and off-road vehicle use (sec. 8.2.3). The extent to which these and other changes represent a shift in emphasis for management of motorized and other recreation is uncertain.

The 109th Congress is considering legislation and conducting oversight on issues pertaining to recreation on federal lands. Several major issues are covered in this report, particularly motorized recreation on BLM and FS lands; use of personal watercraft and snowmobiles in certain National Park System units; overflights of national park units; and expansion of the National Trails System. Other issues addressed cover recreation within the National Wildlife Refuge System; recreation at federal (Corps and Bureau) water sites; recreation fees; and Colorado River management within Grand Canyon National Park.

While this report focuses on recreation issues on federal lands, it does not cover additional issues affecting these lands comprehensively. For background on federal land management generally, see CRS Report RL32393, *Federal Land Management Agencies: Background on Land and Resources Management*, coordinated by Carol Hardy Vincent. Overview information on numerous natural resource use and protection issues is provided in CRS Report RL32699, *Natural Resources: Selected Issues for the 109th Congress*, coordinated by Nicole Carter and Carol Hardy Vincent. For information on NPS issues, see CRS Issue Brief IB10145, *National Park Management*, coordinated by Carol Hardy Vincent. Information on BLM and Forest Service lands is contained in CRS Issue Brief IB10076, *Bureau of Land Management (BLM) Lands and National Forests*, coordinated by Ross W. Gorte and Carol Hardy Vincent. For information on appropriations for federal land management agencies, see CRS Report RL33399, *Interior, Environment, and Related Agencies: FY2007 Appropriations*, coordinated by Carol Hardy Vincent and Susan Boren.

CURRENT ISSUES

Motorized Recreation on BLM Land (by Carol Hardy Vincent)

Background. The growing and diverse nature of recreation on BLM lands has increased the challenge of managing recreation and other land uses, and managing different types of recreation. Access to BLM lands for a variety of recreational purposes is viewed as important for fostering public health, public support for land management, and a stable economic base for communities that depend on recreation and tourism. It also has enhanced interest in protecting the ecological integrity of federal lands from environmental harm as a result of recreational use.

Motorized OHV use, including use of dirt bikes and all-terrain vehicles, is a major recreational use of BLM lands that has been controversial. While motorized user groups often have opposed restrictions on OHV use, many environmentalists have been concerned about harm to natural and cultural resources. In some areas, OHV use may conflict with other types of recreation, such as hiking, that seek quiet and solitude on agency lands. There are also differing views on how effectively OHV authorities are being enforced. While BLM employs a variety of means of enforcement, including monitoring, law enforcement, signing and mapping, and emergency closures of routes, enforcement may be impeded in some locations due to their remoteness, insufficient signage, lack of sufficient staff and resources, and other factors.

Administrative Actions. Guidance on OHV use on BLM lands is provided in law, executive orders, and agency regulations and policies. Under agency regulations (43 C.F.R. 8340), BLM has been designating public lands as open, limited, or closed to OHV use. As of October 31, 2005, the following designations had been made: open, where OHV use is permitted anywhere, 81.1 million acres; limited, where OHV use is in some way restricted, 126.7 million acres; and closed, where OHV use is prohibited, 11.6 million acres. The remaining 42.1 million acres of BLM land (mostly in Alaska) are not currently designated. Other regulations govern OHV use in particular areas. For instance, on August 18, 2005, BLM issued final supplementary rules for its lands in Oregon and Washington, which include guidance on OHV use.

The FY2007 BLM budget justification describes BLM's "most pressing challenge" as "comprehensively managing travel, off highway vehicles (OHVs), and public access in the West (p. III -128). In FY2007, BLM plans to develop approximately 67 travel management plans, which will identify and designate roads and trails for motorized travel, and to begin implementation when the plans are completed. The agency requested $63.8 million for recreation management generally for FY2007, a 2% reduction from the FY2006 level of $65.1 million. In passing H.R. 5386, the House approved $67.0 million for recreation management in FY2007, a 3% increase over FY2006 and a 5% increase over the Administration's request.

BLM has issued two national strategies dealing with transportation on its lands. The *National Management Strategy for Motorized Off-Highway Vehicle Use on Public Lands* ([http://www.blm.gov/ohv/]) has multiple purposes, including to guide land managers in resolving OHV issues; to promote consistency of OHV decision making; to highlight needed staff and funding for OHV management; to reduce conflicts among land users; to promote responsible OHV use and reduce habitat degradation; and to lead to an update of OHV regulations (which has not occurred to date). The *National Mountain Bicycling Strategic Action Plan* ([http://www.blm.gov/mountain_biking/] addresses mountain bicycling and other muscle-powered mechanical transport. Further, to guide BLM managers in taking actions affecting recreation during FY2003-FY2007, in May 2003 BLM issued *The BLM's Priorities for Recreation and Visitor Services.*

BLM revised its land use planning handbook in 2005 regarding motorized and non-motorized recreation. The agency makes OHV designations during the planning process, on an area-by-area basis, and such designations often have been contentious and complex. Although the agency is in the midst of a multi-year effort to develop and update land use plans, many plans do not currently address OHV use and other relatively recent issues. In some cases, the BLM and FS jointly address OHV use on their lands. For instance, an interagency plan governs OHV use on lands in Montana, North Dakota, and South Dakota. Joint management approaches, where federal lands are intermingled, can promote consistency and public understanding of OHV guidance. However, BLM and FS lands are different, and they are governed by separate authorities, making complete consistency on vehicular travel management difficult to achieve.

Legislative Activity. A July 13, 2005, House Resources joint subcommittee hearing examined motorized recreational use on federal lands. (See [http://resourcescommittee.house.gov/archives/109/nprpl/071305.htm].) Agency representatives discussed the increased popularity of OHV use on federal lands, development and implementation of travel management plans, and challenges of managing OHVs. Other witnesses testified on availability of federal lands for OHV use, and the effects of OHV use on human health, the economy, the environment, and other forms of recreation.

Some pending measures affect OHV use in particular areas. For instance, H.R. 3603 contains provisions related to OHV use in Central Idaho. They include conveyance of BLM land to the State of Idaho to establish a motorized recreation park, establishment of a special management area on certain BLM and FS lands to provide opportunities for motorized and other recreation, and authorization of up to $1.0 million for the Secretary of Agriculture to grant to the State of Idaho for the off-road motor vehicle program.

Motorized Recreation in the National Forests (by Ross Gorte)

Background. The national forests are managed by the USDA Forest Service (FS) for a variety of uses, including many types of recreation — sightseeing, OHV use, backpacking, etc. — while preserving the productivity of the lands. Recreation use continues to grow, with OHV use among the fastest growing uses. (See *Off-Highway Vehicle Recreation in the United States, Regions and States* (USDA-FS Southern Research Station, June 2005).)

The various uses and values of the national forests sometimes conflict with one another. For example, timber harvesting and OHV use may affect bird watching and sightseeing, and can degrade water quality in certain settings. Decisions about what uses are allowed, and when and where, are made in comprehensive land and resource management plans prepared for each unit of the National Forest System, and at the project level. Because of multiple efforts to modify the planning regulations, many plan revisions were delayed. New planning regulations (70 *Fed. Reg.* 1023, Jan. 5, 2005) have recently been finalized, and plan revisions are now expected to proceed. (See [http://www.fs.fed.us/emc/nfma/index2.html].)

Administrative Actions. Federal guidance on OHV use in E.O. 11644 and E.O. 11989 was incorporated into FS regulations, at 36 C.F.R. Part 295. Despite this guidance, not all forest plans have identified areas as open or closed to OHVs, and local practices as to OHV use vary. In 2004, the FS Chief identified *unmanaged recreation* — "increasing use of the national forests for outdoor activities ... , including the use of off-highway vehicles" — as a threat to the nation's forests and grasslands. In particular, OHV use has created many unauthorized roads and trails, which can be unsafe and harmful to other resources. In response, the FS has finalized new regulations (70 *Fed. Reg.* 68264-68291, Nov. 9, 2005) to *require* forest plans to identify a system of roads, trails, and areas for motorized vehicle use and prohibit the use of OHVs and other motorized vehicles outside the designated system. Implementing directives are expected to be published for public comment during 2006, and decisions governing motorized uses are then to be made in forest planning (with public involvement) over the next four years.

Opinions are divided over the importance and impact of the regulations. Some assert that the regulations do not go far enough, preferring that all OHV uses be prohibited in the national forests, because OHVs can (and sometimes do) damage national forest lands and resources. Others counter that the regulations penalize the majority of OHV users that obey the current rules and restrict off-highway uses at a time when other landowners and other federal and state agencies are reducing recreational access to their lands.

The FY2007 FS budget proposes cutting recreation funds. Recreation management would be funded at $250 million, a $7.9 million (3%) reduction from the FY2006 level of $258.8 million. Trails funding would be $60.3 million, a $13.9 million (19%) reduction from the FY2006 level of $74.2 million, with a greater reduction (in dollars and percentage) in trails construction than in maintenance.

Legislative Activity. The House-passed FY2007 Interior appropriations bill, H.R. 5386, restored or increased FS recreation and trails funding, compared to the request. Recreation management was approved at $262.0 million, $3.2 million (1%) above FY2006 and $11.1 million (4%) above the request. Trails funding was approved at $73.4 million, $0.8 million (1%) below FY2006 (all in construction) and $13.1 million (22%) above the request (increasing both construction and maintenance).

On July 13, 2005, two subcommittees of House Resources held a joint hearing to examine motorized recreation use on federal lands. (See "Legislative Activity" under BLM, above.) To date, no comprehensive legislation addressing OHV use in national forests generally has been introduced in the 109th Congress.

Personal Watercraft (PWC) (by Kori Calvert)

Background. PWCs are high-speed, very shallow draft, and highly maneuverable watercraft "operated by a person or persons sitting, standing, or kneeling on the vessel rather than within the confines of the hull" (36 C.F.R. §1.4). Often used to perform stunt-like maneuvers, PWCs include watercraft known by their brand and generic names as jet ski, sea doo, surf jet, water sled, wavejammer, wetjet, waverunner, and wet bike. While PWCs represent a small segment of the recreational boat market, the number of PWC accidents has raised concerns. Critics of PWC use cite environmental issues, including noise, air, and water pollution; damage to land, plants, and wildlife; and public safety. Supporters of access for PWCs argue that technological advances enable manufacturers to produce cleaner, more efficient machines, and point to the economic benefits to communities serving users. PWC users assert that in park units that allow motorized boating generally, PWCs also should be allowed. Recent controversies have focused on regulatory actions that would restrict recreational use or "access" of these vehicles, often in specific park units.

Administrative Actions. The NPS currently is evaluating PWC use in several of its 390 units. That effort began in 2000 when the agency issued a rule prohibiting PWC use in 66 of the 87 units where motorized boats were allowed (65 *Fed. Reg.* 15077, effective April 20, 2000). The rule allowed PWC use to continue until April 22, 2002, at the remaining 21 areas while the NPS evaluated whether to permanently authorize PWC use and develop special regulations. The rule recognized that certain National Recreation Areas (NRAs), such as Lake Mead and Glen Canyon, might choose to continue PWC use because their establishing legislation emphasized motorized water-based recreation as a primary purpose. An April 2001 negotiated settlement of a lawsuit by Bluewater Network and Earth Island Institute over the PWC rule prohibited PWCs from the 21 areas unless the Park Service initiated park-specific rules and environmental assessments. PWCs could continue to operate during the rulemaking process, but only until specified "grace period" deadlines.

The NPS has been working on such park-specific rules and analyses for the 21 areas. The NPS has lifted PWC bans and authorized their use in 11 designated areas: in 2003, Lake Mead and Glen Canyon (Lake Powell) NRAs, and Assateague National Seashore; in 2004, Lake Meredith, Lake Roosevelt, Amistad, and Chickasaw NRAs; in 2005, Bighorn Canyon NRA, Fire Island National Seashore, and Pictured Rocks National Lakeshore; and in 2006, Gulf Islands National Seashore. Five areas are working on environmental reviews and special regulations on PWC use, and the NPS has proposed rules to allow PWCs in three: Cape Lookout National Seashore (Dec. 29, 2005), Gateway NRA (Feb. 24, 2006), and Curecanti NRA (March 17, 2006). The agency prohibited PWC use in another 5 of the 21 areas (effective April 22, 2002) that had completed an environmental review process and favored PWC bans: the Cape Cod and Cumberland Island National Seashores, Delaware Water Gap and Whiskeytown NRAs, and Indiana Dunes National Lakeshore.

Draft NPS Management Policies include revisions concerning PWCs (sec. 8.2.3.3). The draft replaces existing language stating that "(PWC) use is prohibited unless it has been identified as appropriate for a specific park" and is consistent with visitor use criteria (sec. 8.2), with revised wording stating that "(PWC) use may be permitted through special regulations and when this use has been identified as appropriate for a specific park." Whether these changes would have a substantive impact on PWC management is unclear.

Legislative Activity. On May 10, 2006, the House Appropriations Committee adopted by voice vote an amendment to the FY2007 Interior appropriations bill urging NPS to complete PWC rulemakings "in an efficient and timely manner." (See "Administrative Actions," above; and H.Rept. 109-465.) A March 15, 2006, House Government Reform subcommittee hearing examined NPS rulemaking efforts governing PWC use, status of park-specific rules, and reasons for and impacts of rulemaking delays. (See [http://reform.house.gov/RA/Hearings/ EventSingle.aspx?EventID=40886].) On May 4, 2005, a House Resources subcommittee oversight hearing considered PWC use in the National Park System. (See [http://resourcescommittee.house.gov/archives/109/nprpl/ 050405.htm].)

Snowmobiles (by Kori Calvert)

Background. Proposals to regulate recreational snowmobile use in NPS units have been controversial, with debate often mirroring the preservation/use conflict within the NPS mission. On April 27, 2000, the NPS announced the strict enforcement of long-standing regulations on snowmobile use, which would have prohibited recreational snowmobiling throughout the Park System. Limited exceptions to this new enforcement policy included Yellowstone and Grand Teton National Parks, park units in Alaska, Voyageurs National Park (MN), and access to private land within or adjacent to a park. By July 2000, the Interior Department had backed away from its strict enforcement stance with a clarification: snowmobiles would not be banned in the 43 park units permitting such use prior to the April 2000 announcement, pending formal rulemaking and public comment period. To date, NPS has taken no further action on a general policy for snowmobiles.

Administrative Actions. Since the summer of 2000, regulatory and judicial actions to restrict or allow snowmobile use have centered on Yellowstone and Grand Teton National Parks and the connecting John D. Rockefeller, Jr., Memorial Parkway. The Clinton Administration issued final rules (66 *Fed. Reg.* 7260, Jan. 22, 2001) to incrementally eliminate snowmobile use in these three park units, with limited exceptions, in favor of multi-passenger "snowcoaches" by the 2003-2004 winter season. However, a June 2001 Bush Administration lawsuit settlement with the International Snowmobile Manufacturers Association (ISMA) and the state of Wyoming required NPS to revisit the snowmobile ban and consider any additional information on "cleaner, quieter" snowmobile technology. The new NPS final rule (68 *Fed. Reg.* 69267, Dec. 11, 2003) reversed the snowmobile ban in favor of daily entry limits, use of trained guides, snowmobile emission standards, and an "adaptive management strategy" allowing park managers to take remedial action if monitoring indicates unacceptable impacts from air and noise pollution.

Subsequent legal challenges effectively split the 2003-2004 winter season into two sub-seasons, each managed under different rules with significantly different limits on daily snowmobile entries. These conflicting rulings created confusion for park visitors, local communities, and businesses, with many unsure whether they could visit the park in winter and what winter use rules were in effect. Subsequently, NPS issued a final rule (69 *Fed.Reg.* 65348, Nov. 10, 2004) to implement a temporary winter use management plan effective for three winter seasons, through 2006-2007. (See [http://www.nps.gov/yell/press/04114.htm].) The interim rule allows up to 720 commercially guided Yellowstone snowmobile entries daily. Commercial guides are not required for the 140 daily snowmobile entries to Grand Teton and the Rockefeller Parkway. The plan includes, with limited exceptions, Best Available Technology (BAT) requirements to reduce snowmobile emissions and noise, but no "adaptive management strategy" component.

The interim rule's intent is to provide certainty to gateway communities, businesses, and park visitors while NPS completes long-term environmental impact analyses of motorized oversnow vehicles on the three area parks, and develops a new long-term plan to manage winter recreational use. The agency anticipates releasing a draft Environmental Impact Statement (EIS) by fall 2006. The EIS will evaluate several alternative winter use scenarios, each with varying mass-transit snowcoach and snowmobile entry levels, commercial guiding requirements, and Best Available Technology standards for snowcoaches and snowmobiles. (See [http://www.nps.gov/yell/planvisit/winteruse/index.htm].) Meanwhile, the 2005-2006 winter use statistics show 19.9% and 15.3% increases in snowmobile and snowcoach visitors, respectively, over the previous winter season.

Judicial proceedings also continue. On October 14, 2005, Judge Clarence Brimmer, Federal District Court for Wyoming, ruled against the Wyoming Lodging and Restaurant Association's challenge of the NPS interim rule, calling it "...the best compromise currently available." (See [http://www.nps.gov/yell/ technical/planning/winteruse/plan/wlraorder.pdf].) (For background information on snowmobiles in park units generally, see CRS Report RL31149, *Snowmobiles: Environmental Standards and Access to National Parks*, by James E. McCarthy.)

The recently released NPS draft Management Policies add new language to cover both snowmobiles and oversnow vehicles (sec. 8.2.3.2). It states that "Routes and areas may be designated for snowmobile and oversnow vehicle use by special regulation on routes and water surfaces that are used by motor vehicles or motorboats during other seasons. Such routes or areas shall be designated only when determined to be an appropriate use."

Legislative Activity. The FY2007 Interior Appropriations bill (H.R. 5386, Sec. 124) contains language to ensure that the three Yellowstone area parks remain open to snowmobiles throughout the 2006-2007 winter use season. The FY2005 and FY2006 Interior appropriations laws (P.L. 108-447 and P.L. 109-54) included similar language to ensure that judicial rulings could not deny snowmobiles entry during the 2004-2005 and 2005-2006 winter use seasons, respectively. On April 12, 2005, a House Resources subcommittee held an oversight hearing on snowmobile use and restrictions in the National Park System and their economic impact on local communities. (See [http://resourcescommittee.house.gov/archives/109/nprpl/041205.htm].)

Aircraft Overflights (by Carol Hardy Vincent and Kori Calvert)

Background. The NPS is to provide for the public enjoyment of parklands while protecting resources, while the Federal Aviation Administration (FAA) controls airspace and aircraft overflights. This has created a conflict between resource management and aviation access authorities and their constituencies. Grand Canyon National Park has been the focal point of a conflict between groups seeking to limit overflights of national parks due to concerns about noise and safety, and air tour operators whose economic stability, with ripple effects on local businesses, may depend on providing overflights. The National Parks Overflights Act of 1987 (P.L. 100-91) directed NPS to recommend a flight control plan for Grand Canyon that would provide a "substantial restoration of the natural quiet" and prohibited flights below the canyon's rim. It required an NPS study of the effects of all aircraft overflights, which was submitted to Congress in 1994.

The National Parks Air Tour Management Act of 2000 (Title VIII, P.L. 106-181, hereafter "Air Tour Act") regulates commercial air tours at other park units. It requires the FAA and NPS to create management plans for air tours at individual park units and within a half-mile of their boundaries. Each plan could prohibit or limit air tours, such as by route and altitude restrictions. The act also requires the FAA to establish "reasonably achievable" requirements for quiet aircraft technology for the Grand Canyon within one year and to designate, by rule, Grand Canyon routes or corridors for aircraft and helicopters using quiet technology. Quiet aircraft would not be subject to existing caps on canyon overflights.

Administrative Actions. Several actions have been taken to achieve the substantial restoration of natural quiet at Grand Canyon. First, a *limitations rule* capped the annual number of commercial air tour overflights at Grand Canyon (65 *Fed. Reg.* 17708, effective May 4, 2000). Second, the *airspace rule* expanded flight-free zones and restrictive routing over the canyon. East end Special Flight Rules Area (SFRA) airspace changes were delayed until February 20, 2011 (71 *Fed. Reg.* 9439). Third, the FAA issued a final rule establishing a standard for quiet technology for certain aircraft in commercial air tour operations over Grand Canyon (70 *Fed. Reg.* 16084, March 29, 2005). The rule identifies which aircraft meet the standard. In future rulemaking, the FAA will address the establishment of routes or corridors for commercial air tour operations that use the quiet technology. Fourth, data on the natural ambient sound level is being collected and used, together with air tour reported flight operations data and radar tracking data, to model air tour traffic and aircraft noise at the park.

The model is being used to measure success in restoring natural quiet. Most recently, the FAA and NPS published a notice of intent to prepare an environmental impact statement on options that could be taken to restore natural quiet at Grand Canyon (71 *Fed. Reg.* 4192, Jan. 25, 2006). There is a public comment period through April 27, 2006.

Other regulatory actions affect commercial air tours at park units. The Air Tour Act final rule (67 *Fed. Reg.* 65661, Oct. 25, 2002) requires air tour operators to apply for authority to fly over national park and abutting tribal lands. The FAA received applications for commercial air tours over 107 of the 388 park units, and has granted interim operating authority to applicants. Application triggers development of an Air Tour Management Plan (ATMP) by the FAA and NPS for each unit where none exists. (See [http://www.atmp.faa.gov/default.htm].) The purpose of a plan is to mitigate or prevent any harm by commercial air tours to natural and cultural resources, visitor experiences, and tribal lands. Development of an ATMP requires an environmental analysis under the National Environmental Policy Act of 1969 (NEPA, U.S.C. § 4321-4370f). The FAA and NPS currently are developing their first ATMPs for six areas. On September 30, 2005, the FAA and NPS released an implementation plan for the development of the ATMPs that sets out the roles and responsibilities of the two agencies in developing ATMPs.

A Government Accountability Office (GAO) report (GAO-06-263, Jan. 27, 2006) addressed the impact of the delay in implementation of the Air Tour Act. The report concludes that the delay has had little effect on park units, but has limited the ability of tour operators to make major business decisions. The agency identified four issues for Congress and the agencies to address to improve implementation, relating to the lack of flexibility for determining which parks need plans, an absence of NPS funding for plan development, limited ability to verify and enforce the number of air tours, and inadequate FAA guidance on the act's safety requirements. A more recent GAO report (GAO-06-468, May 11, 2006) addresses NPS collection of air tour fees.

The FAA is developing a final rule to provide safety standards for commercial air tours nationally, including over Grand Canyon and other park units (68 *Fed. Reg.* 60572). The proposed rule seeks to increase air tour safety by requiring certification of tour operators and by establishing safety standards, including regarding low-level flights, over-water flights, and visibility limits. Opponents assert that the cost of compliance would make it infeasible for many to continue operating, existing regulations are sufficient to keep tours safe, and the proposed merger of helicopter and airplane traffic increases the chance of collisions. The agency expects to issue a final rule by fall of 2006.

As part of an overall review of its management policies, the NPS has proposed changes on overflights and aviation uses (sec. 8.4) and on soundscape management (sec. 4.9). One proposal would delete existing language stating that the NPS "will preserve, to the greatest extent possible, the natural scoundscapes of parks." Another change would replace "adverse effects" of overflights with "unacceptable impacts" in a number of places. Such changes could be regarded as having a substantive effect on management of overflights.

Legislative Activity. To date, general legislation on aircraft overflights has not been introduced in the 109th Congress. P.L. 108-176 directed the Secretary of Transportation to issue a final rule establishing standards for quiet technology that are reasonably achievable at Grand Canyon. The FAA issued the final rule on March 29, 2005. The law also established a mediation process for rulemaking disputes. Conferees stated that they were "greatly disappointed with the lack of progress" in managing the noise in parks from air tours, and directed the agencies to develop ATMPs expeditiously and collaboratively and to determine environmental impacts of air tours.

The National Trails System (by Sandra L. Johnson)

Background. The National Trails System Act (P.L. 90-543), authorizing the National Trails System (NTS), became law on October 2, 1968. (See [http://www.nps.gov/nts/].) The federal portion of the trails system consists of 24 national trails (8 scenic trails and 16 historic trails, both of which must be designated by Congress) covering almost 50,000 miles, more than 900 recreation trails, and 2 connecting and side trails. Issues involve the funding, quality, and quantity of trails.

Administrative Actions. On June 1, 2006, the Secretary of the Interior announced the designation of 36 new National Recreation Trails (NRTs). Since 2001, the Bush Administration has designated 164 National Recreation Trails, totaling more than 4,200 miles. These designations do not require an act of Congress and are part of an ongoing effort to promote community partnerships and to foster innovative ways to encourage physical fitness.

The Bureau of Land Management (BLM) manages more miles of National Historic Trails than any other federal agency. On February 13, 2006, the BLM released its first National Scenic and Historic Trails Strategy and Work Plan for congressionally-designated trails under its jurisdiction. The 10-year plan provides guidance to establish a coordinated and consistent trails-focused administrative infrastructure; develop national policies to protect and sustain trail resources within BLM's multiple-use mandate; manage trail resources to enhance visitor experiences and promote "appropriate public access;" and maintain and advance BLM's partnerships with trail organizations and other agencies. (See [http://www.blm.gov/nlcs/nsht/NSHTSWfinalSig.pdf].)

Legislative Activity. Many trail projects became eligible to receive federal highway program funds with the passage of the Intermodal Surface Transportation Efficiency Act of 1991 (ISTEA; P.L. 102-240), reauthorized as the Transportation Equity Act for the 21st Century (TEA-21, P.L. 105-178). The Recreational Trails Program (RTP), originally a six-year program authorized under ISTEA and reauthorized under TEA-21, provides funds to states to develop and maintain recreational trails and trail-related facilities for motorized and non-motorized recreational trail uses. On August 10, 2005, President Bush signed into law the Safe, Accountable, Flexible, Efficient Transportation Equity Act: A Legacy for Users (P.L. 109-59, SAFETEA-LU). SAFETEA-LU authorizes funds for the Recreational Trails Program at $370 million over five years ($60 million for FY2005, $70 million for FY2006, $75 million for FY2007, $80 million for FY2008, and $85 million for FY2009). The measure sets a specified level of $840,000 annually for administrative expenses.

Legislation (H.R. 690) introduced on February 9, 2005, would add National Discovery Trails as a new category of long-distance trails within the National Trails System, and designate the American Discovery Trail (ADT) as the nation's first coast-to-coast National Discovery Trail. The ADT would connect several national scenic, historic, and recreation trails, as well as many other local and regional trails. Two "willing seller" bills (H.R. 2332, S. 974) would provide federal authority to acquire land from willing sellers to complete nine national scenic and historic trails. These proposals would not commit the federal government to purchase any land or spend any money, but would allow managers to purchase land to protect the national trails as opportunities arise and funds are appropriated.

Measures introduced in the 109th Congress to designate, study, or extend specific components of the National Trails System are shown in the following table. The table includes bills that could involve management by the NPS or other agencies. Bills related to the system more generally are not included.

Also, on July 26, 2005, a House Resources subcommittee conducted an oversight hearing on the implementation of the National Trails System Act. Issues covered by agency and other witnesses included trail designations, maintenance, and management; land acquisitions; private landowner concerns; and public-private initiatives and collaborative efforts. (See [http://resourcescommittee.house.gov/archives/109/nprpl/072605.htm].)

Bill Number	Type	Title	Status
H.R. 690	Desig.	National Discovery Trails Act	Introduced
H.R. 1250 S. 588	Study	Arizona Trail Feasibility Study Act	Introduced Hearing held
H.R. 1796	Study	Mississippi River Trail Study Act	Introduced
H.R. 2053 S. 958	Desig.	Star-Spangled Banner National Historic Trail	Introduced Passed Senate
H.R. 2361 H.R. 2588 S. 336 HR5466 S. 2568	Study Desig. Desig.	Captain John Smith Chesapeake National Historic Trail	P.L. 109-54 Introduced Hearing held Introduced Ordered reported
H.R. 2964	Study	Chisholm Trail and Great Western Trail	Introduced
H.R. 3085 S. 1970	Study	Trail of Tears National Historic Trail	Introduced Reported (S.Rept. 109-239)
H.R. 3615	Study	1855 Treaty Trail	Introduced
H.R. 5053	Extend	Lewis and Clark National Historic Trail Extension Act of 2006	Introduced
S. 54	Study Extend	Amends the National Trails System Act to require the Secretary of the Interior to update the feasibility and suitability studies of four national historic trails, and for other purposes	Passed Senate

Other Issues

The 109th Congress is evaluating several other recreation issues affecting federal land. These include recreation within the National Wildlife Refuge System; recreation at federal water sites (Bureau of Reclamation and Army Corps of Engineers); recreation fees; and Grand Canyon Colorado River management.

Recreation in the National Wildlife Refuge System. (by M. Lynne Corn) The National Wildlife Refuge System (NWRS) is dedicated primarily to conserving animals and plants. Other uses — hunting, fishing, recreation, timber harvest, grazing, etc. — are permitted only to the extent that they are compatible with the purposes for which the individual refuges were created. Some have characterized the NWRS as intermediate in protection between the BLM and FS lands on the one hand and NPS lands on the other, but this is not entirely accurate. The NWRS resembles the FS or BLM lands in allowing some commercial uses, but in certain cases, uses (e.g., public access) can be substantially more restricted than for NPS lands. For example, some refuges (especially island refuges for nesting seabirds) may be closed to the public — more restrictive than for an NPS area, given the NPS mandate to provide for public enjoyment of park resources.

Recreational conflicts within the NWRS were more frequent before the 1997 enactment of the National Wildlife Refuge System Improvement Act (16 U.S.C. 668dd). A key provision of this law designates "compatible wildlife-dependent recreational uses involving hunting, fishing, wildlife observation and photography, and environmental education and interpretation as priority public uses of the refuge system." It also requires that priority public uses must "receive enhanced consideration over other general public uses in planning and management within the System." The law continues the statutory policy that activities that are not wildlife-dependent (e.g., grazing, growing hay, etc.) may be permitted, provided they are wildlife-compatible. Final regulations for determining compatibility were published on October 18, 2000 (65 *Fed. Reg.* 62457). Some interest groups contended that the regulations did not allow for sufficient public access for some forms of recreation, such as use of off-road vehicles or personal watercraft. Others felt that the regulations struck a proper balance among user groups.

A recent controversy concerns applications for amateur radio operators to have access to three remote island refuges (Farallon, Navassa, and Desecheo) to transmit from these locations. To protect the refuges' seabird colonies and vegetation, FWS does not allow access or consider radio transmission a priority or compatible use. Two bills would require the Interior Secretary to open these refuges for at least one period each year under special use permits. H.R. 298 applies to the three refuges, while H.R. 1183 (reported on Dec. 6, 2005; H.Rept. 109-320) applies only to Navassa and Desecheo. Supporters include radio operators but also those who favor wider public access to federal lands in general. Opposition includes scientists and environmental groups based on risk to the colonies through human interference, introduction of invasive species, and precedent for wider access to sensitive islands.

Recreation at Federal Water Sites. (by Nicole Carter and Nic Lane) Much of the recreation on federally owned or managed waters and adjacent lands occurs at U.S. Army Corps of Engineers ("Corps," in the Department of Defense) and Bureau of Reclamation ("Bureau," in DOI) sites, primarily at federal reservoirs. These agencies' more than 4,000 recreation areas attract nearly 500 million visits per year (400 million at Corps-managed areas; 90 million at Bureau sites). While these federal reservoirs often are operated primarily for irrigation, navigation, hydropower, and/or flood control, they also provide recreation and other benefits. Reservoir operations can be contentious because decisions on water releases often represent tradeoffs among the multiple reservoir and river uses and among different types of recreation, such as bird watching, boating, fishing, hunting, sightseeing, swimming, and whitewater activities.

Bureau of Reclamation. An ongoing issue involves the Bureau's Lake Berryessa in Sonoma County, California. Formed when the Bureau built Monticello Dam in 1957, the lake is a popular recreation area where the Bureau has let long-term contracts with seven concessionaires who provide recreation support services. Six of these contracts, which have been in place for 40 plus years, will expire in 2008-2009. The seventh, an interim contract, expired at the end of 2005. The Bureau is considering significant changes to contract structure upon renewal, including actions that will affect long-term camping (trailer parking) at the lake. This is contentious for the concessionaires and current occupants of long-term sites. (See [http://www.usbr.gov/mp/berryessa/faqs.html].) A Record of Decision clarifying the Bureau's intent for the management of long-term camp sites at the lake is expected to be released this summer.

Corps of Engineers. The 109th Congress is considering questions related to the maintenance of recreational facilities (under constraints on recreational spending), relative priority of multiple reservoir uses, and policies for recreational development and land use at Corps and Bureau projects. Two authorization bills include changes to Corps recreation. The House version of a Water Resources Development Act (WRDA, H.R. 2864) would adjust the existing user fee authorization. The Senate version (S. 728) would make more extensive changes. One provision of S. 728, which is similar to the Administration proposal from the FY2006 and FY2007 budget requests, would require the Corps to implement recreation admission fees. User and admission fees collected would be available directly to the Corps. This contrasts with the deposit into general Treasury accounts of current collections from Corps user fees. A second provision in S. 728 would allow the Corps to enter into a contract with public or private entities to provide visitor services.

Recreation Fees. (by Carol Hardy Vincent) The 108th Congress established a new recreation fee program for the four major federal land management agencies (NPS, BLM, FWS, and FS) as well as the Bureau of Reclamation. Provisions of P.L. 108-447 (Division J, Title VIII) provide guidance on establishing entrance, standard, expanded, and special recreation permit fees. They outline criteria for establishing fees, and prohibit charging fees for certain activities or services. The law provides for public input in setting fees, including establishing Recreation Resource Advisory Committees to make fee recommendations. It authorizes the creation of an interagency national recreation pass and of regional multi-entity passes. Each agency can spend the revenue collected without further appropriation. In general, not less than 80% of the fees are to be spent at the collecting site, but that amount can be reduced to not less than 60%. The balance of the collections is available to be used agency-wide. The collections can be used for specified purposes, such as repair, maintenance, and facility enhancement. The agencies are to report to Congress on the program every three years, and the program is to terminate 10 years after enactment.

DOI and the Department of Agriculture are implementing the new law. They are developing long-term fee guidance and the America the Beautiful Pass, which will cover entrance and standard fees for the five agencies. During the transition to the new program, the agencies have agreed that existing passes will be honored, no new fee areas will be created, and existing fees will be evaluated against the criteria and prohibitions set out in the new law. The agencies (excluding the Bureau of Reclamation) anticipate collecting about $208 million in fees in FY2006 and $240 million in fees in FY2007, with NPS collections accounting for about two-thirds of the totals. The 109th Congress is overseeing agency efforts to establish, collect, and spend recreation fees under the new program. On February 17, 2005, a Senate subcommittee held a hearing on NPS implementation of the program, with a focus on the development of the America the Beautiful Pass. On October 26, 2005, a Senate subcommittee held a hearing on the implementation of the new fee program.

Grand Canyon Colorado River Management. (by David Whiteman) The NPS regulates and manages river-running boat trips on the Colorado River inside Grand Canyon

National Park to protect river resources and ensure a high-quality visitor experience. The 277-mile river canyon is a popular destination for multi-day raft trips, one of the most iconic of national park experiences. Decades of conflict have ensued over motorized boating, helicopter flights used to ferry commercial boating passengers in and out of the canyon, and the proportion of commercial outfitters versus noncommercial private boaters. Historically, about 70% of river access permits have gone to commercial concessioners, with about 30% to noncommercial self-guided private boaters. These activities have been opposed by groups favoring the preservation of wilderness-like values in the river corridor. Commercial river trip outfitters assert that access for motorized boating does not harm resources and is the only practical way to offer popular short-duration trips.

In late 2005, the NPS proposed a new Colorado River Management Plan (CRMP) governing recreational river use for at least 10 years and establishing goals and objectives for a longer time frame. The NPS analyzed nearly 20,000 comments before completing a Final Environmental Impact Statement and issuing a Record of Decision on March 23, 2006. The new management plan alters the allocation of river access between commercial and noncommercial users, with more access for the self-outfitted sector and a shorter season for commercial trips. The waiting list for noncommercial users is to be phased-out and replaced by a "hybrid" weighted lottery system. Complaints thus far contend that, even though noncommercial users have more overall access, they are largely relegated to off-season periods and are allowed less time on the river. Also, some interests fear that accommodations for motorized use could jeopardize long-pending prospects for wilderness designation.

On February 16, 2006, a coalition of conservation groups filed suit in federal court to force Interior to re-evaluate its approach to river canyon ecosystem recovery. They cite continuing damage to beaches, vegetation, unique species, and cultural resources from the operation of the Glen Canyon Dam, and contend that the new CRMP does not adequately protect park resources from user impacts. Another coalition of conservation and boating groups filed a separate suit on March 28, 2006, over motorized use and perceived inequities of the new river use plan.

In: Public Lands: Use and Misuse
Editor: William E. Neeley, pp. 99-125

ISBN: 978-1-60021-352-6

Chapter 7

The National Forest System Roadless Areas Initiative*

Pamela Baldwin

Summary

The roadless areas of the National Forest System have received special management attention for decades. In part to recognize the importance of national forest roadless areas for many purposes and in part because making project decisions involving roadless areas on a forest-by-forest basis was resulting in controversy and litigation that consumed considerable time and money, the Clinton Administration established a new nationwide approach to the management of the roadless areas in the National Forest System. A record of decision (ROD) and a final rule were published on January 12, 2001, that prohibited most road construction and reconstruction in 58.5 million acres of inventoried forest roadless areas, with significant exceptions. Most timber cutting in roadless areas also was prohibited, with some exceptions, including improving habitat for threatened, endangered, proposed, or sensitive species, or reducing the risk of wildfire and disease. With some exceptions, the new prohibitions would have applied immediately to the Tongass National Forest in Alaska.

The Bush Administration initially postponed the effective date of the roadless area rule, then decided to allow it to be implemented while proposing amendments. However, the Federal District Court for Idaho preliminarily enjoined its implementation. The Ninth Circuit reversed the Idaho district court, but on July 14, 2003, the Federal District Court for Wyoming again permanently enjoined implementation of the Rule. This holding is still on appeal to the 10th Circuit, but now may be moot. A final rule "temporarily" exempting the Tongass National Forest (Alaska) from the roadless rule was published December 30, 2003. On July 16, 2004, a new general roadless rule was proposed and a new final rule was published on May 13, 2005. The new rule eliminates the need for a separate Tongass rule, and replaces the Clinton roadless rule with a procedure whereby the governor of a state may petition the Secretary of Agriculture to promulgate a special rule for the management of roadless areas in that state, and make recommendations for that management. The new rule contains no standards by which the Secretary is to review a state's recommendations, and does not address the weight to be given to the views of local residents versus those of out-of-state residents with an interest in the public lands.

---

* Excerpted from CRS Report RL30647, Updated May 19, 2005

A new final forest planning rule was also published on January 5, 2005. The rule does not address roadless areas at all, but does require review of areas that might be suitable for wilderness designation when plans are revised.

This chapter traces the development and content of the roadless area rules and directives, describes the statutory background, reviews recent events, and analyzes some of the legal issues.

THE ROADLESS AREAS AND RELATED INITIATIVES — BACKGROUND

The Clinton Administration undertook a series of actions affecting the roadless areas of the National Forest System (NFS).[1] More particularly, new rules were finalized with respect to: (1) the roadless areas as such; (2) the NFS roads that make up the Forest Development Transportation System, and (3) the planning process of the Forest Service (FS). The provisions of these three new rules were intertwined and each part affected the others. The new roadless area rules were issued in light of the importance of the roadless areas for many forest management purposes and to the American public, and because addressing projects in roadless areas on a forest-by-forest basis as part of the usual planning process was resulting in controversy, conflict, and the expenditure of time and money on appeals and litigation, such that national-level guidance regarding projects in roadless areas was deemed advisable.

The Clinton Administration roadless area proposals were praised by some, criticized by some for not being far-reaching enough, and criticized by others as being too restrictive, creating "de facto wilderness," and being procedurally flawed. Several lawsuits were filed challenging the adequacy of the information provided the public, the opportunity to comment, and other aspects of the rulemaking. The Bush Administration initially postponed the effective date of the roadless area rule, but then decided to implement it while considering changes. Implementation of the rule was enjoined on May 10, 2001, but this district court decision was reversed and remanded by the 9th Circuit. However, the rule was again enjoined by the Wyoming District Court on July 14, 2003, on NEPA grounds and because the court concluded it created de facto wilderness. This decision was appealed by intervenors to the 10th Circuit, but may now be moot.

The Bush Administration put into effect an initial set of interim directives regarding roadless area management, solicited comments retroactively on the interim directives and on the management of roadless areas in general, and finalized a directive altering the requirements for preparation of NEPA documents in some instances. A to exempt the Tongass National Forest was then published, pending other possible rules to address the application of the roadless rule in Alaska. On July 16, 2004, new roadless rules were proposed that would eliminate the previous rule and provide a new procedure for the governor of a state to petition the Secretary of Agriculture for a state-wide rule on the management of roadless areas. In the meantime, roadless areas would be managed under the interim direction, with some modifications. New final forest planning rules were published on January 5, 2005, and a new round of interim directives was published. A new final roadless area rule was published on May 13, 2005.[2]

This report focuses on the roadless areas initiative, describes the statutory background, summarizes and provides citations for the various rules and subsequent actions, and analyzes some of the legal issues in connection with the roadless areas.

Roadless Areas. On October 13, 1999, President Clinton directed the Secretary of Agriculture, acting through the Forest Service, to develop regulations to provide "appropriate long-term protection for most or all of the currently inventoried 'roadless' areas, and to determine whether such protection is warranted for any smaller roadless areas not yet inventoried."[3] A Notice of Intent to complete an environmental impact statement (EIS) on alternatives for protection of NFS roadless areas was published on October 19, 1999;[4] a draft EIS (DEIS) was issued in May, 2000, and accompanying regulations were proposed on May 10, 2000;[5] and a final environmental impact statement (FEIS) was issued on November 13, 2000. A record of decision (ROD) and final rules were issued on January 12, 2001, to be effective on March 13, 2001.[6] The rules were issued in light of the importance of the roadless areas for various forest management purposes and to the American public, and because addressing projects in roadless areas on a forest-by-forest basis as part of the planning process was resulting in controversy, conflict, and the expenditure of a great deal of time and expense on appeals and litigation, such that national-level guidance was deemed advisable.[7]

The ROD and final rule would have: (1) prohibited, with significant exceptions, new roads in inventoried roadless areas; (2) prohibited most timber harvests in the roadless areas, but allow cutting under specified circumstances; and (3) applied the same prohibitions to the Tongass National Forest in Alaska, but allowed certain road and harvest activities already in the pipeline to go forward. The details of the final rule will be discussed below.

Roads. In related actions, the Forest Service on January 28, 1998, issued an Advance Notice of Proposed Rulemaking to revise its Forest Development Transportation System regulations related to roads in the NFS,[8] and also proposed an interim rule to temporarily suspend road construction and reconstruction in certain NFS unroaded areas.[9] On February 12, 1999, the agency published a final interim rule that temporarily suspended road construction and reconstruction in unroaded areas, and provided certain procedures related to such areas.[10] A proposed rule[11] and proposed administrative policy[12] regarding the Forest Development Transportation System were published on March 3, 2000. Final Roads rules (36 C.F.R. §212) and a transportation policy were published on January 12, 2001, both effective on that date.[13] (Note that the final roadless area management rule also was published on that date.) Certain terms were changed in the final rule,[14] and the policy provided new direction to be contained in the Forest Service Manual that emphasizes the maintenance and decommissioning of existing roads rather than the construction of new roads. The policy addressed when and how to conduct roads analyses, required that a compelling need for a new road be demonstrated, and also required an economic analysis that addressed both initial and long-term costs, a scientific analysis, and a full EIS before a road could be built in roadless areas. The new final policy was to supersede the interim policy except with respect to roads in the Tongass National Forest, in which forest the interim policy would continue to govern the activities that are permitted to go forward. These policies and interim direction have now been changed under the Bush Administration.

Under 36 C.F.R. § 212.5(b),[15] the focus is on providing and maintaining the minimum forest transportation system needed for safe and efficient travel and for the administration, utilization, and protection of NFS lands. This is to be determined by science-based roads analysis at the appropriate scale and is to minimize adverse environmental impacts. Unneeded roads would be decommissioned and the roadbeds restored. The economic and ecological effects of roads would be analyzed as part of an interdisciplinary, "science-based" process in which the public would be engaged. Until the new road inventories and analyses are completed, interim requirements would pertain and a compelling need for new roads would have to be demonstrated. These rules are still in effect, though new rules have been proposed.

Planning. On a third track, the Forest Service on November 9, 2000, issued final new planning regulations, effective on that date.[16] However, new planning regulations were again proposed on December 6, 2002, and the date for compliance with the 2000 planning regulations was extended,[17] — which had the effect of restoring the 1982 planning regulations until new planning regulations were finalized. New regulations were published on January 5, 2005.[18]

ROADLESS AREAS — STATUTORY BACKGROUND

In considering the roadless area initiatives, a review of the most relevant portions of the statutes that govern the management of the NFS may be helpful.

The principal forest management statutes relevant to analysis of the Roadless Area Initiative are the Organic Act of 1897,[19] the Multiple-Use Sustained-Yield Act of 1960,[20] and the National Forest Management Act of 1976.[21] The 1897 Act directs that the national forests be managed to improve and protect the forests or "for the purpose of securing favorable conditions of water flows, and to furnish a continuous supply of timber for the use and necessities of citizens of the United States ...."[22] The 1897 Act also authorizes the Secretary to issue regulations to "regulate the occupancy and use of the forests and to preserve them from destruction ...."[23]

Over the years, many uses of the national forests in addition to timber and watershed management have been allowed administratively. Statutorily, the Multiple-Use Sustained-Yield Act of 1960 (MUSYA) expressly recognizes and authorizes the "multiple use" of the forests, a term MUSYA defines as the management of all the various renewable surface resources of the national forests "in the combination that will best meet the needs of the American people" and recognizes that "some land will be used for less than all of the resources ... without impairment of the productivity of the land, with consideration being given to the relative values of the various resources, and not necessarily the combination of uses that will give the greatest dollar return or the greatest unit output."[24] MUSYA states that the national forests are established and shall be administered for their original purposes and also for "outdoor recreation, range, timber, watershed, and wildlife and fish purposes"[25] and that "[t]he establishment and maintenance of areas of wilderness are consistent with the purposes and provisions of [the act.]"[26] This latter language, which preceded enactment of the 1964 Wilderness Act ,[27] recognized that the FS had been managing some forest areas as administrative wilderness or natural areas. What constitutes the most desirable combination of uses for a forest has been hotly debated for decades.

MUSYA also requires "sustained yield," which is defined as the "achievement and maintenance in perpetuity of a high-level annual or regular periodic output of the various renewable resources of the national forests without impairment of the productivity of the land."[28] How much is a "high-level annual or regular periodic output" of forest resources that does not impair the productivity of the land has also been the subject of much debate.

The National Forest Management Act of 1976 (NFMA) set out additional provisions on the management of the national forests that include direction for developing land and resource management plans. NFMA directs that regulations be adopted to guide forest planning and accomplish specific goals set by the Congress, including insuring consideration of the economic and environmental aspects of various systems of renewable resource management including "silviculture and protection of forest resources; to provide for outdoor recreation (including wilderness), range, timber, watershed, wildlife, and fish; and providing for diversity of plant and animal communities."[29]

The roadless areas in the National Forest System have long received special management attention. Beginning in 1924, long before the enactment of MUSYA, the FS managed many forest areas as natural, primitive, or wilderness areas — a practice expressly approved in MUSYA. More permanent, congressionally approved statutory wilderness areas were provided for in the 1964 Wilderness Act,[30] which established the National Wilderness Preservation System. The Wilderness Act directed review of FS-designated primitive areas and other larger roadless areas to consider their suitability for inclusion in the national wilderness system. This review was carried out and expanded (with respect to the national forests) in the Roadless Area Review and Evaluation or "RARE" studies, which expanded on studies begun before enactment of the 1964 Wilderness Act. Roadless areas inventoried either as part of the RARE studies or as part of subsequent reviews during the NFMA planning process are the "inventoried" roadless areas referred to in the October 19, 1999 Notice. Congress has designated many additional wilderness areas since 1964, but, under the statutes summarized above, especially the MUSYA, the FS may still manage parts of the national forests as natural, primitive, or wildlife areas, which might be characterized as "administrative wilderness" areas.

The management of the roadless areas of the NFS is of great interest to both wilderness proponents and to opponents of additional natural or wilderness area protection. Proponents of additional protection point to the many purposes the roadless areas serve, including water quality protection, backcountry recreation, and habitat for wildlife; opponents assert that the formal congressional wilderness review and designation process sets aside adequate natural areas and the remaining areas should be available for timber harvesting, mining, developed recreation, and other uses.

The FS identified approximately 58.5 million acres of inventoried roadless areas, roughly one-third of all NFS lands. Road building is not allowed in 20.5 million acres of this total under current plans. Roads are also currently prohibited in an additional 42.4 million acres of Congressionally-designated areas such as Wilderness or Wild and Scenic River corridors. There are approximately 386,000 miles of FS and other roads in the NFS. The explanatory material in the final rulemaking states that roadless areas provide significant opportunities for dispersed recreation, are sources of public drinking water, and are large undisturbed landscapes that provide open space and natural settings, serve as a barrier against invasive plant and animal species, are important habitat, support the diversity of native species, and provide opportunities for monitoring and research.[31] In contrast, the explanatory material continues, installing roads can increase erosion and sediment yields, disrupt normal water flow processes, increase the likelihood of landslides and slope failure, fragment ecosystems, introduce non-native species, compromise habitat, and increase air pollution.[32]

The Final Clinton Administration Roadless Area Rule

The final roadless area rule put in place by the Clinton Administration was more restrictive in several respects than was either the proposed roadless rule or the preferred alternative set out in the FEIS. With some exceptions, the final rule imposed immediately-effective, national-level, Service-wide, limitations on new road construction and reconstruction in the inventoried roadless areas throughout the NFS, and also imposed nationwide prohibitions on timber harvesting in those areas, with some exceptions. The regulations were to apply immediately to the Tongass National Forest in Alaska, although certain activities already in the planning stages in that Forest were allowed to go forward.

The final rule prohibited new road construction and reconstruction, but with some significant exceptions. The exceptions were if:

> (1) A road is needed to protect public health and safety in cases of an imminent threat of flood, fire, or other catastrophic event that, without intervention, would cause the loss of life or property;
>
> (2) A road is needed to conduct a response action under the Comprehensive Environmental Response, Compensation, and Liability Act (CERCLA) or to conduct a natural resource restoration action under CERCLA, Section 311 of the Clean Water Act, or the Oil Pollution Act;
>
> (3) A road is needed pursuant to reserved or outstanding rights, or as provided for by statute or treaty;
>
> (4) Road realignment is needed to prevent irreparable resource damage that arises from the design, location, use, or deterioration of a classified road and that cannot be mitigated by road maintenance. Road realignment may occur under this paragraph only if the road is deemed essential for public or private access, natural resource management, or public health and safety;
>
> (5) Road reconstruction is needed to implement a road safety improvement project on a classified road determined to be hazardous on the basis of accident experience or accident potential on that road;
>
> (6) The Secretary of Agriculture determines that a Federal Aid Highway project, authorized pursuant to Title 23 of the United States Code, is in the public interest or is consistent with the purposes for which the land was reserved or acquired and no other reasonable and prudent alternative exists; or
>
> (7) A road is needed in conjunction with the continuation, extension, or renewal of a mineral lease on lands that are under lease by the Secretary of the Interior as of January 12, 2001 or for a new lease issued immediately upon expiration of an existing lease. Such road construction or reconstruction must be conducted in a manner that minimizes effects on surface resources, prevents unnecessary or unreasonable surface disturbance, and complies with all applicable lease requirements, land and resource management plan direction, regulations, and laws. Roads constructed or reconstructed pursuant to this paragraph must be obliterated when no longer needed for the purposes of the lease or upon termination or expiration of the lease, whichever is sooner.

Maintenance of classified roads was permissible in inventoried roadless areas.

The cutting, sale, or removal of timber from inventoried roadless areas also was prohibited unless one of specified circumstances exists, and the expectation was expressed that cutting would be infrequent. The proposed regulations had allowed timber to be cut for "stewardship" purposes, but the final regulation eliminated the use of that ambiguous term in favor of specifying the purposes for which cutting could be allowed. Cutting of small diameter trees was permissible if doing so would maintain or improve one or more of the roadless area characteristics and would:

> improve habitat for species that are listed as threatened or endangered under the Endangered Species Act or are proposed for listing under that Act, or which are sensitive species; or maintain or restore ecosystem composition and structure, such as to reduce the risk of uncharacteristic wildfire effects.[33]

Other cutting could be permitted if incidental to the implementation of a management activity that was not otherwise prohibited; if needed and appropriate for personal or administrative use in accordance with 36 C.F.R. § 223 (the regulations on sale and disposal of timber); or if roadless characteristics had been substantially altered in a portion of an inventoried roadless area due to the construction of a classified road and subsequent timber harvest before January 12, 2001. In this last instance, timber could only be cut in the substantially altered portion of the roadless area.[34]

The new roadless area rule expressly would not have revoked, suspended, or modified any permit, contract, or other legal instrument authorizing the occupancy and use of NFS lands that was issued before January 12, 2001, nor would it have revoked, suspended, or modified any project or activity decision made prior to January 12, 2001.[35] The rule would not have applied to roads or harvest in the Tongass National Forest if a notice of availability of a draft environmental impact statement for the activities had been published in the Federal Register before January 12, 2001.[36] These provisions would have grandfathered the activities addressed, but otherwise the new rule would have applied to the Tongass immediately.[37]

The explanatory material accompanying the Clinton Administration's planning rule of November 9, 2000, indicated that it was very similar to the proposed roadless area rule and also stated that the "final planning rule clarifies that analyses and decisions regarding inventoried roadless areas and other unroaded areas, other than the national prohibitions that may be established in the final Roadless Area Conservation Rule, will be made through the planning process articulated in this final rule. Under this final rule, the responsible official is required to evaluate inventoried roadless areas and unroaded areas and identify areas that warrant additional protection and the level of protection to be afforded."[38]

Therefore, possible *additional* restrictions on use of the roadless areas beyond those provided by the national rule would be developed as part of the planning process. The materials also compared particular parts of the proposed roadless areas rule with the final planning rule. It appears that the final planning regulations are less specific with respect to roadless area reviews than were the proposed regulations. As noted, the final rule eliminated the separate treatment of roadless area reviews within that rule.

CAN "DE FACTO" WILDERNESS AREAS BE CREATED ADMINISTRATIVELY?

Some have asserted that the management changes involved in the roadless area initiative would amount to "de facto" wilderness, and that only Congress can designate wilderness areas.

The explanatory material with the final Clinton roadless area regulation stated that the regulation preserves "multiple use" management and that a wide range of multiple uses were permitted in inventoried roadless areas subject to the management direction in forest plans before the roadless rule, and that a wide range of multiple uses would still be allowable under the new rule.

> Under this final rule, management actions that do not require the construction of new roads will still be allowed, including activities such as timber harvesting for clearly defined, limited purposes, development of valid claims of locatable minerals, grazing of livestock, and off-highway vehicle use where specifically permitted. Existing classified roads in inventoried roadless areas may be maintained and used for these and other activities as well. Forest health treatments for the purposes of improving threatened, endangered, proposed, or sensitive species habitat or maintaining or restoring the characteristics of ecosystem composition and structure, such as reducing the risk of uncharacteristic wildfire effects, will be allowed where access can be gained through existing roads or by equipment not requiring roads ....
>
> The Roadless Area Conservation rule, unlike the establishment of wilderness areas, will allow a multitude of activities including motorized uses, grazing, and oil and gas development that does not require new roads to continue in inventoried roadless areas ....[39]

Certainly, only Congress can designate areas for inclusion in the National Wilderness Preservation System.[40] However, the MUSYA (enacted before the 1964 Wilderness Act), expressly provides for the administrative management of national forest lands for fish and wildlife, outdoor recreation, and watershed purposes, as well as for timber, and states that "the establishment and maintenance of wilderness areas is consistent with [MUSYA's] purposes."[41] The NFMA (enacted after the Wilderness Act), directs that forest plans "assure ... coordination of outdoor recreation, range, timber, watershed, wildlife and fish, and *wilderness* ...."[42] Therefore, it appears that, as a general matter, some new prohibitions on activities in roadless areas could lawfully be imposed administratively and the roadless rule might be defended as appropriate management of non-timber resources for multiple use purposes (such as outdoor recreation, mineral development, game and other wildlife), yielding those benefits without permanent impairment of the lands. However, it also is possible that, as applied, restrictions that were severe and extensive might be challenged as violating the "sustained yield" aspects of the MUSYA.

Some of these issues have been raised in suits challenging the roadless area rule, and on July 14, 2003, Judge Brimmer of the Federal District Court for Wyoming permanently enjoined the roadless rule, in part on NEPA grounds and in part on the ground that it was a "thinly veiled attempt to designate 'wilderness areas' in violation of the clear and unambiguous process established by the Wilderness Act for such designation."[43] The court equated the roadless areas with de facto wilderness, noted the severity of the restrictions under the roadless rule, which the court characterized as restrictive, or more so, than that of congressionally designated wilderness areas,[44] and that the argument that the roadless rule permits multiple uses (such as motorized uses, grazing, and oil and gas development) to proceed so long as roads were not constructed "fails because all of those uses would, in fact, require the construction or use of a road."[45] Because it felt that the roadless areas under the new rule were tantamount to wilderness areas, the court concluded that the rule was "in violation of the clear and unambiguous process established by the Wilderness Act for such Designation."[46] The court did not reach Wyoming's assertions that the roadless rule also violated NFMA and MUSYA, but did mention that the Wilderness Act "provides protection for a use of the National Forests that was not contemplated by either the Organic Act or the MUSYA ...,"[47] and repeatedly equated roadless areas generally with congressionally designated wilderness.

As discussed above, both MUSYA and NFMA mention wilderness as a use of the national forests, a point the Brimmer opinion did not discuss. Furthermore, in the compromise "release" language in state-by-state wilderness acts since the mid-1980s, Congress repeatedly declined to direct that roadless areas that were not designated as part of the National Wilderness Preservation System when forest management plans were revised be managed for only non-wilderness uses, but instead permitted their management for uses that might maintain their wilderness attributes. The court noted part of the legislative history of the Wilderness Act to the effect that "the statutory framework of the Wilderness Act would ... assure that no further administrator could arbitrarily or capriciously either abolish wilderness areas that should be retained or make wholesale designations of additional areas in which use would be limited."[48] The validity of the assertion that the roadless rule was "in violation of the clear and unambiguous process established by the Wilderness Act for such [Wilderness] Designation,"[49] would seem to depend on whether one agrees that management of the roadless areas under the roadless rule would be as restrictive as that under the Wilderness Act, and on how one views the references to wilderness in MUSYA and NFMA and the actions of Congress in continuing to allow management of the roadless areas that maintains wilderness characteristics on national forest lands.

Administrative Actions and Litigation Since January 20, 2001

The "Card" Memorandum. Immediately after President Bush took office, his Chief of Staff, Andrew Card, issued a memo that directed, among other things, that the effective date of regulations that had been published in the Federal Register, but had not yet taken effect, be postponed for 60 days, unless a department head appointed by President Bush had reviewed and approved the regulatory action.[50] The roadless area regulation was covered by this language, since although it was published as a final rule on January 12, 2001, it was not to be effective until March 13, 2001.[51] The delay was because the roadless rule was determined to be a "major" rule under the Congressional Review Act, under which Congress is given a certain amount of time to possibly take action to disapprove the rule.[52] If Congress had disapproved the roadless area rule and the President had signed the resulting act, that new legislated direction, of course, would have been binding, but Congress did not take action.

Effective Date Postponed. On February 5, 2001, notice was published in the Federal Register[53] postponing for 60 days the effective date of the roadless area rule from its previous effective date of March 13, 2001, to May 12, 2001.[54] The Administration then decided to implement the rule, but to consider amending it.

Implementation Enjoined — Part 1. The state of Idaho sued for a declaratory judgment and to enjoin implementation of the roadless rule for violation of NEPA, NFMA and the APA, and other suits in other states also were filed.[55] The court in the Idaho case found that plaintiffs were likely to succeed on their assertion that the FS had not provided the public an opportunity to comment meaningfully on the rule in that there was inadequate identification of the inventoried roadless areas (the court noting that statewide maps were not made available until after the public comment period had ended), inadequate information was presented during the scoping process (FS employees were alleged to be ill-prepared), and the period for public comment was not adequate (all of the public meetings in Idaho occurred within 12 business days of the end of the first 60-day comment period and many of the public comments were received within the last week of the time given and no responses were provided). The court characterized the comment period as "grossly inadequate" and an "obvious violation" of NEPA. The court further found that the FEIS did not consider an adequate range of alternatives, since all but the "no action" alternative included "a total prohibition" on road construction and the EIS did not analyze whether other alternatives might have accomplished protection of the environmental integrity of the roadless areas. In addition, the court concluded that FS did not analyze possible mitigation of negative impacts of the alternatives it did study.

The Bush Administration did not defend the rule, but did ask the court to postpone ruling on the motion for preliminary injunction until it had had an opportunity to complete a full review of the rule, arguing that an injunction was not necessary because the rule was not to be implemented until at least May 12, 2001.

The court reserved its ruling until on or after May 4th, the day that the Administration was to submit a status report on its review and findings. On May 4th, the Administration filed its status report with the court and announced that it would implement the Roadless Rule, but would take additional actions to address "reasonable concerns raised about the rule" and ensure implementation in a "responsible common sense manner," including providing greater input at the local planning level.[56]

However, on May 10th, Judge Lodge granted a preliminary injunction to prevent implementation both of the Roadless Rule and of the portion of the Planning Rule that relates to prescriptions for the roadless areas (36 C.F.R. § 219.9(b)(8)). The court found the Government's "vague commitment" to propose amendments to the Rule indicative of a failure to take the requisite "hard look" that an EIS is expected to perform, leaving the court with the "firm impression" that implementation of the Roadless Rule would result in irreparable harm to the National Forests. The court concluded that the government's response was a "band-aid approach" and enjoined implementation of the Rule while the agency goes forward with its new study and development of proposed amendments.

The United States did not appeal this decision, but environmental groups who had been granted intervenor status did appeal. Several other lawsuits raising various issues have been filed, including suits in North Dakota, Idaho, Alaska and the District of Columbia. The Ninth Circuit reversed the district court and remanded the case to the district court, as will be discussed further below.

Advance Notice of Proposed Rulemaking on Roadless Area Management. On July 10, 2001, the Forest Service published an Advance Notice of Proposed Rulemaking and asked for public comment on ten questions relating to "key principles" involving management of the roadless areas. Comments were due by September 10, 2001, on such questions as: what is the appropriate role of local forest planning in evaluating roadless management; what are the best ways to work collaboratively; how to protect the forests, including protection from severe wildfires; how to protect communities and homes from wildfires on federal lands; how to provide access to nonfederal properties; what factors the FS should consider in evaluating roadless area management; what activities should be expressly prohibited or allowed in roadless areas through the planning process; should roadless areas protected under a forest plan be proposed to Congress for wilderness designation or should they be maintained under a specific roadless management regime; how should the FS work with individuals and groups with strongly competing views; and what other concerns relate to the roadless areas.

Interim Management of Inventoried Roadless Areas I. The final Clinton administrative policy on National Forest System roads published on January 12, 2001,[57] provided interim direction on the management of roadless areas and the construction of roads in roadless areas that was to apply until a roads analysis was completed and incorporated into the relevant forest plans. This direction was in the Forest Service Manual (FSM) and contained considerable detail that would have permitted new roads only if the Regional Forester determined there was a compelling need for the road and both an EIS and a science-based roads analysis had been completed. Examples of instances that constituted compelling need were provided. The management direction was to apply to both inventoried roadless areas and to areas of more than 1,000 acres that were contiguous to inventoried roadless areas (or certain other areas) and met stated criteria. Exceptions were provided to the applicability of the interim guidelines.

Interim Management of Inventoried Roadless Areas II. Pending expected publication of proposed new roadless area rules, the Bush Administration issued a series of Interim Directives affecting roadless area protection and management. The first Directive was effective May 31, 2001, but was not published until August.[58] On June 7, 2001, additional new interim roadless area management direction was provided. On that date, the new Chief of the Forest Service issued a memorandum addressing protection of roadless areas and requiring his approval for some proposed roads or timber harvests in inventoried roadless areas pending completion of forest plan revisions or amendments.

Interim Directive 1920-2001-1 issued December 14, 2001, was published on December 20, 2001.[59] This December directive appears to substantially replace much of the previous directives. However, the Notice did not clearly indicate which provisions were being replaced or the precise extent of revisions. The published explanatory material states that affected material is set out and unaffected material is not. Yet some of the earlier provisions are neither shown nor discussed and therefore, might still have been in effect. However, the final text of new FSM §1925 did not show these undiscussed earlier provisions — as though they were superseded. Therefore, it is not clear which of the previous materials were still in effect. For example, some of former FSM §7712.16 (that contained many specific details on permissible road construction) is expressly revised in the December Directives (notably the former requirements for protection of contiguous areas and the requirement for preparation of an EIS for projects in roadless areas are eliminated) and the explanatory materials state that the revised provisions are then moved to appear in the Planning part of the Manual as new §1925. Yet other provisions that were in §7712.16 were neither discussed as superseded or modified, nor set out in new §1925. One example is that the previous requirement for a "compelling need" for the road project has disappeared without comment.[60] These ambiguities make analysis of and comment on the December Directives difficult. These ambiguities are relevant because this December directive has now been reinstated, as will be discussed below.

As with earlier directives, the December directive was already in effect (as of December 14, 2001) when published, but retroactive comment was invited — to be considered if final directives are developed. However, the interim directive was only to be in effect for 18 months, unless this time is extended to 36 months, and also apparently was to cease to apply once a forest plan was revised or amended.

As noted, the December directive moved some provisions that more directly address roadless area management into the planning part of the Manual. Only inventoried roadless areas were subject to the interim requirements. The December Directive reserved, as did the earlier ones, authority to the Chief to approve or disapprove certain proposed timber harvests in inventoried roadless areas until a plan revision or amendment is completed "that has considered the protection and management of inventoried roadless areas pursuant to FSM 1920." It also provided that the Chief could designate an Associate Chief, Deputy Chief, or Associate Deputy Chief on a case-by-case basis to be the responsible official. This delegation authority was changed to also include Forest Supervisors in the reinstated and amended directive.

The Regional Forester was to screen timber harvest projects in inventoried roadless areas for possible referral to the Chief. The Chief was to make decisions regarding harvests *except* for those that were: (1) generally of small diameter material, the removal of which is needed for habitat or ecosystem reasons (including reducing fire risk), (2) incidental to a management activity not prohibited under the plan; (3) needed for personal or administrative use; or (4) in a portion of an inventoried roadless area where harvests had previously taken place and the roadless characteristics had been substantially altered. Decisions as to these harvests were to be made by forest officers normally delegated such authority under existing FSM §2404.2. (These delegations included Forest Service line officers.)

The December 2001 directive stated that the Chief's authority with respect to timber harvests did not apply if a Record of Decision for a forest plan revision was issued as of July 27, 2001 — as was true of the Tongass National Forest — and would otherwise terminate when a plan revision or amendment that has considered the protection and management of inventoried roadless areas was completed.[61]

The Chief's authority with respect to road construction was to remain in effect until a forest-scale roads analysis was completed and incorporated into each forest plan, at which point it terminated.[62] The Regional Forester was to make many decisions on road construction projects under new §1925.04b. There was no express provision in that section for termination of the authority of the Regional forester. However, the general policy section, 1925.03, keyed termination of the special provisions to completion of a roads analysis and its incorporation into the relevant forest plan:

> Inventoried roadless areas contain important environmental values that warrant protection. Accordingly, until a forest-scale roads analysis (FSM7712.13b) is completed and incorporated into a forest plan, inventoried roadless areas shall, as a general rule, be managed to preserve their roadless characteristics. However, where a line officer determines that an exception may be warranted, the decision to approve a road management activity or timber harvest in these

> areas is reserved to the Chief or the Regional Forester as provided in FSM 1925.04a and 1925.04b.[63]

Under FSM 1925.04a, the Chief had approval authority over all road construction and reconstruction except those decisions delegated to the Regional Forester. Under FSM 1925.04b, the Regional Forester was to screen proposed road projects, forward certain of them to the Chief for approval, but be the deciding officer for many decisions on road projects in inventoried roadless areas, such as when a road is needed:

> to protect public health and safety in cases of an imminent threat of flood, fire, or other catastrophic event that, without intervention would cause the loss of life or property
>
> to conduct a Superfund response or to conduct a natural resources restoration action under Superfund, §311 of the Clean Water Act, or Oil Pollution Act
>
> in conjunction with the continuation extension, or renewal of a mineral lease on lands under lease as of January 12, 2001
>
> pursuant to reserved or outstanding rights or as provided by statute or treaty
>
> for critical resource restoration and protection
>
> to prevent resource damage by an existing road that is deemed essential for public or private access, management, or public health or safety, and where such damage cannot be corrected by maintenance; or
>
> to restore wildlife habitat.

Note that the December Directive apparently eliminated the requirement that there be a *compelling* need for a road and also eliminated the requirements for a science-based analysis and a full EIS in all cases. In addition, the applicability of the interim direction to certain important contiguous areas also was eliminated. Although the responsible official could still do an EIS and could protect contiguous areas, and a compelling need for a road might exist in some instances, less protection to roadless areas could result because while the new directive *permitted* protection, it did not contain the higher thresholds for approval of activities and more formalized documentation requirements of the previous direction.

This interim directive expired on June 14, 2003. However, as discussed under the heading "2005 Roadless Areas Regulations" below, the directive, renumbered and with certain changes, was later reinstated.

Changes to "Categorical Exclusions." Changes to agency NEPA documentation requirements also could significantly affect the roadless areas. Under NEPA, agencies must prepare an EIS for proposed actions that might have a significant effect on the human environment. If it is not clear whether if an action might have such an effect, the agency is to prepare an environmental assessment (EA) to determine if an EIS is necessary. Depending on what the EA finds, preparation of an EIS may then follow, or the agency may issue a Finding of No Significant Impact (FONSI), in which case no further analysis is required. However, some actions have been shown to have so little effect on the environment that not even an EA is necessary. An agency may indicate what these clearly non-harmful actions are through its articulation of "categorical exclusions" — actions that are excluded from preparation of even an EA.[64]

Several agency actions have expanded the activities that may be conducted as categorical exclusions, and have replaced previous categorical exclusions on timber sales. Joint Forest Service/Bureau of Land Management categorical exclusions were finalized for hazardous fuels reduction projects that can include mechanical treatments on up to 1,000 acres.[65] A categorical exclusion was also finalized for smaller FS timber sales.[66] In addition, certain silvicultural treatments may proceed as categorical exclusions under Title IV of the Healthy Forests Restoration Act.[67]

Previously, the categorical exclusions portion of the FS Handbook set out types of activities that normally would be excluded from NEPA documents — unless extraordinary circumstances are present. One of the listed extraordinary circumstances was the presence of inventoried roadless areas. Extraordinary circumstances were defined as "conditions associated with a normally excluded action that are identified during scoping as *potentially* having effects which *may* significantly affect the environment." (Emphasis added.) The presence of an extraordinary circumstance arguably removed the proposed action from qualifying as a categorical exclusion and required the preparation of an EA in order to probe further the possible environmental effects. This is the interpretation of the Handbook section and its legislative history in a Seventh Circuit case.[68]

New interim guidance was proposed[69] and finalized,[70] such that the presence of circumstances previously considered "extraordinary" do not necessarily preclude an action from being a categorical exclusion if the responsible official, based on scoping, determines there would be no significant environmental effects. Indeed, under the new directive, a circumstance *is* "extraordinary" only if the responsible official determines it is because the proposed action may have a significant effect on the environment, in which case an EIS is to be prepared. Or, if the responsible official is uncertain whether the proposed action may have a significant effect on the environment, an EA is to be prepared. Under this approach, the presence of circumstances that previously were per se "extraordinary" now are merely "resource conditions" that must specifically be considered in determining whether an action may have a significant effect. "It is the degree of the potential effect of a proposed action on these resource conditions that determines whether extraordinary circumstances exist."[71] This is a significant change from the previous text.

In defense of the proposed changes on explanatory circumstances, the explanatory material asserted that there is a split in the decisions of the circuits on the effects of the presence of extraordinary circumstances, and that the Ninth Circuit has held that an agency may issue a categorical exclusion even where a certain resource condition, such as the presence of threatened or endangered species, is found.[72] However, the cited case involved a salvage sale under §2001 of the Rescissions Act,[73] a statute that sets out a very narrow scope of judicial review of environmental decisions and a very broad range of discretion in the Secretary to determine the adequacy of any environmental reviews. In contrast, the Seventh Circuit opinion, which analyzed the wording and derivation of the current categorical exclusion provisions was not so contextually limited, and hence is arguably more on point.[74] Under the final directive, some timber sales could be conducted as categorical exclusions in roadless areas (and possibly in a roadless area with endangered or threatened species) if the official determines, without the necessity of written documentation of the underlying analysis relied upon, that there would be no significant environmental effects.

Comments on Possible Roadless Changes. On June 26, 2002, the Forest Service released its summary report dated May 31, 2002, on the public comments received in response to the Advance Notice of Proposed Rulemaking. The Forest Service received approximately 726,000 responses, said to be mostly form letters to the 10 questions, but which included 52,432 original responses. The report includes appendices that describe the system used to analyze the comments, and urges caution in relying on the gist of the comments received, in that "respondents are self-selected; therefore their comments do not necessarily represent the sentiments of the entire population. The analysis attempts to provide fair representation of the wide range of views submitted, but makes no attempt to treat input as if it were a vote." Appendix E indicates that the overwhelming number of "organized" responses were in favor of the Roadless Rule.[75]

Ninth Circuit Decision on 1st Injunction. On December 12, 2002,[76] the Ninth Circuit reversed the Idaho district court stating:

> We hold that the district court had discretion to permit intervention, under Fed. R. Civ. P. 24(b), and intervenors now can bring this appeal under Fed. R. Civ. P. 24(b); that plaintiffs have standing to challenge the Roadless Rule; and, assessing the merits, that the district court abused its discretion in granting [sic] preliminary injunction against implementation of the Roadless Rule.[77] . . . . Because of its incorrect legal conclusion on prospects of success, the district court proceeded on an incorrect legal premise, applied the wrong standard for injunction, and abused its discretion in issuing a preliminary injunction.[78]

Idaho's petitions for panel rehearing was denied on April 4, 2003.

In reaching its conclusions, the Ninth Circuit reviewed the substantive grounds considered by the district court and disagreed that plaintiffs had demonstrated a likelihood of success on the merits, finding instead that the Forest Service did adequately comply with NEPA in its provision for public comment on the Roadless Rule because the maps provided did not suffer from the grave inadequacies alleged by plaintiffs, plaintiffs had actual notice as to the roadless areas that would be affected, and at most possibly inadequate maps would only affect the propriety of the Rule on the 4.2 million acres added during the EIS process. The court also found that the Forest Service had provided more than the minimum required amount of time for comment, the time allowed was adequate,[79] and that the EIS considered an adequate range of alternatives.[80] Because it felt that the district court wrongfully found that plaintiffs were likely to succeed on the merits, the appellate court concluded that the district court accepted only a minimal showing of irreparable harm and incorrectly issued the injunction.

Most of the unfavorable response to the decision has focused on whether it was proper for the intervenors to bring the appeal when the government did not. It will be recalled that the case came forward in an unusual context: although several statutes were initially involved in the lawsuits, the district court decision focused on the inadequacy of the federal defendants' NEPA compliance, a decision the federal defendants did not appeal. Certain environmental groups had been granted intervenor status and appealed the district court's ruling. The decision of the Ninth Circuit raises significant issues relating to whether the intervenor groups could appeal NEPA-compliance rulings when the federal defendants — the only ones who could comply with NEPA — did not.

Under Rule 24 of the Federal Rules of Civil Procedure, a potential intervenor must meet certain criteria to intervene, either as of right under Rule 24(a) or with the permission of the court under Rule 24(b). Earlier cases, including two in the Ninth Circuit, have held that only the federal government can defend the adequacy of its NEPA compliance,[81] and the dissenting opinion questions whether the majority adequately established that the appealing intervenors fit within even permissive intervention under Rule 24(b). The majority held that the district court erred to the extent it permitted intervention under Rule 24(a), but found intervention proper under Rule 24(b). In reaching this conclusion, the court quoted from a leading treatise which seems to postulate generous grounds for allowing intervention.[82] In a search for "independent jurisdictional grounds" sufficient to support intervention to pursue an appeal abandoned by the other parties, the court looked to the standing of the intervenor applicants. The court determined that the applicants need not show that they independently could have sued the party who prevailed in district court, but need allege only a threat of injury stemming from the order they seek to reverse, an injury which would be redressed if they win on appeal.[83] The court stated that "intervenors asserted their interests related to the Roadless Rule in moving to intervene,"[84] but did not clearly set out what those interests were. Possibly, they are the "interest in the use and enjoyment of roadless lands and in the conservation of roadless lands in the national forest lands subject to the roadless Rule" the court mentioned previously. The court also discussed the fact that the district court expressly noted the magnitude of the case and that "the applicants' intervention will contribute to the equitable resolution of this case," to which opinion the appellate court added that the presence of intervenors would "assist the court in its orderly procedures leading to the resolution of this case, which impacted large and varied interests."[85] This approach echoes another Ninth Circuit opinion that had applied a generous approach to intervention saying: "[a] liberal policy in favor of intervention serves both efficient resolution of issues and broadened access to the courts. By allowing parties with a practical interest in the outcome of a particular case to intervene, we often prevent or simplify future litigation involving related issues; at the same time we allow an additional interested party to express its views before the court."[86] This same court approached the 'interest' test of Rule 24(b) generously as "primarily a practical guide to disposing of lawsuits by involving as many apparently concerned persons as is compatible with efficiency and due process."[87] The Ninth Circuit denied Idaho's petition for rehearing, and the case was remanded to the district court to reconsider its previous reasoning and injunction in light of the opinion of the appellate court. Several of the other lawsuits challenging the Roadless Rule were stayed pending the decision by the Ninth Circuit.

Interim implementation; Tongass. It will be recalled that the Clinton Administration on January 12, 2001, had issued interim direction for the management of roadless areas until a roads analysis had been completed and incorporated into relevant forest plans. This interim direction was followed by other interim directives issued by the Bush Administration in light of the injunction. This interim direction on management of roadless areas expired on June 14, 2003, but was later reinstated with modifications, as will be discussed.

On June 9, 2003, the Bush Administration indicated that it would "retain" the roadless rule and would not renew the interim management directives. However, the roadless rule would be modified to exclude the Tongass National Forest as part of a settlement of the lawsuit filed by the State of Alaska. A proposed rule to exclude the Tongass from the broader protection of the roadless rule was published on July 15[88] and an Advance Notice of Proposed Rulemaking to exclude both the Tongass and the Chugach National Forest (also in Alaska) was also published on the same day.[89] A final rule "temporarily" exempting the Tongass from the roadless rule was published on December 30, 2003.[90] Specifically, the roadless area restrictions on road construction, road reconstruction, or the cutting, sale, or removal of timber in inventoried roadless areas do not apply on the Tongass National Forest. The explanatory material indicates that the exemption is temporary — until an Alaska-wide roadless rule is finalized. The exemption means that roadless areas protected under the Revised Land Management Plan for the Tongass would remain protected, but an additional 300,000 acres of currently roadless area will be available for logging under that plan.

Implementation Enjoined — Part 2. On July 14, 2003, Judge Brimmer of the Federal District Court for Wyoming permanently enjoined the Roadless Rule, in part because of NEPA defects, and in part because he concluded it created de facto wilderness in violation of the Wilderness Act.[91] (See discussion of the wilderness issues, *supra*.) The court concluded that 1) the FS's decision not to extend the scoping comment period was arbitrary and capricious; 2) the FS's denial of cooperating agency status to Wyoming and other states was arbitrary and capricious; 3) the FS's failure to rigorously explore and objectively evaluate reasonable alternatives to the Roadless Rule was contrary to law; 4) the FS's failure to adequately analyze cumulative effects was a clear error in judgment; and 5) the FS's decision not to issue a supplemental EIS in light of new information on updated roadless area inventories was arbitrary and capricious, and contrary to law.[92] The court stated that the agency drove the rule "through the administrative process in a vehicle smelling of political prestidigitation"[93]in its "rush to give President Clinton lasting notoriety in the annals of environmentalism"[94] — and concluded that the agency must "start over."[95] This decision is on appeal to the 10th Circuit Court of Appeals.

New Proposed Roadless Regulations. On July 16, 2004, a new proposed roadless rule was published.[96] Under the proposed changes to 36 C.F.R. §394, no protections of roadless areas would be prescribed in the rule. Instead, a new procedure would be put in place under which there would be a window of time within which the governor of a state could petition the Secretary of Agriculture to promulgate a state-specific rule on the management of roadless areas. The comment period on the proposed rule was extended to November 15, 2004.[97]

Interim Management of Inventoried Roadless Areas III. Effective upon publication of the proposed rules in the Federal Register, and for the duration of the time allowed for the state petition process, the FS reinstated the December 2001 directive 1920-2001-1, renumbered as ID 1920-2004-1 and modified it in two respects.[98] This reinstatement put in place again the provisions described above that allow the Chief of the FS to make decisions affecting inventoried roadless areas involving 1) road construction — until a forest-scale roads analysis is completed and incorporated into a forest plan or a determination is made that a plan amendment is not needed; and 2) the cutting of timber until a forest plan is in place that "considers" the protection and management of roadless areas.

ID 1920-2004-1 differs from the previous one in that it allows the Chief to grant project-specific exceptions to allow a Regional Forester or a Forest Supervisor, for good cause, to exercise the authority to conduct projects in roadless areas. The addition of forest supervisors to those who can conduct projects in roadless areas is an expansion of the previous ID that arguably could make it easier to approve projects in those areas. Secondly, FSM 1925.04b is changed to allow the Regional Forester to make decisions on road construction and reconstruction in an inventoried roadless area for lands associated with any mineral lease, license, permit or approval for mineral leasing operations.

Publication of the final roadless area rules states that the July 16, 2004 interim directive will remain in place until January 16, 2006, but may be renewed for an additional 18 months.[99]

New Forest Planning Regulations

New regulations on National Forest System land management planning were published on January 5, 2005.[100] A separate rule repealed the 2000 planning regulations at 36 C.F.R. § 219, Subpart A, but did not repeal the roadless area management rule at 36 C.F.R. § 294, Subpart B, which remained on the books, but enjoined.

New § 219.7(a)(5)(ii) of the new rules basically retains a provision from the 2000 rules[101] and provides that:

> Unless otherwise provided by law, all National Forest System lands possessing wilderness characteristics must be considered for recommendation as potential wilderness areas during plan development or revision.

Depending on how 'wilderness' characteristics and evaluation criteria might be defined, this provision could require many roadless areas to be reviewed for possible wilderness designation as part of the cyclical plan revision process. However, no management guidance for inventoried roadless areas that are not recommended for inclusion in the National Wilderness Preservation System is provided.[102] Another section indicates that, initially at least, all forest lands generally will be considered to be available for multiple uses going into the planning process.[103] "Roadless area" and "inventoried roadless area" are removed from the definitions section because the terms are not used in the rule. Comments raising concerns about protection for roadless areas were submitted when the planning regulations were proposed and the response was that the "Responsible Official considers these values during the planning process for the plan's desired conditions and objectives, which will involve local, regional, and national interests, and use the best available local information." This response seems to indicate that roadless values will be only one factor among many to be considered in managing the forests.[104]

The new planning regulations stress that plans are not decisional in nature, but rather are aspirational only, setting out goals for the management of forest units. Nor do they contain much detail on how to manage the forests, leaving that to the Forest Service Manual, Handbooks, and directives. In particular, the explanatory material states that guidance about special area concerns, such as roadless areas are more properly included in Forest Service directives.[105] In response to another comment that special protection for roadless areas was lost in the new regulations, the materials point only to the provision on wilderness evaluations quoted above, and state that additional guidance on roadless *wilderness evaluations* will be forthcoming in directives.[106]

Several publications of interim directives with solicitation of comments occurred since the publication of the final planning rules, principally the 12 IDs published on March 23, 2005.[107] However, as has been true of previous directives, it is difficult to find the texts in question[108] and to ascertain the current status of a particular management issue — in this case the management of inventoried roadless areas. In addition, the relationship of the March

23rd ID to the previous interim directive on roadless area management is not clear. It may be recalled that ID 1920-2001-1 (issued December 14, 2001, and expired June 14, 2003) was reinstated and renumbered as ID 1920-2004-1 "to provide guidance for addressing road and timber management activities in inventoried roadless areas until land and resource management plans are amended or revised."[109] (Again, although that July 16, 2004, publication indicates the ID is available at [http://www.fs.fed.us/im/directives], it in fact is not — but see the discussion of it in the preceding section of this report.) The March 23rd interim directives include ID 1920-2005-1, which states that it does not supersede any previous IDs. The new 1920 series directive does not address the previous directive bearing that number, nor address roadless area management at all, except to indicate that part 1925 of the Forest Service Manual is "reserved" for IDs and field management guidance on the Management of Inventoried Roadless Areas — with no indication that there is in fact already such a directive in effect that is not referenced. Therefore, it was not clear whether there was any direction in effect with regard to management of roadless such areas pending revision of plans under the new planning regulations. The new final roadless area rule states that the plans and the July 14, 2004 interim direction are to apply.

2005 Roadless Area Regulations

New final roadless area rules were published on May 13, 2005.[110] The final roadless area regulations are very similar to the proposed regulations. A procedure is established to permit a Governor of a state to submit a petition to the Secretary regarding roadless areas in a state, and to make recommendations as to management of such areas. Petitions are required to provide specified information, including 1) a description of the particular lands for which the petition is made; 2) particular management recommendations; 3) identification of the circumstances and needs intended to be addressed by the petition, including conserving roadless value, protecting health and safety, reducing hazardous fuels, maintaining dams, providing access, etc.; 4) information on how the recommendations differ from the relevant federal plans and policies; 5) how the recommendations compare to state land policies and management direction; 6) how the recommendations would affect fish and wildlife and habitat; 7) a description of any public involvement efforts undertaken by the state during development of the petition; and 8) a commitment by the state that it will participate as a cooperating agency in any environmental analysis for the rulemaking.

Petitions must be submitted not later than November 13, 2006, but the explanatory material mentions that petitions for rulemaking or amendment after that time could be filed under 7 C.F.R. § 1.28. If the Secretary approves a petition, the FS must coordinate development of the proposed rule with the state, but the Secretary or the Secretary's designee is to make the final decision on any rule.

The rule does not include any standards on the scope or balance required for public participation in the development of a state's recommendations, or for how a state is to gather its information about an area's resources and values. There also are no requirements or standards for the Secretary's review and approval of a petition, and, perhaps most importantly, no statement as to the relative weight to be given to a state's recommendations versus the preferences of non-state residents who may express an opinion on the desired management of these national lands.[111]

The background materials accompanying both the proposed and final rule refer to the importance of collaborating with partners, including state governments, stating: “strong State and Federal cooperation regarding management of inventoried roadless areas can facilitate long-term, community-oriented solutions.”[112] The materials review the promulgation of the original roadless rule and note that “concerns were immediately expressed by those most impacted by the roadless rule’s prohibitions” and that the new rule is proposed in response to those concerns.[113] This latter comment raises interesting questions about the role of public input in the rulemaking in that only approximately 4% of the extraordinary number of comments received on the original roadless rule opposed or expressed concerns about its protections. Similarly, the overwhelming number of responses to the new roadless rule favored continuing protection. The explanatory materials justify taking a different approach by stating that “every comment received is considered for its substance and contribution to informed decisionmaking, whether it is one comment repeated by tens of thousands of people or a comment submitted by only one person. The public comment process is not intended to serve as a scientifically valid survey process to determine public opinion.”[114]

Advisory Committee Established. Also on May 13, 2005, a Roadless Area Conservation National Advisory Committee was established by the Secretary under the Federal Advisory Committee Act, to provide advice and recommendations on the implementation of the state petitions for special roadless area management rules.[115] Nominations for this Committee must be received in writing by June 27, 2005. The Committee is to consist of 12 members representing a “balanced group of representatives of diverse national organizations who can provide insights into the major contemporary issues associated with the conservation and management of inventoried roadless areas.” The Committee is to operate “in a manner designed to establish a consensus of opinion.”

CONCLUSION

Roadless areas of the National Forest System have received special management for decades and more recently have been addressed by two administrations through a complex series of interrelated actions on roads, roadless areas, and forest planning. A new nationwide rule providing protections and use restrictions on inventoried roadless areas was promulgated in January 12, 2001, in an effort to standardize management of such areas and avoid persistent litigation. However, a federal court enjoined implementation of the Clinton Administration’s roadless rule, and although this decision was later reversed, another federal district court has again permanently enjoined implementation of the rule. A new roadless area rule has been finalized that replaces previous protections with a new process by which a governor of a state may petition the Secretary to promulgate a state-specific rule for the management of roadless areas. A petition would also contain recommendations for the management of the areas. The proposed rule does not contain details on how the public is to be involved in the development of a state petition, or how the state’s recommendations are to relate to the preferences expressed by non-state residents regarding the same public lands.

During the time allowed for the new process, previous interim direction for the management of the roadless areas was reinstated, with some modifications, to govern the management of these areas during the time allowed for the new process. This direction allows the Chief of the FS to make decisions as to roads and timber cutting, but to delegate that responsibility in some circumstances, including to authorize forest supervisors to conduct projects in roadless areas. The interim provisions would be in effect until January 16, 2006 (unless extended for 18 additional months), a statewide rule is finalized, or a forest unit plan "considers" roadless areas.

New final planning regulations published on January 5, 2005, appear to presume that roadless areas are basically available for a variety of uses, including timber harvests, subject to unit-by-unit planning processes. Other administrative changes regarding categorical exclusions and extraordinary circumstances now appear to allow certain actions to be taken in roadless areas without written environmental analyses.

In summary, the regulatory direction for the management of the remaining National Forest System inventoried roadless areas arguably has gone from embodying a special recognized status with nationwide protections to having no special status or even separate mention in the new forest-by-forest planning regulations. Also, a new petition process has been established under which a Governor of a state may seek a special statewide rule regarding roadless areas. What management protections, if any, may apply to roadless areas in the future is not clear.

REFERENCES

[1] The NFS includes the national forests and national grasslands and is administered by the Forest Service in the Department of Agriculture. Roadless areas within the NFS have long received special management. Beginning even before enactment of the 1964 Wilderness Act, larger (generally 5,000 acres or more) roadless areas were "inventoried" to consider their wilderness characteristics, and later their suitability for inclusion in the National Wilderness Preservation System. These are the "inventoried" areas referred to in the Administration's initiative and in this report. A discussion of the roadless area initiative and many of the related documents are available on the Forest Service website at [http://www.roadless.fs.fed.us/].

[2] 70 Fed. Reg. 25,654.

[3] Memorandum from President William J. Clinton to the Secretary of Agriculture on Protection of Forest 'Roadless' Areas, Oct. 13, 1999.

[4] 64 Fed. Reg. 56,306.

[5] 65 Fed. Reg. 30,276.

[6] 66 Fed Reg. 3,244 (January 12, 2001), adding 36 C.F.R. § 294, Subpart B..

[7] *Id.*, at 3,246.

[8] 63 Fed. Reg. 4,350, regarding regulations at 36 C.F.R. § 212.

[9] 63 Fed. Reg. 4,354.

[10] 64 Fed. Reg. 7,290 (Feb. 12, 1999).

[11] 65 Fed. Reg 11,680 (Mar. 3, 2000).

[12] 65 Fed. Reg. 11,684.

[13] 66 Fed. Reg 3,206 and 3,219 respectively.

[14] "Forest development roads" is changed to "National Forest System roads" and "forest transportation plan" is changed to "forest transportation atlas." Other new definitions also are added, e.g. to clarify "road construction" and "road reconstruction." 66 Fed. Reg. 3,216-3,217.

[15] 66 Fed. Reg. 3,230.

[16] 65 Fed. Reg. 67,514. Revising the planning regulations has been a contentious issue for the Forest Service for quite some time.

[17] The compliance date was extended in an interim final rule, 66 Fed. Reg. 27,552 (May 17, 2001). Compliance with the 2000 regulations was later postponed until new planning regulations are finalized. 67 Fed. Reg. 35,431 (May 20, 2002). See also extension of compliance for projects implementing plans, 68 Fed. Reg. 53,294 (September 10, 2003).

[18] 70 Fed. Reg. 1,023.

[19] Act of June 4, 1897, ch. 2, 30 Stat. 34.

[20] P.L. 86-517, 74 Stat. 215.

[21] P.L. 94-588, 90 Stat. 2949, primarily amending P.L. 93-378.

[22] 16 U.S.C. § 475.

[23] 16 U.S.C. § 551.

[24] 16 U.S.C. § 531.

[25] 16 U.S.C. § 528.

[26] 16 U.S.C. § 529.

[27] P.L. 88-577, 78 Stat. 890.

[28] 16 U.S.C. § 531.

[29] 16 U.S.C. § 1604(g). Note that "wilderness" management is again mentioned, twelve years after enactment of the Wilderness Act.

[30] P.L. 88-577, *supra.*

[31] 66 Fed. Reg. 3,245 (Jan. 12, 2001).

[32] *Id.*, at 3,246.

[33] New 36 C.F.R. § 294.13(b)(1), 66 Fed. Reg. 3,273.

[34] *Id.*, § 294.13(b)(2)-(4).

[35] *Id.*, § 294.14(a) and (c).

[36] *Id.*, § 294.14(d).

[37] The *proposed* rule would not have applied the prohibitions on new road construction to the Tongass National Forest in Alaska. Rather, decisions on whether the prohibitions should apply to any or all of the inventoried roadless areas in the Tongass would have been considered at the time of the five-year review of the April 1999 revised Tongass Plan (i.e. in 2004). In contrast, the preferred alternative in the FEIS would have applied the road and timber prohibitions to the Tongass in April 2004.

[38] 65 Fed. Reg. 67,529.

[39] 66 Fed. Reg. 3,249.

[40] P.L. 88-577, 78 Stat. 890.

[41] P.L. 86-517, 74 Stat. 215, 16 U.S.C. § 529.

[42] 16 U.S.C. § 1604(e).

[43] Wyoming v. U.S. Department of Agriculture, 277 F. Supp. 2d 1197, 1239 (D. Wyo 2003).

[44] The court reviewed the exceptions by which roads could be allowed in roadless areas under the rule, but did not mention that Federal Aid Highways could be permitted in some instances (p. 1236). On the other hand, the court noted that the roadless rule was more constrained with respect to constructing roads in roadless areas in order to combat problem conditions than was the Wilderness Act, in that the Wilderness Act allows

roads "to control fire, insects, and diseases," while the roadless rule only allows roads in the case of an "imminent flood, fire, or other catastrophic event that, without intervention, would cause the loss of life or property." (Comparing 16 U.S.C. 1133(d)(1) with 36 C.F.R. § 294.12(b)(1).

[45] *Id.* .

[46] *Id.* at 1239.

[47] *Id.*, at 1234.

[48] *Id.*, at 1233, quoting from H.Rept. 88-1538.

[49] *Id.*, at 1239.

[50] Memorandum for the Heads and Acting Heads of Executive Departments and Agencies, Andrew H. Card, Jr. January 20, 2001. Exceptions are also made for rules that are subject to statutory or judicial deadlines, or rules the Office of Management and Budget Director deems are excepted because they are needed for an emergency or other urgent situation relating to health and safety.

[51] Several dates surround the roadless rule: the 60-day delayed effectiveness date in the rule itself — which derives from the Congressional Review Act (CRA)(Subtitle E of the Small Business Regulatory Enforcement Act of 1996, Pub. L. No 104-121, 110 Stat. 857-874, 5 U.S.C. §§801 *et seq.*); the 60-day delay resulting from the President's directive; and the usual 30-day delay that might otherwise apply under the Administrative Procedure Act (APA)(5 U.S.C. 501 *et seq.*). Normally, the 30-day APA delay period and the 60-day CRA delay period run concurrently.

[52] Under 5 U.S.C. § 804(2), a major rule is one that "has resulted in or is likely to result in — (A) an annual effect on the economy of $100,000,000 or more; (B) a major increase in costs or prices for consumers, individual industries, Federal, State, or local government agencies, or geographic regions; or (C) significant adverse effects on competition, employment, investment, productivity, innovation, or on the ability of United States-based enterprises to compete with foreign-based enterprises in domestic and export markets" other than rules under the Telecommunications Act of 1996. Under the Review Act, a rule that has been determined to be a major rule cannot become effective for at least 60 days after publication. This delay period is to give the Congress time to consider the rule and to address legislatively issues raised by it. A major rule will take effect the later of the date occurring 60 days after the date on which — (1) Congress receives the report submitted pursuant to § 801(a)(1); or after the rule is published in the Federal Register, if it is; (2) if the Congress passes a joint resolution of disapproval which is subsequently vetoed by the President, then the earlier of when one House votes and fails to override the veto, or 30 session days after Congress receives the veto message from the President; or (3) the date the rule would otherwise have taken effect if not for the review requirement. 5 U.S.C. § 801(a)(3). Other provisions allow a major rule to become effective earlier under certain circumstances, such as those involving an imminent threat to health or safety or other emergency circumstances, national security, etc., or if either House votes to reject a joint resolution of disapproval. When, as in this instance, a rule is published and/or reported within 60 session days of adjournment of the Senate or 60 legislative days of adjournment of the House through the date on which the same or succeeding Congress first convenes its next session, that Congress may consider and pass a joint resolution of disapproval during a period of 60 session or legislative days after receiving the reported rule. A

held-over rule takes effect as otherwise provided; but the opportunity for Congress to consider and disapprove it is extended. The *usual* effective date of a regulation under the APA is 30 days after publication, during which time affected persons may prepare for and adjust to the impending effects of the rule. The 30-day period is intended as a minimum, and an agency may set a longer interval if that appears advisable, and longer times have been afforded in circumstances when it is anticipated that economic adjustments must be made in response to the new regulatory requirements. However, there are exceptions to the applicability of the APA, one of which is that the usual rulemaking procedures do not apply to rules relating to agency management or public property. However, in 1971, Secretary of Agriculture Hardin partially waived the APA exemption for rules related to public property (36 Fed. Reg. 13804 (July 24, 1971). The Hardin Order subjects Department of Agriculture rulemaking to the public notice and comment requirements prescribed by 5 U.S.C. 553(b) and (c), subject to exceptions for good cause. However, the Order does not appear to subject Department rules to the 30-day delay requirement of § 553(d), or to other APA provisions beyond § 553(b) and (c), a fact which may be relevant to options available to change the rule. Many Forest Service rules, including the new Planning rule and the Roads rule, are effective immediately upon being finalized. Under the APA, interested persons have the right to petition for issuance, amendment, or repeal of a rule, even during the 30-day delay period, although by what procedures an agency may accomplish changes in response to such a petition during the delay period is not totally clear. As noted above, however, the roadless rule does not appear subject to these provisions. Even if it were, the roadless rule is a final published rule, even though it is not yet in effect, and at least one court has held that an agency cannot simply "repeal" such a regulation, but rather may need to modify or revoke the final regulation through commensurate procedures (Consumer Energy Council of America v. Federal Energy Regulatory commission, 673 F. 2d 425 (D.C. Cir. 1982)) — here those that may be required by the NFMA and other agency regulations.

[53] 66 Fed. Reg. 8,899.

[54] The postponement notice stated that the action was exempt from notice and comment either because it is a procedural rule or for good cause shown: "[t]o the extent that 5 U.S.C. section 553 applies to this action, it is exempt from notice and comment because it constitutes a rule of procedure under 5 U.S.C. section 553(b)(A). Alternatively, the Department's implementation of this rule without opportunity for public comment, effective immediately upon publication today in the Federal Register, is based on the good cause exceptions in 5 U.S.C. section 553(b)(B) and 553(d)(3). Seeking public comment is impracticable, unnecessary and contrary to the public interest. The temporary 60-day delay in effective date is necessary to give Department officials the opportunity for further review and consideration of new regulations, consistent with the Assistant to the President's memorandum of Jan. 20, 2001. Given the imminence of the effective date, seeking prior public comment on this temporary delay would have been impractical, as well as contrary to the public interest in the orderly promulgation and implementation of regulations. The imminence of the effective date is also good cause for making this rule effective immediately upon publication."

[55] Idaho v. Dombeck, CV01-11-N-EJL (D.C. Id. 2001); Kootenai Tribe of Idaho et al v.Dombeck, CV01-10-N-EJL. (D.C. Id. 2001) Colorado and Alaska have joined Idaho in the suit and Utah also has filed suit.

[56] USDA News Release No. 0075.01.

[57] 66 Fed. Reg. 3,219.

[58] The first of these (I.D. No. 7710-2001-1) was actually published on August 24, two days after the second of these directives (I.D. No. 7710-2001-2 and I.D. No. 2400-2001-3, both issued July 27, 2001), even though the first one had been in effect since May 31. See 66 Fed. Reg. 44,590 (August 24, 2001) and 66 Fed. Reg. 44,111 (August 22, 2001).

[59] I.D. No. 7710-2001-3 and I.D. No. 1920-2001-1, both effective December 14, 2001. 66 Fed. Reg. 65,796.

[60] Another example is §7712.16b, paragraph 3, which distinguished between classified and unclassified forest roads and stated that environmental mitigation and environmental restoration of unclassified roads are appropriate in inventoried roadless and contiguous unroaded areas and must follow NEPA-based decisionmaking processes. However, reconstruction or maintenance of unclassified roads in inventoried roadless and contiguous unroaded areas is inappropriate, other than to prevent or correct resource damage, as such activity would lead to de facto road development.

[61] FSM §1925.04a. 66 Fed. Reg. 65,801-65,802. Therefore, if the interim direction did not apply to Tongass, and the new roadless area rule were enjoined, arguably the usual forest line officers could approve timber harvests in that forest under the procedures and provisions in place before a the new final roadless area management rule and in accordance with the plan for that forest.

[62] *Id.,* at 65,801.

[63] 66 Fed. Reg. 65,801.

[64] 40 C.F.R. 1508.4.

[65] 68 Fed. Reg. 33,814 (June 5, 2003).

[66] 68 Fed. Reg. 44,598 (July 29, 2003).

[67] P.L. 108-148, 117 Stat. 1887.

[68] Rhodes v. Johnson, 153 F. 3d 785 (7th Cir. 1998).

[69] 66 Fed. Reg. 48412 (September 20, 2001).

[70] 67 Fed. Reg. 54622 (August 23, 2002).

[71] FSH 19909.15 — Environmental Policy and Procedures Handbook, § 30.3b.2.

[72] Southwest Center for Biological Diversity v. U.S. Forest Service, 100 F. 3d 1443, 1450 (9th Cir. 1996).

[73] P.L. 104-19, 109 Stat. 194, 240-247.

[74] Rhodes v. Johnson, 153 F. 3d 785 (7th Cir. 1998).

[75] The Report on the Public Comments can be reached via the June 26, 2002 News Release at [http://www.roadless.fs.fed.us]. The Ninth Circuit pointed out that the Attorney General of Montana had asserted that nationally “96% of commenters favored stronger protections.” Kootenai Tribe of Idaho v. Veneman, 313 F. 3d 1094 (9th Cir. 2003).

[76] 313 F. 3d 1094 (9th Cir. 2003).

[77] *Id.* at 1104.

[78] *Id.* at 1126.

[79] *Id.* at 1118-1119.
[80] *Id.* at 1120-1121.
[81] An earlier Ninth Circuit case, Churchill v. Babbitt, 150 F. 3d 1072, as amended by 158 F. 3d 491 (9th Cir. 1998) held that the district court in that instance did not err in allowing intervenors under Rule 24(a) to intervene only as to the remedial part of the case. In Portland Audubon Society v. Hodel, 866 F.2d 302 (9th Cir. 1989) the court held that environmental intervenors did not qualify under Rule 24(a) to intervene as of right to defend a NEPA challenge although they evidently were allowed intervenor status on other claims. This latter case referred to an earlier Seventh Circuit case (Wade v. Goldschmidt, 673 F. 2d 182 (7th Cir. 1982)) in which the court denied intervenor status to an applicant because it failed to assert an interest sufficient to warrant intervention as of right under Rule 24(a) in the context of a NEPA challenge, stating: "In a suit such as this, brought to require compliance with federal statues regulating governmental projects, the governmental bodies charged with compliance can be the only defendants." (Wade, at 185.) Furthermore, the court found that "as it should be clear from our discussion of intervention of right," the applicants did not have "a question of law or fact in common" to satisfy the requirement for permissive intervention under Rule 24(b).
[82] Kootenai, at 1109.
[83] *Id.*
[84] *Id.* at 1111.
[85] *Id.*
[86] Forest Conservation Council v. Forest Service, 66 F. 3d 1489, 1496 n.8 (9th Cir.1995)(citation omitted).
[87] *Id.* at 1497.
[88] 68 Fed. Reg. 41865 (July 15, 2003).
[89] 68 Fed. Reg. 41864 (July 15, 2003).
[90] 68 Fed. Reg. 75136 (Dec. 30, 2003).
[91] Wyoming v. United States Department of Agriculture, 277 F. Supp. 2d 1197 (D. Wyo. (2003)).
[92] *Id.* at 1231 - 1232.
[93] *Id.* at 1203.
[94] *Id.* at 1232.
[95] *Id.* at 1239.
[96] 69 Fed. Reg. 42,636 (July 16, 2004).
[97] 69 Fed. Reg. 54,600 (September 9, 2004).
[98] 69 Fed. Reg. 42,648.
[99] 70 Fed. Reg. 25,658.
[100] 70 Fed. Reg. 1,023.
[101] 36 C.F.R. § 219.27(b)(2004).
[102] *Id.*, at 1,044.
[103] Section 219.12 at 1,059.
[104] Supplemental Response to Public Comments on the 2002 Proposed Planning Rule, at 31.
[105] *Id.*, at 1,044.
[106] *Id.*

[107] 70 Fed. Reg. 14,637.

[108] Although directives purportedly are available at [http://www.fs.fed.us/im/directives/], the actual text of the new directives is unavailable at that site as of April 19, 2005. If a citizen visits the directives site mentioned in the Federal Register [http://www.fs.fed.us/emc/nfma/], the text of the new interim directives is available, but the sequence of the relevant IDs is not evident and the relationship between previous and current IDs is not clear.

[109] 69 Fed. Reg. 42,648 (July 16, 2004).

[110] 70 Fed. Reg. 25,654.

[111] See CRS Report RL32436, *Public Participation in the Management of Forest Service and Bureau of Land Management Lands: Overview and Recent Changes*, by Pamela Baldwin.

[112] 70 Fed. Reg. 25,654.

[113] *Id.*

[114] 70 Fed. Reg. 25,656.

[115] 70 Fed. Reg. 25,663.

In: Public Lands: Use and Misuse
Editor: William E. Neeley, pp. 127-133
ISBN: 978-1-60021-352-6

Chapter 8

LAND AND WATER CONSERVATION FUND: CURRENT STATUS AND ISSUES*

Jeffrey A. Zinn

SUMMARY

The Land and Water Conservation Fund (LWCF) has been the principal source of monies for four federal agencies — the National Park Service, Bureau of Land Management, Fish and Wildlife Service, and Forest Service — to acquire recreational lands since 1965. The LWCF also funds a matching grant program to assist states (and localities) in acquiring recreational lands and developing facilities. The fund accumulates $900 million annually from designated sources. Congress allocates these funds through appropriations each year.

Current congressional issues include (1) deciding the amount to appropriate each year to each of the four federal agencies, and to the state grant program; (2) identifying which lands should be acquired; and (3) determining whether LWCF funds should be appropriated for additional related purposes. The primary context for debating these issues is Interior appropriations legislation, which is tracked in CRS Report RL32893.

INTRODUCTION

The Land and Water Conservation Fund (LWCF) was created in 1964 and took effect January 1, 1965.[1] It has been the principal federal source of funds for acquiring new recreation lands. Some supporters assert that it was originally intended to be a revolving fund, but it has never operated as one. The fund's basic purpose has not been altered even though the authorizing legislation has been amended, mainly in the early years, most notably to raise the funding ceiling and to mandate that offshore oil and gas leasing revenues should make up any shortfall from other specified financing sources.

Appropriations have been made for (1) federal land acquisition; (2) grants to states; and (3) related purposes (starting in FY1998). Most federal lands are acquired (and managed) by four agencies — the Forest Service (FS) in the Department of Agriculture, and the National

* Excerpted from CRS Report RS21503, Updated June 10, 2005

Park Service (NPS), Fish and Wildlife Service (FWS), and Bureau of Land Management (BLM) in the Department of the Interior, using funds appropriated from the LWCF.[2] These four agencies manage about 94% of all federally owned lands. These agencies have used LWCF funds to acquire approximately 4.5 million acres, an area slightly smaller than New Jersey. (Viewed in a different way, 4.5 million acres is less than 1% of the almost 672 million acres owned by the federal government.) Another portion of the LWCF, administered by the NPS, provides matching grants to states for recreation planning, land acquisition, and facility development. These grants have funded about 38,000 state and local projects. Recipients have acquired approximately 2.3 million acres and have developed recreation facilities at about 27,000 of these projects. Acquisitions funded through LWCF grants must remain in recreation use in perpetuity. A final portion has been appropriated for other related federal purposes since FY1998.

How the Fund Works

The LWCF is a "trust fund"[3] that accumulates revenues from federal outdoor recreation user fees, the federal motorboat fuel tax, and surplus property sales. To supplement these sources to reach the annual authorized level of $900 million, it accumulates revenues from oil and gas leases on the Outer Continental Shelf (OCS). During the past decade, the OCS revenues have accounted for more than 90% of the deposits each year (and almost 100% in most recent years).

The LWCF is not a true trust fund in the way "trust fund" is generally understood in the private sector. The fund is credited with revenues totaling $900 million annually, but Congress must appropriate funds; unappropriated funds remain in the U.S. Treasury and can be spent for other federal activities. Interest is not accrued on the accumulated unauthorized balance that has been credited to the LWCF account. In addition, the LWCF is subject to earmarks and other directions from Congress during the annual appropriations process. From FY1965 through FY2005, $28.1 billion has been credited to the LWCF. However, only about half that amount — $14.3 billion — has been appropriated.

Funding History

The $14.3 billion appropriated from the fund has been unevenly allocated among the states, the four federal land management agencies, and for other purposes, as shown on the chart on the next page. States have received less than 30% of the total, about $3.7 billion. In the early years, more funds went to state grants than to the four federal agencies combined. State grants have declined as a portion of the total since the early 1980s and received no appropriations from FY1996 through FY1999. The four federal agencies have received about two-thirds of the total, divided as follows: the NPS has received $4.0 billion; the FS has received almost $2.5 billion; the FWS has received almost $2.2 billion; and the BLM has received around $0.7 billion. The remainder, about $1.3 billion, has been appropriated for other purposes, starting in FY1998.

Total annual appropriations from the LWCF have fluctuated widely over the past 35 years (see chart above). Except during the Carter Administration (FY1977-FY1980), when appropriations exceeded $500 million each year, they have only approached or exceeded the authorized level of $900 million in FY1998 and FY2001. Except for the earliest decade, the lowest years were FY1996 and FY1997, when appropriations totaled $138 million and $159 million, respectively.

Over the past decade, total annual appropriations have risen and fallen in multi-year periods. Between FY1996 and FY2001, the total generally rose, with spikes in FY1998 and FY2001. FY1998 was the first year that appropriations exceeded $900 million; they included $270 million in the usual funding titles for the four land management agencies, an additional $627 million in a separate title, funding both the acquisition of the Headwaters Forest in California and New World Mine outside Yellowstone National Park, and $72 million for other activities that did not involve land acquisition. The total (and, in general, the funding levels for each federal agency and the state grant program) has declined every year since FY2001. The table below lists appropriations from FY2001 to FY2005 and shows this decline for each federal agency and the state grant program.

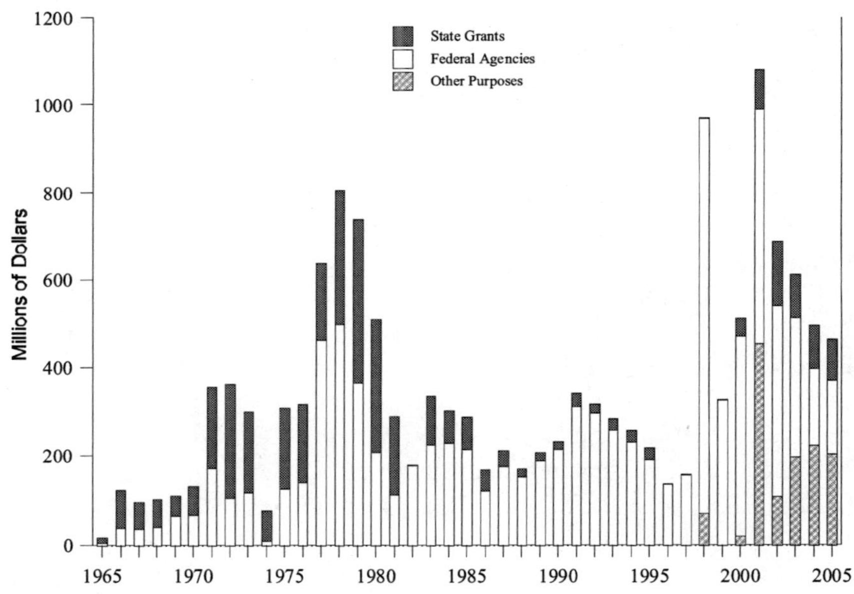

Source: Data through FY2002 compiled by the National Park Service Budget Office, May 1, 2002. Date since FY2002 from conference committee reports and Interior appropriations laws.

Total LWCF Appropriations: FY1965-2005

LWCF Appropriations for Land Acquisition and State Grants, FY2001-FY2005 (in millions of dollars)

Agency	FY2001	FY2002	FY2003	FY2004	FY2005
Forest Service	$150.9	$149.7	$133.8	$66.8	$61.0
National Park Service	$215.1	$274.1	$172.5	$141.5	$146.3
(State Grants)	($88.8)	($144.0)	($98.0)	($94.4)	($91.2)
Fish and Wildlife Service	$121.5	$99.1	$73.4	$43.3	$37.0
Bureau of Land Management	$47.3	$49.9	$33.5	$18.5	$11.2
Total	$534.5	$572.8	$413.2	$270.0	$255.5

Sources: Data for FY2001 and FY2002 from National Park Service Budget Office, May 1, 2002, and data for FY2003 through FY2005 from conference committee reports.
Note: Appropriations for purposes other than land acquisition are not included in the table.

Congress appropriated LWCF funds for purposes other than land acquisition in FY1998 and each year since FY2000. Appropriations for other purposes were much higher in FY2001 than any other year, when they were used to fund programs in the Clinton Administration's Lands Legacy Initiative proposal. Most recently, for FY2005, Congress provided approximately $204 million. The FWS has received more than $850 million of the $1.3 billion appropriated for other purposes since FY1998. The amounts and purposes, by year, include:

- In FY1998, $72 million for critical maintenance needs to the four land management agencies, and to the FS for the Beartooth Highway (Montana) rehabilitation and maintenance;
- In FY2000, $20 million for programs administered by the NPS and FS;
- In FY2001, $456 million for several federal and state programs, such as the Historic Preservation Fund and the Payment-in-Lieu-of-Taxes Program;
- In FY2002, $135 million for three FWS programs;
- In FY2003, $197 million for four FWS programs;
- In FY2004, $223 million, predominantly for FWS and FS programs; and
- In FY2005, $204 million, predominantly for FWS and FS programs.

Congress is considering the Bush Administration's FY2006 request for LWCF appropriations. This overall request is for additional reductions. It includes $40.0 million for the FS (a reduction of $21.0 million), $54.5 million for the NPS (a reduction of $91.9 million in total, which includes a reduction of $89.6 million for state grants and a reduction of $2.3 million for federal land acquisition), $41.0 million for the FWS (an increase of $4.0 million), and $13.4 million for the BLM (an increase of $2.2 million). For information on appropriations in the current fiscal year, see CRS Report RL32893, which is tracking these accounts through each step of the FY2006 appropriations process.

CURRENT ISSUES ASSOCIATED WITH APPROPRIATIONS

Appropriation Levels. Between FY1998 and FY2002, funding for land acquisition generally returned to higher levels not seen since the Carter Administration. It has subsequently declined each of the past four years, and is now closer to average funding levels historically (when appropriations for other purposes is not included), as shown in the figure on page 3. However, even if Congress started to provide $900 million annually, and only for land acquisition, it would take more than a decade to address the backlog of identified acquisitions, recently estimated to exceed $10 billion for the three DOI agencies alone.

The concept of the fund enjoys widespread bipartisan support, led by resource protection advocates who seek higher appropriations levels as well as stable and predictable funding. These advocates join together to seek higher appropriations in general. Many of them have more specific priorities, such as higher funding for one of the four federal agencies or the state grant program, or for a specific site or area.

Others oppose higher levels based on concerns about further acquisition of privately owned land by the federal government either generally or at specific sites, especially in the West, where federal ownership is already concentrated. These concerns involve preferences for private ownership, limits that federal agencies may place on uses of their lands, and reduced local tax revenues that result from public ownership. Some opponents believe that maintaining (and rehabilitating) the land and facilities that federal agencies already own should take priority over further acquisitions. Since federal agencies can not use LWCF funds for maintenance, supporters of this priority favor more funding to other accounts that can be used for maintenance and less for LWCF.

Since the early 1990s, the appropriations debate has grown more complicated as perspectives on resource protection have changed. One change is that alternatives to acquisition that may provide potentially lower levels of protection but at less cost (such as easements) have become more widely used by federal agencies. A second change is that resource protection is discussed increasingly for either larger areas with multiple land owners — such as ecosystems, landscapes, or watersheds — or for managing systems where only a portion of the land is in public ownership. In these complex situations, success depends on cooperation and partnerships, and the LWCF may be less critical.

Which Lands to Acquire. The annual budget submission from each of the four federal agencies includes proposals of which lands the agencies seek to acquire with requested funds. The four FY2006 requests, for example, identify a total of 54 sites. Section 7 of the LWCF Act (16 U.S.C. 460*l*-9) provides that federal funds may be used to acquire lands in national park, national forest, and national wildlife system units, and for water development projects with recreational benefits. The large backlog of potential acquisitions at these sites where LWCF spending is authorized provides each agency with many options in its annual request. Congress reviews agency requests, then determines the appropriations level and earmarks almost all appropriations to specific sites. In recent years, Congress also has provided each agency with small amounts for "emergencies," "inholdings," "hardships," and "exchanges," and a larger amount for acquisition management. (Appropriations to the state grant program, by contrast, almost never include earmarks or other directions to the NPS to guide how these funds should be distributed or spent.)

Spending for Other Purposes. Starting in FY1998, Congress has allocated some LWCF appropriations to federal agencies for purposes other than land acquisition, and in the past few years, the Bush Administration has requested LWCF funds for other programs. The FY2006 budget request continues this trend. Section 7 (16 U.S.C. 460*l*-9) on allocation of the fund for federal purposes, states that "moneys appropriated from the fund for federal purposes shall, unless otherwise allotted in the appropriations Act making them available, be allotted by the

President for the following purposes and subpurposes." The listed purposes define which lands are eligible. Traditional fund beneficiaries have expressed concern about expanding the uses of appropriations if it reduces the amount available for federal land acquisition and state grants.

LWCF FUNDING IN RECENT LEGISLATION

Legislation to fully fund the LWCF and to make it operate like a private sector trust fund was first introduced near the end of the 105th Congress. Such proposals were revised and reconsidered by every subsequent Congress. These proposals sought to divert offshore oil and gas revenues to a Conservation and Reinvestment Act (CARA) Fund and to permanently appropriate receipts credited to the LWCF, among other related purposes, with total annual funding of approximately $3 billion in many of the proposals. In the 106th Congress, one CARA bill, H.R. 701, passed the House, the only time either Chamber has approved it. That version would have provided an additional $900 million annually from the CARA Fund to the LWCF, giving it a total of $1.8 billion annually. (For details on the history of congressional deliberations of CARA, see CRS Report RL30444, *Conservation and Reinvestment Act (CARA) (H.R. 701) and a Related Initiative in the 106th Congress.*, by Jeffrey Zinn and M. Lynne Corn.)

When it became clear that CARA legislation would not be enacted in 2001, as the 106th Congress was drawing to a close, it included aspects of CARA in FY2001 appropriations legislation. These provisions established the Conservation Spending Category (CSC), and some referred to it as "CARA lite." The LWCF is a major component in the CSC. The CSC provisions set a target for total funding for all the component programs in FY2001 at $1.6 billion, including $1.2 billion through Interior appropriations and $400 million through Commerce appropriations. Under law, the target increases each year until it reaches $2.4 billion in FY2006. However, while the Interior Appropriations bill authorized the CSC through FY2006, the Commerce Appropriations bill authorized it for only FY2001. (For more information on the CSC, including funding by program, see CRS Report RS20471, *The Conservation Spending Category: Funding for Natural Resource Protection*, by Jeffrey Zinn.)

Many LWCF proponents continue to support legislative proposals that would provide full and certain funding to the LWCF each year both because the annual appropriations process continues to be unpredictable, and because the maximum benefit could be achieved with full funding. Opponents of these proposals believe that these monies should be appropriated for other priorities, that further federal land acquisitions should be limited, or that this funding should not be exempt from the annual appropriations process. However, support for considering the CARA legislation appears to have declined and the gap between the CSC target and actual funding has expanded, possibly because of growing concern about federal budget deficits in future years or other priorities such as the war on terrorism.

REFERENCES

[1] Act of Sept. 3, 1964; P.L. 88-578, 78 Stat. 897. 16 U.S.C. 460*l*-4, *et seq*.

[2] For an introduction to these agencies and their responsibilities, see CRS Report RL32393, *Federal Land Management Agencies: Background on Land and Resource Management.*

[3] LWCF is technically a special account, rather than a trust fund, but in federal budgeting, the only difference is the allocation of interest on unappropriated balances — interest on a trust fund accrues to the fund, while interest on a special account accrues to the General Treasury.

INDEX

N

O

P

R

S

T